DICTIONARY OF ARCHITECTURE

DICTIONARY

OF

ARCHITECTURE

HENRY H. SAYLOR

Editor, Journal of The American Institute of Architects
Fellow of The American Institute of Architects
Fellow of The Royal Geographical Society
Architect registered in the State of New York

John Wiley & Sons, Inc., New York

11 12 13 14 15

ISBN 0 471 75601 6

Library of Congress Catalog Card Number: 52–8260

PRINTED IN THE UNITED STATES OF AMERICA

With deep respect and affection

to

THE AMERICAN INSTITUTE OF ARCHITECTS

PREFACE

Approximately every half century someone writes a dictionary of architecture. Frequently the text is expanded to cyclopedic form, as in the five-volume *Dictionary of Architecture* issued in 1892 by the Architectural Publication Society of London, or as in the three-volume *Encyclopedia of Architecture and Building* of Russell Sturgis published in 1901.

In our own time, with the rapid development of building techniques, new materials, and the necessity of seeking new forms to express new social needs, the encyclopedia becomes more an historical record than an aid to vocabulary. Sturgis' eight-page explanation of the term "iron construction," for example, is now but a quaint picture of the beginnings of the steel-frame technique. Then, too, we now have a flood of specialized books, year by year, keeping pace with our knowledge of building techniques, and we look to them rather than to an encyclopedia for up-to-date information.

The immediate need, it would seem, is for a handy volume in which one can find the spelling, pronunciation (if unusual), and concise definition of the terms met in the study, historical reading, and practice of architecture. For such a need the general dictionaries, even the least abridged, will not suffice. The vocabulary of the architect has gathered many words from other languages, and a reading of architectural history will uncover numerous words that have since disappeared from common—or even uncommon—speech, so that the lexicographers have ruled them out.

In the preparation of an architectural dictionary such as outlined above, the greatest difficulty lies in deciding where to stop. Today's practice of architecture calls for a knowledge of far more than construction and the disposition of space. To confess ignorance of hydraulics, acoustics, heating, ventilation, electricity, hygiene, economics, climatology, painting, sculpture, and art in general—such confession would automatically infer lack of competence as a practising architect. The proper scope of a dictionary of architecture would seem almost boundless unless we recognize the fact that, although an architect should have a general and fundamental knowledge of hydraulics and many other sciences and arts, he cannot be expected to be an expert technician in any one of these subsidiary fields. Nor is he expected to be letter-perfect in their individual technical vocabularies. Therefore, reminding ourselves frequently that this is an *architectural* dictionary brings the scope and size of such a work within measurable limits. Technical terms that might be used, for example, by an engineer of heating and ventilation in discussing with an architect a project on which the two are collaborating should be included in our dictionary; all technical terms used by the same engineer in discussing ways and means with his own technicians are not necessarily included.

With the purpose of saving space and the reader's time, the adjective, verb, and adverb forms are usually omitted when the noun is listed. Where the verb or adjective is more commonly used in the architectural vocabulary, it is given instead of the other forms.

As to pronunciation, it has seemed desirable to avoid the use of diacritical symbols. After one has turned to the front pages to find out how *a* with two dots over it is pronounced, he is then confronted in the same word by a *u* with a small circle over it, and decides that, after all, he is disinclined to enroll for the course and would rather use his own guess as to the pronunciation. The use of phonetic spelling has here been adopted in the full realization that it is unscientific and often inaccurate, particularly in an attempt to convey in English the sound of a word in French, German, or Italian. Undoubtedly, our system falls far short, for instance, in designating the pronunciation of *salon* as "sah lonh," but the shortcomings will perhaps be less annoying to the reader than a shower of strange diacritical symbols. Phonetic interpretation, even though used sparingly, will irritate the reader in the case of a word he knows, but he should bear in mind that the lad from China or Peru, in the United States to study architecture, really needs a helping tongue.

The needs of the student just beginning his quest for knowledge of architecture—which quest, although he may not realize it, will engage him all the years of his life—have been particularly influential in prompting the sporadic labors, extending over ten years, in the writing and illustrating of this book. In this period of transition, when the forms of past epochs seem to have little practical bearing upon the architectural problems of the twentieth century, the student is tempted to fix his eyes on the future and pay little attention to the road behind. And yet he must soon realize that even so forward-looking a pioneer as Einstein could not hope to move ahead into the uncharted fields of knowledge without an understanding appreciation of what has been done along the road behind by such men as Archimedes, Francis Bacon, Isaac Newton, Kant, Descartes—even as far back as the discoverer of the wheel. *The past is prologue.*

In the interests of economy of space, illustrations have been restricted to objects that are difficult or impossible to describe in words alone. Instead of illustrating an object on the page with its definition, where it would appear as a detached entity of uncertain significance and arbitrary scale, the group-assembly method has been followed in general in the plates at the end of the dictionary. Surely it is better to picture an apophyge in its proper relationship to a column shaft than to depend upon conveying its meaning by a small curved line—even at the inconvenience of turning to a numbered plate in the back of the book.

There is no doubt whatever that errors and omissions are sure to be observed in these pages. Human fallibility being what it is and always has been, these must be expected. It is hoped that the defects will be not merely pardoned but corrected. Those who maintain that the compilation of a dictionary should never be entrusted to one man will doubtless find in these pages abundant evidence to confirm their reasoning. It should be a source of some satisfaction, therefore, to bring errors or omissions to the attention of the publishers. We shall, perhaps, be permitted the hope that this first edition will form the basis for a dictionary of architecture that will, with periodic revisions, serve as a modest and convenient aid to those who would know the vocabulary of this mother of the arts.

There remains the privilege of publicly acknowledging with deep gratitude the help of friends and professional acquaintances in specialized fields. Without their gracious suggestions and their verification and correction of lists of words, this dictionary would have been conspicuous for many more shortcomings. My heartfelt thanks, then, to:

Romer Shawhan, Managing Director of the Marble Institute of America, for descriptions of marbles.

D. W. Kessler, National Bureau of Standards; M. J. Morgan, President of the Indiana Limestone Institute; C. W. Chamberlin, Public Buildings Service; and D. G. Runner, formerly of the U. S. Department of the Interior, Bureau of Mines, for help with the limestones and sandstones.

Dr. Eloise Gerry, U. S. Department of Agriculture, Forest Products Laboratory, for her indispensable help with the names of woods.

Harold H. Fletcher, of the H. E. Fletcher Company; the Granite Manufacturers Association; J. W. Strohman, Public Buildings Service; and W. P. Van Fleet, of the Stone Publishing Company, for help with the granites.

Stanley B. Parker, for clarification of terms relative to perspective drawing.

And, finally, to Audrey Teele for her painstaking, patient, and mighty labors in transforming a heterogeneous manuscript into final typescript for the publisher.

HENRY H. SAYLOR

Washington, D.C.
June, 1952

Numbers in parentheses refer to illustrations at the end of the dictionary. The italic letters refer to particular sections of the illustrations.

A

Aaron's rod (airuns rod), a molding of rounded section bearing vines, leaves, and tendrils. 2. a rod from which leaves spring or around which a serpent twines.

abaciscus (abba sis'kus), a small abacus. 2. a stone or tile in mosaic. *See also* abaculus.

abaculus (abbak'youlus), a unit tile in a geometrical-pattern surface.

abacus (ab'akus), the top member of a capital upon which the object supported rests (11*j*).

abamurus (abba mew'rus), a block of masonry, in buttress form, for the support of a structure.

abate (ab bate'), to cut away, as in stonework, or to beat down, as in metalwork, so as to leave parts in relief.

abat-jour [Fr.] (abba zhure), a contrivance, as a skylight, used to deflect light downward. 2. a sloping cover, as for a window, opening upward to prevent those within from seeing what is outside and below.

abat-sons [Fr.] (abba sonh), a contrivance for the purpose of directing sound vibrations downward.

abattoir (abba twar), a building for the slaughter of cattle.

abat-vent [Fr.] (abba vanh), a contrivance to break the force of, or prevent the entrance of, wind, as in a louver or chimney cowl.

abat-voix [Fr.] (abba vwah), a reflector of sound.

abbadia, or **badia** [It.] (abbah dee'ah, badee'ah), an abbey church.

abbatial (ab bay'shal), pertaining to an abbey or an abbot.

ab'bey, the group of buildings forming the dwelling place of a society of monks or nuns. 2. a place of worship connected now or formerly with a monastic establishment. 3. a dwelling now or formerly the residence of an abbot or abbess.

ab'beystead, or **ab'beystede,** the land on which an abbey stands.

abbazzo [It.] (ab bot'zo), a rough sketch, draft, or model, as distinguished from a finished work.

aboudik'ro, *see* sapele.

abraum (ab'rawm), a red ocher, used to color mahogany.

abreuvoir [Fr.] (ab brew vwahr), a joint or chink in masonry, to be filled with mortar.

abura (ah burr'ah) (*Mitragyne ciliata*), a West African wood used for veneers, having a light brown color with a pink tinge.

abut' (intransitive verb), to touch at the end or boundary line; to be contiguous.

abut'ment, a supporting or buttressing structure.

acacia (ah case'yah) (*Acacia* spp.), a wood of the tropical regions of the world, most of which is not important commercially as lumber or veneer.

acajou [Fr.] (ak azhu), the French word for mahogany.

acanthine (akan′theen), like an acanthus.

acan′thus, a conventionalized representation of an acanthus leaf, that of a perennial herb in some of the warmer regions of the Old World. It is a distinguishing characteristic of the Corinthian capital (14*a*, *c*).

access door (ak′sess), provision to reach concealed plumbing or the like without disturbing plaster or fixtures.

accolade (akko laid′), a decorative use of molding over a door or window, in which two ogee curves meet centrally at the top.

accouplement [Fr.] (ak koop le manh), that which couples or is coupled together, as two columns wholly or partly joined.

accra (ak′kra) (*Entandrophragma* sp.), a wood from the African Gold Coast, used for fine veneers, having a dark red mahogany color, sometimes with a curled grain.

aceitillo (assi til′yo), a term loosely used for numerous woods. *See also* satinwood.

achech (at check′), a fabulous animal of Egyptian antiquity, half lion and half bird.

acle (ak′lee) (*Albizzia acle*), a wood from the Philippines used for fine veneers, similar to walnut in color but with a coarser grain and irregular ribbon stripe.

acoustic tile (akoos′tik), tile-shaped blocks of sound-absorbent material used as ceiling or side-wall facing.

acoustics (akoos′tiks), the branch of physics which treats of the phenomena and laws of sound. 2. the qualities of an enclosed space with respect to the clear transmission of distinct sounds.

acoustom′eter, an apparatus for the measurement of acoustic values.

acrolith (ak′rolith), a statue, in Greek art, having head and extremities of stone, with a trunk usually of wood, draped with textiles.

acropodium (akro po′deum), a pedestal for a statue, specifically of large size and with enrichment.

acrop′olis, the citadel of an ancient Greek city, usually a high plateau.

acrote′rion (plural, **acroteria**), a pedestal upon the ends or apex of a pediment to support a statue or other ornament; also the statue or ornament itself.

Adirondack sandstone, *see* Malone sandstone.

adit, or **aditus** (add′it or add′i tus), in ancient classical architecture, the entrance or approach to a building.

adobe (ad doe′bee), a sun-dried brick of earth, with straw as binder, used in Mexico and southwestern U.S.A. Often shortened to ’dobe.

adytum (ad′itum), the innermost shrine in some ancient places of worship.

ædes (eye′dees), in Roman antiquity, a building, as distinguished from a temple, set apart for worship without formal consecration by the augurs.

ædicula (eye dik′you lah), in Roman antiquity, a small house, or shrine, or votive offering, representing a temple. 2. a niche for an image or urn.

ægicrames (eye′gee krames), in classic sculpture, the heads or skulls of rams.

Æginetan Marbles (eye gin nee′tan), a collection of sculptures, the most important of which originally decorated the pediments of the Temple of Aphæa in the island of Ægina, built about 475 B.C. Discovered in 1811, they are preserved in the Glyptothek at Munich. They have given their name to a style of Greek sculpture of the period of transition between the archaic and the fully developed.

ærarium (eye rare′eum), a public treasury in ancient Roman times.

aerodrome (air′o drome), a building in which aircraft are stored and tested.

ærugo (eye roo′go), verdigris on old bronze; the patina.

æsymnium (eye sim′neum), the building erected by Æsymnus the Megarean by suggestion of the Delphic Oracle.

ætiaioi (eye tee eye oy′), in ancient Greece, the slabs forming the tympanum of a pediment.

ætoma (eye toe′mah), or **ætos** (eye′toss), ancient Greek term for the tympanum of a pediment.

afara, *see* limba.

affleuré [Fr.] (af fleu ray), made flush with the surface, as an inlaid medallion or mosaic.

afhus (af′hoos), a small building adjoining a Norse temple in which the altar, idols, etc., were placed.

afong (af fong′), a Bontoc dwelling, in the Philippine Islands.

ag′ba (*Gossweilerodendron balsamiferum*), a wood from West Africa, used for veneers, having a pale, cedar-brown color and resembling mahogany.

ag′ger, in ancient Roman work, a rampart of earth or a stone-faced embankment.

ag′gregate, that which, added to cement and water, makes concrete. Aggregate is said to be fine or coarse according to whether it is sand or the larger stone, gravel, etc.

agiasterium (aggie as tee′reum), the sanctuary in a basilica.

ag′nus, the lamb used as a Christian emblem; Agnus Dei, Lamb of God.

ag′ora, in ancient Greece, an open space, often the market place.

agraffé [Fr.] (agg raf fay), a cramping iron.

A.I.A., The American Institute of Architects. Members are permitted the use of the letters following their names. Fellows use F.A.I.A.

aileron (eye′le ron), a wing wall to mask the aisle of a church.

air brick, brick perforated with holes to allow ventilation through a wall.

air conditioning, a process of controlling for indoor use the distribution and physical properties of air: temperature, humidity, motion, and sometimes dust content.

airlock, an airtight chamber, under water or land as in caisson or tunnel excavation, serving to graduate the air pressure between adjacent atmospheres.

air′shaft, an unroofed area within the walls of a high building, not necessarily starting from the ground level; windows open upon it.

aisle (ile), a passageway between seats. 2. the portion of a church flanking the nave and separated from it by a row of columns or piers (7*g*).

aiwan (eye′wan), a reception hall, as in ancient Parthian buildings.

ajarcara [Sp.] (ah har car′a), brickwork in ornamental relief.

à jour [Fr.] (ah zhure), carving pierced to transmit light.

ajutage [Fr.] (as you tahz), the nozzle of a fountain or *jet d'eau.*

ala (allah), in ancient Roman architecture, a small room, recess, or alcove adjoining a larger room.

Alabama marble, a fine-grained white variety, the chief attractiveness of which is due to its life and warmth of coloring—for the most part a cream white rather than the bluish white common to Italian white marbles. Some of the commercial grades are: Clouded "A," Cream "A," Selected Cream, Madre Clouded, Madre Cream, Madre Vein, Veined Cream.

al′abaster, a white, translucent variety of gypsum, used for decorative screens and for sculpture.

alameda [Sp.] (allah meh′dah), an allée, or sheltered garden walk or drive.

albarium (al bare′eum), a white lime used for stucco, produced by calcination of marble.

Al′berene, trade name for a dense and massive soapstone, blue-gray in color, quarried in Virginia.

al′bronze, alloy of copper and aluminum.

alcazar [Sp.] (al cah′sar), a Moorish or Spanish citadel.

al′cove, an offset or recess in an interior, larger than a niche.

alder (awl′der) (*Alnus rubra*), a red wood of the Pacific Coast, with heartwood and sapwood a pale, pinkish brown; used for interior work, sometimes in imitation of mahogany or walnut.

alectorium (alek toe′reum), in ancient Roman architecture, a room for dice players.

alerce′ (*Fitzroya cupressoides*), a wood from Chile which somewhat resembles California redwood and is used for carpentry and furniture. *See also* sandarac, thuja burl.

alette′, a minor wing of a building. 2. side of a pier under the impost of an arch. 3. a door jamb.

Alexandri′num opus, the third division of the medieval mosaic art, from the time of Constantine to the thirteenth century.

Alham′bra, a palace in Granada, Spain, famous example

of medieval Moorish architecture.

alhauna [Sp.] (allow'na), a niche or other recess.

alipterion (allip tee'reun), in ancient Roman architecture, a room used by bathers for anointing themselves.

alkoranes (al'ko rains), minarets of a mosque.

allée [Fr.] (al lay), a sheltered garden walk or drive.

allége [Fr.] (alayzhe), a thinning of part of a wall, as in a spandrel under a windowsill.

al'ley, a subordinate street; sometimes a narrow passageway.

almemar (al mee'mar), reading desk in a synagogue.

almena [Sp.] (al may'na), a turret or pinnacle. 2. an indented battlement, usually trapezoidal, found in the south and east of Europe.

al'mery, aum'bry, or **am'bry,** a recess or built-in receptacle for the sacred vessels of the Mass.

almique (al mee'keh) (*Manilkara jaimiqui* = *M. bidentata*), a red or reddish brown wood from the Guianas and Cuba, used chiefly for inlay.

almon (am'mon) (*Shorea eximia*), a light-colored wood that darkens; from the Philippines, where it is plentiful and is used for furniture and fixtures.

almond (ah'mond), a cut-glass pendant as used in crystal chandeliers.

almonry (ah'mon ree), a receptacle or a house for the reception of alms, and, if a building, for their dispensing.

almshouse (ahms'house), a building for the reception and maintenance of the indigent.

alor'ing, *see* alure. 2. the parapet walls of a church (7*g*).

Alps Green, a brecciated serpentine marble from Italy, in many varieties. All have the same geological formation but vary considerably in appearance, running from a very deep to a very light green mass, infiltrated with calcite. This causes light green and white veins, which spread at times into broader veins and patches.

al'tar, a table form, originally the place where sacrifices were offered; now the center of most liturgical places of worship.

al'tarpiece, the pictorial composition on the reredos.

al'tar rail, a railing across the chancel, or in front of the altar.

al'tarscreen, the screen behind an altar, usually richly treated in stone, sometimes in wood.

altera'tion, any project involving change of, or addition to, an exisiting building.

al'ternating current, abbrev. a.c., an electric current which reverses the direction of its flow at regular intervals, usually 60 cycles per second.

alto-rilievo (alto rilly a'vo), high relief in panel sculpture. *See also* rilievo.

alure', a passage or gallery, as on the top of a wall.

alveated (al'vee ated), beehive-shaped.

am'aranth (*Peltogyne* sp.), also called purpleheart. A South American wood, used for fine veneers, having a dull brown color that oxidizes when cut to a rich purple, and a mottle figure.

ambe, or **ambi** (am'bay or am' bee), a pulpit or rostrum.

ambitus (am bee'tus), sacred space surrounding a tomb.

am'bo (plural, **am'bones**), a reading desk or pulpit in early Christian churches.

amboy'na burl (*Pterocarpus* sp.), a wood from the East Indies, used for fine veneers, having a rich brown color streaked with red or yellow.

am'bry, an almery or aumbry; a cupboard or niche near the altar of a church, to hold sacred vessels.

ambulacrum (am bu lay'krum), a promenade shaded by trees.

ambulatio, *see* pteroma.

ambulatory (am'bu lah toe ree), a covered walk; a term usually applied to the gallery or corridor leading behind an altar from one side to the other.

Amherst sandstone, a light gray or light buff, or variegated stone, quarried in Lorain County, Ohio.

A.M.I.C.E., associate member of the Institute of Civil Engineers.

A.M.I.E.E., associate member of the Institute of Electrical Engineers.

am'pere, the unit of measure indicating the intensity of current flow through an electrical circuit, the flow resulting from one volt pressure against a resistance of one ohm.

amphidis'tyle-in-antis, in a Greek temple, having two columns between antæ at both front and rear.

amphipro'style, with columned portico at front and rear but no columns at sides; applied to the classic temple.

amphithalamus (amfi thal a' muss), in the early Greek dwelling, an anteroom off a bedchamber.

amphithe'ater, originally an arena encircled by tiers of seats; now usually semicircular.

amphithu'ra, in ecclesiastic antiquity, the curtain, parted in the middle, which separated the chancel from the main body of the church.

amugis (ah moo'giss) (*Koordersiodendron pinnatum*), a hard, heavy, reddish brown wood from the Philippine Islands.

anaglyph (an'na gliff), sculpture or other ornament in relief more pronounced than bas-relief.

anaglyph'a, vessels of metal embossed in relief.

analo'gion, or **analo'gium,** a lectern or ambo.

analytique [Fr.] (anna lit teek), a problem in design which calls for the study of architectural elements.

anchor (ang'kor), a tie rod with plain or decorative end washers, to prevent bulging or separation of elements. 2. a metal bar attached to wood as a lag screw or to masonry by the expansion of its embedded end.

ancien [Fr.] (ah see anh), a senior student in a French atelier.

ancillary (ann'silary), a subordinate, auxiliary building in a group composition; a dependency.

ancon, ancone (an′kone), or crossette, a console form at the top of the architrave jamb, to support the cornice or over-door; sometimes merely a widening of the architrave as an "ear" at the top of the jamb (2*i*).

anco′na [It.], a formally set picture or group of pictures, as for an altarpiece. 2. a framed and architecturally important recess for a piece of sculpture.

andiroba (andy roe′bah) (*Carapa guianensis*), also called crabwood and carapa; a South American wood used for veneer, having the red-brown color of mahogany and a stripe figure when quarter-sawn.

and′iron, one of a pair of movable supports for logs in a fireplace.

an′dron, the part of a house, church, or monastery set apart for the use of men.

androsphinx (ann′dro sfinx), sculptured lion with human head, used in Egyptian art; the Sphinx at Ghizeh is an example of great size.

angan (ahn′gan), bedroom of an Igorot dwelling.

angelim amargoso (anje′leem am mar go′suh) (*Vatairea guianensis*, related to *Andira* sp.), a Brazilian wood, yellow when cut, becoming yellow-brown or somewhat reddish, with fine stripes.

ange′lim pedra (*Hymenolobium* sp.), Brazilian woods, pale red-brown with white streaks, darkening on exposure; close-textured with numerous pores; likely to be riddled with worm holes.

angelique (ahn je leek′) (*Dicorynia paraensis*), a heavy wood, resembling teak, from British, French, and Dutch Guiana, red-brown in color, clean and even in grain, moderately hard, tough, strong, elastic, and not difficult to work.

Angevin (ahn zhe vanh), the medieval style developed in Anjou, France.

Angkor-Vat (ahng′kor vaht), the architecturally famous ancient city of southern Siam.

angle bead (ang′el beed), a vertical member protecting or decorating the salient angle of a wall or partition.

an′gle beam, or **an′gle iron,** a rolled-steel beam of L section, the wings usually at right angles.

angle capital, a capital at the corner where a range of columns turns.

angsena, *see* narra.

Ang′strom, unit of wavelength, equal to a hundred-millionth of one centimeter.

anisomet′ric perspective, a form of orthogonal perspective in which the three main dimensions of objects are respectively at different inclinations to the plane of projection.

anneal′ing, slow cooling of heated glass or metal to decrease brittleness.

an′nex, a supplementary building added to, or used in connection with, a previously existing structure.

an′nular, ringlike. An annular vault is one springing from a pair of walls that are circular in plan and have the same center.

an′nulated column, a group of slender shafts apparently held together by encircling bands.

an′nulet, a fillet molding at the neck of a Doric column, sometimes in groups of three or even five (11*j*).

annun′ciator, an electromagtic device that indicates which of several circuits has been activated.

an′odize, to give an aluminum oxide coating by electrolytic action.

an′ta (plural, **antæ**), a thickening of a wall at its normal termination, as when the lateral walls of a Greek temple were extended beyond the front wall to form, with columns between, the porch. A porch thus arranged was called "in antis."

an′techamber, originally a room adjacent to the bedchamber of royalty or a high official. 2. a room subsidiary to an adjoining one.

an′techapel, that part of a chapel lying between the west wall and the choir screen; it would form the transept if a nave were added to the west.

antechoir (an′ty quire), a space more or less enclosed in front of a choir, especially the space between the inner and outer gates of a choir screen.

ante-cour [Fr.] (anty-kerr), an approach to the main body of a house; often a link with service quarters.

an′tefix (plural, **antefixæ**), an ornamental end for a course of tiles at the eaves line; sometimes also applied to a cresting (16*d*).

an′tenave, a narthex or porch west of the nave.

antepag′menta, the molded jambs of an opening; the corresponding lintel group of moldings was called the supercilium.

antepen′dium, the frontal of an altar.

antepo′dium, the seat for the clergy behind the podium in a choir.

anterides (anta ride′ees), in ancient architecture, the buttresses of a wall.

an′teroom, or **an′techamber,** a room of secondary use, often serving as a waiting-room or reception room to a space of greater importance.

anthemion (an thee′me un), conventionalized, decorative designs based on the honeysuckle or palmette, common in Greek architecture and minor arts (11*i*).

an′ticum, a porch of a front entrance, as distinguished from posticum, a porch of a rear entrance.

apa (*Afzelia* spp.), light brown woods, that darken on exposure, several species of which are produced commercially for utility lumber of the general character of teak.

apadana (ah pah dah′nah), main hall of a Persian palace.

aparejador (ah paray′hah dor), or **aparigerdor,** Spanish term for clerk of the works.

apart′ment, a suite of rooms. 2. a dwelling unit of a multifamily house.

apaya, *see* avodiré.

a′pex, top or peak of a pyramidal or conical form.

apitong (appee′tong) (*Dipterocarpus grandiflorus*), a wood from the Philippine Islands, red, hard, heavy, straight-grained, and of coarse texture.

apodyterium (appo dee tee′ reum), or **apoth′esis,** the robing-room of ancient public baths.

apophyge (appoff′egee), or **apoph′ysis,** the concave increase in diameter of classical column shaft where it joins base or capital (12).

apothe′ca, in ancient Greek architecture, a storage cellar for wine, oil, and the like.

apoth′esis, *see* apodyterium.

appen′tice, a hood over an entrance, supported by attachment to the wall.

appliqué [Fr.] (applee kay), ornament or enrichment applied or mounted on another material.

apprais′al, an estimate of value or of cost.

appui [Fr.] (ap we), a solid, separate member, as a windowsill or the top member of a parapet or balustrade.

a′pron, the trim member under the projecting interior sill of a window.

apse, or **apsis,** or **absis** (apps, app′sis, or ab′sis), the eastern or altar end of a basilica or church, usually semicircular in plan and vaulted with a half-dome (16*l*).

ap′sidal, containing or resembling an apse.

apsid′iole, a minor or secondary apse.

ap′teral, descriptive of a temple with porches at ends but without columns on the sides.

aquarium (ackware′eum), a container or building for the display of fish in water.

aqueduct (ak′wee dukt), an artificial support and channel for a stream of water, as built for the supply of ancient Rome and many modern cities.

Aquia Creek stone, a light gray and buff cretaceous sandstone quarried in Stafford County, Va.

ara, Roman term for altar.

arabesque (arrah besk′), a decorative pattern combining animal, plant, and, occasionally, human forms, used in Roman and Renaissance design. 2. a decorative pattern of interlaced lines or bands in geometrical forms, developed in Arabian design.

Arabotedesco (arrah′bo tee des′ ko), a modification of Byzantine architectural forms by Arabian or Saracenic motifs.

araca (arah′kah) (*Terminalia januarensis*), a hard and heavy wood from Brazil, used for veneers, having an olive-brown cast with straight, darker brown ribbon stripes.

ar′æostyle, *see* areostyle.

arariba (arrah ree′bah) (*Centrolobium* sp.), a Brazilian wood, commonly called balaustre or canarywood in the U.S.A. Of yellow or orange color, changing to red or brown, often variegated with red or black streaks.

araucaria (arah ka′rea) (*Araucaria araucana*), a tree native to southern Brazil, in England called "monkey puzzle." The wood closely resembles Parana pine in color and grain.

arbitra′tion, the adjudication of matters in dispute between two parties by one or more arbitrators selected by the parties.

ar′bor, a framework, sometimes partly filled in with lattice, for the support of vines.

arc [Fr.], an arch. 2. a division or foil of a trefoil, quatrefoil, cinquefoil, or multi-foil arch (1*r*).

arcade (ar kayd′), a range of arches with their supports. 2. a passageway, one side of which is a range of arches supporting a roof.

arcature (ar′kah chure), a miniature arcade, such as an arched balustrade.

arc-boutant [Fr.] (ark boo tanh), a flying buttress (7*g*).

arc-doubleau [Fr.] (ark doo blo), an arch forming a projection upon the main soffit or intrados of an arch, in section similar to that of a pilaster and its background.

arcella (ar kel′ah), in medieval architecture, a cheese room.

arc formeret [Fr.] (ark for meh ray), the wall arch or wall rib, or the corresponding rib coming next to the arcade between nave and aisle, as in Gothic vaulting.

arch (artch), a form of construction, usually of masonry, in which a number of units span an opening by carrying the downward thrust laterally to the next unit and finally to the abutments or vertical supports. Usually further described by its intrados outline, as round, elliptical, pointed, trefoil, etc. (1, 2).

bell arch, a semicircular arch supported on quarter-round corbels (1*n*).

blind arch, a relieving arch concealed behind a wall facing.

camber arch, an arch with concave intrados approaching the flat.

cinquefoil arch, an arch of five arcs (1*q*).

compound arch, an arch whose archivolt recedes successively from the face plane (2*f*).

drop arch, a form of the lancet arch in which the centers of the two halves are located within the span (1*j*).

Dutch arch, *see* flat arch.

equilateral arch, an arch whose span and radii of the two halves form an equilateral triangle (1*f*).

flat arch, an arch whose intrados is a horizontal line. Also called French arch and Dutch arch, especially when of bricks that are not wedge-shaped (1*a*).

floor arch, a structural vault form supported by longitudinal beams.

four-centered arch, an arch approximating elliptical form in which the intrados is a combination of four arcs of circles in two symmetrically disposed pairs (2*c*).

French arch, *see* flat arch.

horseshoe arch, an arch whose intrados includes more than a semicircle (1*g*).

imperfect arch, a round

arch whose intrados includes less than a semicircle.

inflected arch, an arch the curve of whose intrados reverses to form a point at the top (1*h*).

interlaced arch, a series of arches overlapping horizontally (2*h*).

inverted arch, or ogee arch, an arch used to balance two thrusts from above, instead of distributing a weight between two faces.

keel arch, *see* inflected arch.

lancet arch, a sharply pointed arch (1*i*).

miter arch, an "arch" which is really a lintel with opposed halves at an angle (1*o*).

multi-foil arch, an arch of more than five arcs (1*r*).

ogee arch, *see* inverted arch.

rampant arch, an arch with one abutment higher than the other (2*e*).

relieving arch, a segmental arch, usually a blind arch, above a lintel, for the purpose of relieving the lintel of the weight above (1*c*).

segmental arch, a round arch whose intrados includes less than a semicircle (1*d*, *e*).

stilted arch, an arch in which the center is above the impost line (1*b*).

three-centered arch, an arch approximating elliptical form in which the intrados is a combination of three arcs of circles, one centered between a symmetrically disposed pair (2*b*).

trefoil arch, an arch in several varieties where the radii are differently located (1*k*, *l*, *m*).

trimmer arch, a flat or segmental arch between chimney and a trimmer beam for the support of a hearth.

Tudor arch, an elliptical or pointed elliptical form, usually drawn as a three-, four-, or five-centered arch (2*a*, *b*, *c*, *d*).

Welsh "arch," a keystoned lintel (1*p*).

archaic (ar ka′ik), of or like a period before that of highest development.

arch band, the visible portion of a rib in vaulting.

archeion (ark a′eon), in the ancient Greek temple, a secret place for treasures.

archeology (ar kee ol′ogy), the study of history through artifacts.

ar′chitect, one skilled in the design of buildings and having technical knowledge of their construction.

architectonic (ar kitek ton′nick), having the constructive characteristic of architecture.

ar′chitecture, the art and science of designing and constructing buildings adapted to their purposes, one of which is beauty. 2. the products of architecture.

ar′chitrave, in classic architecture, the member of an entablature resting on the capitals of columns or piers and supporting the frieze (12). 2. the trim of door or window opening.

ar′chivolt, the molding defining the extrados of an arch (1*b*).

archivol′tum, in Medieval architecture, a sewer or cesspool.

arch′way, an opening or passageway spanned by an arch.

arc light, an electric light source depending on a voltaic arc between the ends of two carbon rods.

ar′cograph, an instrument for drawing arcs of a circle without striking them from a center as with a compass.

arcosolium (arko so′leum), an arched niche in the catacombs of Rome.

arcuated construction (ark′ yoo ated), stone masonry in compression, using arch and vault, in contradistinction to trabeated construction, that of the post and lintel.

arcus ecclesiæ (arkus eek lee′ zee eye), in Medieval architecture, the arch dividing nave from choir.

ar′dish, an East Indian form of decoration, achieved by embedding bits of glass in the plaster of walls or ceiling.

area (air′e ah), the surface within specific boundaries. 2. a light-well sunk before windows partly or wholly below grade.

arena (arree′nah), the open exhibition space in the center of an amphitheater.

arenatum (ahren ah′tum), a word used by Vitruvius to signify a kind of plaster or mortar of lime and sand.

areostyle (air′eo stile), one of the intercolumniation spacings used in classical architecture —that of four diameters, or even five. It was considered applicable only to the Tuscan order.

areosystyle (airy o sis′tile), intercolumniation alternately areostyle (four diameters) and systyle (two diameters).

argand burner, a gaslight source consisting of a hollow ring, through the inside face of which gas is emitted through a row of fine holes, forming a cylindrical flame.

argento (ar jen′to) (*Eucalyptus regnans*), another name for mountain ash, from Australia or Tasmania; the wood, used for fine veneers, is creamy white with irregular light brown wide streaks and a cross-fire similar to English harewood.

A.R.I.B.A., Associate of the Royal Institute of British Architects.

Arizona marble, varying to the extent of every color of the spectrum and in a wide scale of veinings. The principal productions are known as Apache Gold, Geronimo, and Navajo Black and Gold.

Arkansas marble, a group name given to several colorful and decorative varieties quarried near Batesville and known as Ozark Famosa, Ozark Fleuri, Ozark Rouge, and St. Clair.

ar′mature, iron bars or framing to help support slender columns, tracery, and the like. 2. in sculpture, similar support for modeling clay or plaster.

armoire (ar mwar), a cupboard or cabinet. 2. an ambry.

armored cable, *see* BX.

ar′mory, a building for the use of a military organization.

aromilla (ahro meel′ah) (*Terminalia amazonia*), also called nargusta; a wood from Mexico and British Honduras, light in color, with an attractive figure of wavy red-brown lines. It is hard to work on account of the cross grain and requires expert dry kilning.

arotelle (ah ro tel′lee), of or bearing circular ornaments.

ar′ras, a tapestry or other woven fabric used as a wall hanging.

arricciate [It.] (arritch e ah′ teh), the middle coat of three-part fresco painting, the first coat being rinzaffato, the final coat, intonaco.

ar′ris, the edge of an external angle. 2. the ridge between adjoining flutes of a Doric column (11*j*).

articled clerk (ar′tikeld), an apprentice by written covenant.

ar′tifact, that which is produced by human art.

artif′icer, a craftsman with art and skill.

artific′ial stone, a substitute for building stone made by casting selected aggregates and cement in molds.

artisan (ar′tizan), a trained workman in industry.

ar′tist, one skilled in any of the fine arts.

Art Nouveau [Fr.] (ar noo vo), a phase of reaction against tradition, originating in France and Germany about 1900, in which designers glorified the curved line.

asarotum (assa roe′tum), a painted pavement used by the Romans before the use of mosaic surfaces.

asbes′tos, a fibrous mineral used as a barrier against fire.

A.S.C.E., American Society of Civil Engineers.

ash (*Fraxinus* spp.), hardwoods of the eastern U.S.A., ranking high in weight, strength, resistance to shock and wear, and ability to hold a formed shape; used in manufacture of doors and other interior woodwork; heartwood warm brown, sapwood white.

European ash (*Fraxinus excelsior*), a term including wood from English, French, and Turkish sources; the English ash resembles olivewood in its grayish white color, showing, in burl veneer, variations of wavy, curly grain.

mountain ash, *see* argento.

ash dump, a receptacle beneath a fireplace into which ashes are dumped through a frame and door in the hearth.

ash′lar, masonry having a face of square or rectangular stones.

asperso′rium, Latin term for a stoup or holy water basin.

asphalt (ass′fault), a bituminous substance used for paving, roofs, etc., in combination with sand and crushed rock.

as′tragal, a molding of half-round profile (12). 2. the molded strip covering the junction of a pair of doors or casements.

astylar (eh sty′lar), lacking column or pilaster.

asylum (as eye′lum), originally a place of sanctuary; now a building for the shelter and care of children or patients with more or less chronic illnesses.

asymmetry (ass sim′etree), lack of symmetry, but possibly with axial balance.

atelier [Fr.] (attel yay), studio of an artist. 2. a studio or drafting-room where design is taught.

Athenian (ah thee′nee an), adjective, characteristic of the center of Greek art, Athens.

atlantes (at lan′tees), male figures corresponding to the more familiar female figures, caryatids, used as masonry supports.

atrium (a′tree um), the open-roofed entrance court of a Roman dwelling.

at′tic, a low story of a building, just under the roof. 2. a low story above the main cornice of a classical building.

Attic (at′tik), characteristic of Attica of ancient Greece.

Attic base, a base for columns commonly used by the Romans, the upper and lower torus with scotia and fillets between.

auditorium (aw dit tor′eum), a room or building designed to meet the needs and comfort of an audience.

aula (aw′lah), in ancient Greek architecture, a court or hall.

aum′bry, *see* almery.

aviary (a′vee airy), a compartment, or whole building, set aside for the keeping of birds.

avocado (ahvo cah′doe) (*Persea americana*), also known as alligator pear; a native tree of the Antilles, Mexico, and Central America but cultivated in all tropical countries, furnishing a handsome cabinet wood, light red-brown in color, fine-textured and easy to work.

avodiré (ahvo deer′ay) (*Turraeanthus africana*), a West African wood also called apaya; used as lumber and for fine veneers, its color ranging from paper white to a light, golden cream shade; fine-textured, strongly figured.

awn′ing, a sheltering screen, often of fabric on a hinged support, over a window, door, outside walk or the like.

axe [Fr.] (ax), axis.

ax′ial, having an axis.

ax′is (*axe* in French), an imaginary line in plan or elevation dividing symmetrical parts.

Ax′minster, a town in England which gave its name to a long-pile hand-tufted carpet.

axonomet′ric perspective, *see* orthogonal perspective.

ayan (eye′an) (*Distemonanthus benthamianus*), also called movingui; a wood from West Africa, the light yellow background resembling satinwood but with a more open grain; used chiefly for veneer.

ayous (eye′use) (*Triplochiton scleroxylon*), a West African wood, known as obeche and by many other names; a clean, creamy white wood with a fairly open, uniform grain; weathers to a light brownish yellow; used for fine veneer.

Az′tec architecture, work of the warlike Aztecs, who for a century before the coming of the Spanish conquerors in 1519 had flourished by capturing and sacrificing the neighboring peoples.

azulejo [Sp.] (assoo leh′hoh), a glazed decorative tile in which blue is prominent.

B

back′band, the outer molding member of casing for door or window.

back filling, the earth and broken stone used to fill that part of an excavation between the outside foundation wall and grade.

back hearth, that part of a fireplace floor between the side walls and behind the face.

back′ing (of a wall), employment of less costly materials and workmanship behind an exterior facing; the backing face itself is usually furred with interior finish of other materials.

back plastering, a coating of plaster on the side of the lath opposite the finished surface.

badia [It.] (bah dee′ah), abbreviation of abbadia, an abbey church.

badigeon (bah dij′on), plastic patching material for minor defects in stonework or in woodwork.

baf′fle, a partial obstruction against direct flow, as in a pipe or duct.

bagnio (bahn′yo), a bath or bathhouse. 2. a brothel. 3. in Turkey, a prison.

bag′tikan (*Parashorea malaanonan*), a hard, heavy, coarse-textured wood from the Philippines; pale white to light red, sometimes with a slight brownish tinge.

baguette (bag et′), a small molding of the astragal type, sometimes embellished by carving (13).

bahay (bah e′), a Philippine Islands dwelling.

bahut (buy ut′), a medieval cupboard. 2. the rounded top course of a masonry wall.

baignoire [Fr.] (bain wahr), one of the lowest tier boxes in a French theater.

bai′ley, the external wall of a feudal castle, or any similar circuit wall.

baked finish, paint or varnish requiring baking at temperatures above 150° F. for the development of desired properties.

baku, *see* makoré.

balaneia (bah lan eye′ah), Greek term for a bath.

balaustre, *see* arariba.

balconet′, the combination of railing and opening as in a balcony, but without the latter's floor space.

bal′cony, a projecting railed platform in front of a window or door, sometimes sheltered. 2. in a theater or auditorium, an upper tier of seats.

baldachin, or **baldachino** [It.] (bal′de kin, or bal de kee′no), a canopy supported or suspended over an altar, throne, or tomb.

balistraria (ballis tray′re ah), in medieval strongholds, an archer's aperture in the form of a cross.

ball catch, a form of friction latch with a small spring-activated ball which engages a slot on the jamb.

ball-flower, an ornament roughly spherical in shape, the front separation of three conventionalized petals revealing an inner ball; usually the ball-flower is one of a series set in a concave molding (9*p*).

ballie pole, a rough-hewn pole used in Iran for structural framework and scaffolding.

ballium (bal'leum), in Medieval architecture, the court or open space within a stronghold.

balloon' frame, the type of timber framing in which the studs are continuous, without a girt for second-floor joists.

ball'room, a large room for social assemblies.

ball valve, a valve controlled by a lever with ball float.

balnea (plural, **balneæ**) (bol'ne ah, bol'ne aye), the Roman public bath, usually plural.

bal'sa (*Ochroma* spp.), known also as corkwood; lightest in weight of all woods, weighs but 7½ pounds per cubic foot when oven dry. The wood is pinkish white, soft, and porous.

bal'samo (*Dalbergia* sp.), pink to purplish red wood with darker, wavy lines of red, shading almost into black; a dense, hard, strong, fine-grained wood used for lumber and fine veneer.

bal'teus, literally, a belt; præcinctio; the band forming the junction of the volutes in an Ionic capital (13). 2. the wide step between tiers of seats in an ancient theater or amphitheater.

bal'uster, a miniature column or other form of upright which, in series, supports a handrail, as in a balustrade.

balustrade', a railing or parapet consisting of a handrail on balusters, sometimes on a base member and sometimes interrupted by piers.

banaba (bah nah'bah) (*Lagerstroemia speciosa*), a Philippine wood, hard, heavy, strong, and durable; ashy rose to reddish brown in color.

banak, *see* virola.

band, band course, or **band molding,** a flat, horizontal member of relatively slight projection, marking a division in the wall plane.

banded column, one with its drums alternately larger in diameter than the shaft proper, or more or less richly decorated; fairly common in the French Renaissance.

bandelet', a small band encircling a column shaft.

ban'derole, a sculptured or painted band, ribbon-like, as for an inscription.

band shell, a bandstand supplied with a sounding board of shell shape.

ban'ister, corruption of baluster.

bank, a building, or occasionally merely a room, in which is conducted a banking business.

ban'quet hall, a large room designed for use on festal or other important occasions.

banquette [Fr.] (bang ket), a sidewalk of about 18″ width.

banuyo (bah nu'yo) (*Wallaceodendron celebicum*), a Philippine wood, light to dark brown in color; hard and heavy; works well for carving.

baptistery, or **baptistry** (bap′ tiss tree), that part of a church set apart for the rite of baptism. 2. the pool for baptism by immersion.

bar, a counter over which refreshments are served, or the room in which the counter is located.

barabara (bar′eh bar′eh), a sod house of Alaska.

barbacan, or **barbican** (bar′ba kan), a watchtower on, or outside of, a stronghold.

B.Arch., abbreviation for the degree of Bachelor of Architecture.

Bardiglio (bar dee′leo), a marble available in several varieties, generally having a bluish gray ground traversed by dark veins. It is quarried at Mont' Alto in southern Tuscany. In one variety, Bardiglio Fiorito, the veining gives a fancied resemblance to flowers.

barge′board, or **verge′board,** the vertical-face board following, and set back under, the roof edge of a gable, sometimes decorated by carving (7*e*).

bargello [It.] (bar zhel′lo), headquarters of an army watch or civil police.

bar joist, a truss form of steel top and bottom members, of plates, channels, or T-sections, with heavy wire or rod web lacing; used for floor and roof supports.

barn, a building for housing cattle or horses, for storage of hay or other crops, or for a combination of such purposes.

Baroque (bar oke′), a style developed during the late Renaissance in reaction from classical forms; characterized by elaboration of scrolls, curves, and carved ornament.

barrab′kie, an Eskimo hut.

bar′racks, a building for the housing of soldiers, police, or groups of workers.

bar′rel vault, semicircular vaulting unbroken by ribs or groins.

bartisan (bar′tizan), a turret for a flagstaff. 2. a turret projecting from a corner of a tower or of a parapet.

barycæ, or **barycephalæ** (barry′ki, barry seffa′li), Greek term for an areostyle temple.

ba′salt, an igneous rock of fine grain, high density, and dark color.

bas′cule bridge, a bridge having a balancing section to form a drawbridge.

base, a lower supporting member; when applied to a building, it is the first clearly defined mass above grade; in a classical column, it is the part between shaft and pedestal (if any) or paving (12, 13).

baseboard, the skirting member at the junction of wall and floor.

base block, the squared block terminating a molded baseboard at an opening.

base course, in masonry, the lowest course, or footing, of a wall or pier.

base′ment, the substructure of a building, partly or wholly below grade.

basilica (bah sill′ikah), in Roman architecture, a hall of justice, rectangular in plan, with a nave and aisles; adopted as a type for early Christian churches (16*l*).

ba′sin, a receptacle for water. 2. in plumbing installations, the lavatory.

basketweave, a checkerboard pattern used in masonry, wood inlay, and painting. (*See* 3*n*, *o* for brick paving.)

bas-relief (bah′releef), sculpture or carving with slight projection from the background.

basse cour [Fr.] (bos cur), the service court or stable court in a château or villa of some size.

basso-rilievo [It.] (bahso rilly a′ vo), bas-relief.

bass′wood (*Tilia americana*), also called linden and, in Europe, limewood; fine-textured, soft, light in weight and easily worked; used for Venetian blinds, furniture, millwork, core material, and plywood.

bastide [Fr.] (bass teed), in the Middle Ages, a town erected by fiat and according to a specified plan.

bastile [Fr.] (bass teel), a fortified tower. Le Bastile de la Porte S. Antoine is the chief state prison of France, built by Charles V.

bas′tion, a projecting mass in a fortification, usually half of a hexagon in plan, from which the adjacent perimeter can better be defended.

bat, half of a broken brick. 2. a unit of flat, wrapped insulation.

bate′ment light, a window with its sill aslant from the usual horizontal; the shape implies abatement of the light.

batete (bah teh′teh) (*Kingiodendron alternifolium*), a wood from the Philippines; reddish brown turning to very dark brown with age or exposure; moderately fine texture and cross-grained.

bath, the tub for human bathing, or the room containing it and other plumbing fixtures, when it is usually called bathroom.

bath′room, a room providing bathing and toilet facilities.

bath′tub, a tub for human bathing, usually a fixed plumbing installation.

batikuling (batty keu′leeng) (*Litsea leytensis*), a tree of the Philippine Islands supplying a light-weight light-colored wood that takes a high polish.

bat′ten, a cleatlike member laid across a series of boards to fasten them together. 2. a narrow strip member covering the vertical joint between two boards.

bat′ter, a slope upward and backward from the perpendicular in wall or pier.

bat′terboard, a horizontal board on stakes outside an excavation, used to support lines indicating foundation walls and levels.

bat′tlement, a parapet, the top of which is broken by slots or embrasures (8*b*).

bay, the portion of a plan or of a building contained between adjacent piers or columns. 2. a bay window.

bay′tree, *see* myrtle burl.

bay window, a window or windows in a wall that projects angularly from another wall and from the ground up. *See also* bow window and oriel window.

bazaar (baz ahr′), a group of retail shops.

bead, or **stop-bead** (beed), a strip, usually of wood and with one edge molded, against which a sash slides or a door closes.

bead-and-reel, a molding having a profile of approximately half a circle or more, in which bead forms, singly or in groups, alternate with disc forms (10*c*).

bead molding, one having a small half-round or half-spherical section, continuous or divided into beadlike forms.

beak, a drip mold.

beak-head molding, one common in Norman architecture, using grotesque heads in a series, all heads terminating in a pointed chin or beak (9*k*).

beak molding, *see* bird's-beak molding.

beam, a horizontal, weight-supporting member of a structural frame.

beamed ceiling, a ceiling in which the beams, cased or uncased, are a purposeful part of the design.

bear′er, a horizontal supporting member across studding; a ribbon.

bear′ing, the support, or surface of same, upon which a structural load rests. 2. the length of bearing given a beam or joist upon a wall.

Bear's Den Gray, a granite of warm gray color, medium grain, quarried **at** Mason, N. H.

beaux-arts [Fr.] (boze ar), fine arts.

École des Beaux-Arts (akole day boze ar), the national school of fine arts in France.

bed, of a stone or other masonry unit, the surface upon which it is laid in the mortar; with a stone, the natural bed is a horizontal cleavage in quarrying.

bed molding, or **bed mold,** the member in a series of moldings on which others are superimposed. In classical architecture, the molding above which the corona projects.

bed′room, a room designed primarily for sleeping.

beech, American (*Fagus grandifolia*), a hard, stiff, strong hardwood with reddish brown heartwood and white sapwood; plentiful throughout eastern U.S.A.; low in resistance to decay; difficult to season because of shrinkage and tendency to warp.

European beech (*Fagus sylvatica*), a wood similar to American beech, but preferred to the American product by furniture makers.

white beech, *see* cooinnew.

bel-étage [Fr.] (bell ay tahzhe), the principal story of a building.

bel′fry, a small bell tower, nearly always a part of a building.

Bel′gian Black, a marble from Belgium of a deep, uniform black, and very hard.

bell, in classical architecture, the bare vase form of the Corinthian capital, around which the acanthus leaves are grouped (14*c*). 2. an electrical device for producing a ringing sound when the electrical circuit is closed. 3. a form made of metal for sounding a musical tone with the aid of a clapper.

bell gable, bell turret, or **bell cot,** a substitute support and shelter for a church bell, common in Early English Gothic, usually topping the gable of the west end.

Bellingham, a medium- to coarse-grained granite, pink, black, and pearl gray with some thin, black lines; quarried in Bellingham, Minn.

belt course, *see* band.

belvedere′, an open pavilion built for a view, either on top of a building or as an independent building.

bema (Gr., a platform) (bee′ ma), the sanctuary or chancel of Eastern or Oriental churches. 2. the open space between the termination of the arcade of a basilica and its eastern wall; perhaps the embryo of the transept.

benatu′ra, the vessel for holy water placed inside the entrances to some churches.

bench mark, a datum point from which differences in level are reckoned.

bench table, a low stone seat on the inner walls or around piers, usually of churches.

bend′ing moment, a measure of the forces tending to break a beam by bending.

benin, *see* tigerwood. African walnut.

bent, a framework support, prefabricated at mill or on the ground, as one of the supports of an overhead pipe line or the like.

Berea sandstone, a fine-grain Ohio sandstone, quarried at Amherst, Ohio, of very light buff, gray, or mixtures of gray and buff; evenly bedded, even texture, easily carved. There is also a Berea Spiderweb, gray with irregular, streaked brownish lines.

berm, a bank of earth, as the piled-up earth along a canal or against a masonry wall.

besant, bezant (bay′zant), or **byzant,** a circular-disc ornament in series upon a molding; common in Norman architecture.

bethabara (betha bar′ah) (*Tabebuia* spp.), woods from South America that are hard, brown, and oily, and resemble teak; used mainly for timber.

béton [Fr.] (bay tonh), concrete.

bev′el, a sloped or canted surface contiguous with a vertical or horizontal one.

beveled siding, *see* siding.

bezant′ee, a molding of the Norman period simulating Byzantine coins or bezants.

bib, bibb, or **bibcock,** a terminal valve in a pipe. 2. a faucet (usually so termed when the pipe carries a liquid).

bibliotheca [Lat.] (bib leo tha′ kah), **bibliothèque** [Fr.] (beeb leo take), library.

bidet [Fr.] (bee day), a bathroom fixture of the sitz-bath group.

bilin′ga (*Sarcocephalus* spp.), woods from the west coast of Africa, yellow to reddish with reddish brown, diagonal stripes; used for veneer.

bil′let molding, a molding used chiefly in Norman architecture (9*q*).

bil'lywebb (*Sweetia panamensis*), a wood from Mexico, Central, and northern South America, light brown and lustrous; used mainly for veneer.

bi'otite, brown or dark green mica, a magnesium iron silicate.

birch (bertch), a wood of northeastern U.S.A., commercially distributed in two varieties, yellow birch (*Betula lutea*) and sweet birch (*Betula lenta*); even-textured, hard, strong wood used for flooring, interior woodwork, and veneer.

Norway burl birch (*Betula alba*), a wood from Norway, Sweden, and Finland, somewhat resembling bird's-eye maple; used chiefly for veneer.

bird's-beak molding, a drip mold found notably in the cap of the anta or pilaster of the Doric order.

bird's-eye, a group of grain patterns visible in many veneers, particularly in maple.

bird's-eye view, or **bird's-eye perspective,** one of which the station point is above the object.

bird's-head molding, a medieval molding using a conventionalized, pendant bird (9*m*).

bishop's throne, the seat of state in a cathedral, formerly *en axe* in the apse; later, generally in the southeast corner of the choir.

bitu'minous, describing cement, mastic, or roofing, indicating a product in which asphalt is a major ingredient.

Black-and-Gold, a marble of which the best quality has a jet-black ground with chain veining of old-gold color in fairly even pattern. It comes from the Isle of Tino, Gulf of Spezia, Italy.

black bean, Australian (*Castanospermum australe*), a coarse-textured, straight-grained wood with texture somewhat resembling chestnut; fairly hard and heavy, resembling teak; used for veneer.

Black Diamond, igneous rock of the gabbro or "black granite" class, with a fine and uniform grain; quarried at Escondido, Calif.

Black Vista, a cross-grained, easily worked granite, classed among the blacks; quarried near San Diego, Calif.

black'wood, African (*Dalbergia melanoxylon*), also called Mozambique ebony or congowood; a hard, close-textured, dark purple wood used chiefly for veneer. There is also an Australian blackwood (*Acacia melanoxylon*) of a deep, reddish brown color.

bleed'ing, the diffusion of coloring matter through a coating from the substrata; also the discoloration arising from such diffusion.

Bleu Belge, a marble having a blue-black ground with thin, straight, pure white veins suggesting in pattern the twigs of a tree. As the name suggests, it comes from Belgium.

blight (blite), in a city or community, an existing area in which the property has deteriorated below acceptable standards.

blind, a window shade. 2. a louvered shutter.

Venetian blind, a screen for door or window, formed of horizontal slats supported on vertical strips of webbing. It is capable of being collapsed into a small space when raised, and the slats are movable to admit or exclude light.

blind arch, *see* arch.

blind nailing, nailing driven in such a way that the nail heads are concealed.

blind′story, a term sometimes applied to a triforium, as contrasting with a clerestory (7*g*).

blocage [Fr.] (blo kazh), coarse, slovenly masonry.

block, the space, and buildings, contained within an unintersected perimeter of streets in the gridiron plan; it may contain alleys or culs-de-sac.

block′house, a fortified structure, usually of hewn logs.

block′ing, internal members of wall furring, or the like, to afford fastening and rigidity for the outside shell. 2. a little-used term for a parapet.

block plan, one that is simplified to the bare essentials.

blue′print, a positive print with white lines on blue background, made on ferroprussiate paper from a translucent drawing as negative, and developed in water.

blue′stone, a bluish gray sandstone of fine texture used for paving, coping, stair treads, etc.

board (bord), a flat piece of wood having a nominal thickness of 1″ or less and a width of 4″ or more. If thicker, but not over 3″, it is usually called a plank; if thicker still, a timber.

board foot, unit of lumber measurement, 1″ x 12″ x 12″.

board measure, the common measure of lumber, of which the unit is the board foot.

boast, to surface a stone with broad chisel (boasting chisel) and mallet.

bob, a plumb bob.

Bois Jourdain (bwah zhurdane), a French fossiliferous marble, dark gray in tone, having white veins with a reddish tinge and small red markings.

Boise sandstone (boy′ze), trade name for an Idaho sandstone of medium grain, varying from light gray and buff to darker tones, often with brown and purple veinings.

bolection molding (bo lek′ shun), originally a panel molding which projected beyond the face of the rails and stiles; hence a molding of unusually large and broad convex projection.

bol′lard, a stone guard against damage to a wall corner by encroaching traffic; also a free-standing stone post to obstruct or direct vehicular traffic.

bolongita (bolong eta) (*Diospyros pilosanthera*), a tree of the Philippine Islands producing a reddish wood streaked with black.

bolster (bowl′ster), a horizontal member used on top of a post or column to lengthen the bearing (16*f*). 2. the cushion-like member joining the volutes of an Ionic column, the balteus (13).

bond, in masonry, the overlapping of joints in successive courses and the employment of units that project laterally into adjacent courses or through the wall.

bonds, in brickwork, *see* Plate 3.

common bond, courses of stretchers, breaking joints, with each sixth course one of headers (3*a*).

Dutch bond, like English bond except at the corners, where a three-quarter brick finishes the stretcher course and the closer is omitted in the header course.

English bond, alternate courses of headers and of stretchers (3*d*).

English cross bond, alternate courses of headers and of stretchers, with the stretcher course breaking joints with its neighboring stretcher courses (3*g*).

English garden wall bond, three courses of stretchers followed by one of headers (3*f*).

Flemish bond, alternate headers and stretchers in each course, breaking joints as illustrated (3*b*).

Flemish diagonal bond, alternating headers and stretchers in a course, followed by a course of stretchers, arranged as illustrated (3*h*).

Flemish double-stretcher bond, a header alternating with two stretchers, breaking joints as illustrated (3*e*).

Flemish garden wall bond, a header followed by three or four stretchers, the courses breaking joints in various ways, one of which is illustrated (3*i*).

garden wall cross bond, a header followed by three stretchers, alternating as a course with one of stretchers (3*c*).

heading bond, a wall brick-length in thickness, with all headers on both faces.

bonjon, *see* tepesuchil.

bon′net tile, or **hip tile,** a roofing tile of approximately semicylindrical shape, used for covering the roofing along a hip.

book′lift, a small elevator, usually in public libraries, for service between bookstacks and delivery points.

book′stack, a tier of shelving for a library.

booth, an open-front stall in a market. 2. a compartment for an individual, as a ticket-seller's booth, or a telephone booth.

bor′ing, a drilling into the earth to bring up samples of the soil to be found at various depths, with the purpose of estimating the load-carrying capacity of the soil.

bosquet [Fr.] (bos kay), a small clump of trees.

boss (bahss), an ornamental form, usually with considerable projection, at the intersection of groin ribs or in the center of a panel or coffer (8*c*).

bossage (bahs′age), a stone in the rough left projecting from a wall, to be sculptured later. 2. coursed ashlar with a roughly dressed or projecting face.

bosse, *see* guarea.

Boston lap, a method of finishing the ridge of a shingled roof with a shingle course having overlapping vertical joints (7*f*).

Botticino (botty chee′no), an Italian marble of two kinds: Light, having a light coffee color with lighter, creamy-white patches, and also characterized by slender, wavy, golden-brown veins and very thin, hardly noticeable veins of calcite; Botticino Dark, a brownish cream or light brown ground color with clouds of darker shade scattered through the mass, and with very small hairlike veins of yellow.

boudoir (boo′dwar), a lady's dressing-room.

bouldering (bowl′dering), paving with cobblestones.

bouleuterion (boo loi tee′reon), in ancient Greece, the house of the Senate.

bow compass (bo kom′pas), a drafting instrument for drawing small circles, its radius adjusted by a setscrew working against a spring.

bow-string truss, a truss form in which both upper assembly and bottom chord are convex with their projections above the horizontal.

bowtell, or **boutell** (bo tell′), a Gothic molding resembling the classical torus.

bow window (bo win′do), a projecting window, or group of windows, the wall beneath which extends to the ground, and the face of which is an arc in plan.

box, a private compartment seating a group of persons in a theater or opera house.

boxed gutter, a roof gutter sunk behind the eaves so as to be concealed.

box girder (gur′der), a girder having a hollow, rectangular cross section.

boziga (bo zee gah), old term for a dwelling.

brace, any oblique member set to hold steady one of the principal members of a frame or other structure.

brack′et, a supporting member for a projecting floor or shelf, sometimes in the shape of an inverted L and sometimes as a solid piece or a triangular truss.

bracket capital, a capital having bracket forms projecting as a continuing support of the lintel; found particularly in Hindu, Saracenic, and early Spanish Renaissance work (15*c*).

brack′eted stair, one in which the exposed ends of steps bear a decorative scroll-bracket form.

brand′rith, a rail or fence enclosing a well.

brass, an alloy of copper and zinc, with decorative and wearing qualities. Movable parts of much hardware are of brass. 2. a generic term given inscription plates countersunk in the face of tombs, and the like.

brat′tishing, battlement, parapet, or cresting.

Brazil nut (*Bertholletia excelsa*), a wood resembling walnut and often used as a substitute therefor.

break (brake), a change in direction, as of a wall.

break ground, to start an excavation.

break joints, to arrange a course of masonry so that its vertical joints are not in line with those of the course just below.

breakfast-room (brek'fst), a room designed for the serving of the morning meal.

breast (brest), a projecting portion of a wall, usually in connection with a chimney.

breast-summer, a summer beam along the top of, and flush with, a curtain wall or partition which affords the beam no support.

breccia [It.] (bretch'ea), stone in which angular pieces are imbedded in a matrix of the same or another composition. Many of the marbles are breccias.

breeze'way, *see* dogtrot.

bretesse (bre tess'), a crenelated tower or bay of wood in medieval fortifications.

Briar Hill sandstone, an Ohio stone with decided variegations in the marking of its general buff color, blending from a golden buff to mottled and banded markings of deeper shades.

brick, a masonry unit, commonly about 2″ x 4″ x 8″, of a kiln-burned clay mixture.

brick nog'ging, filling of brickwork in timber framing.

brick veneer, an outer covering of 4″ brick wall tied to a wood-frame wall.

brick'work, masonry of brick, either structural or paving.

bridge, a structure spanning a trench, ravine, river, or the like.

bridg'ing, diagonal bracing set in a row across a series of parallel joists, or the like. In England it is called strutting.

bri'dle iron, a support by which the end of one beam is carried by another, usually at right-angles to the first. Also called stirrup iron or stirrup (4*e*).

bright tin plate (brite), sheet steel coated with tin. Terne plate is a similar roofing material with a coating over the steel of 20% tin and 80% lead.

brightness, of color, the quantitative aspect of the mental image. Quality factors in color are hue, saturation, and brightness.

Brignoles (brin yo les), a family name for three marbles of French origin: Jaune de Brignoles, having a light yellowish and gold ground, streaked with interlacing veins of vivid pink and red, and also bearing spots, streaks, and clouds of crystalline white; Rose de Brignoles and Violet de Brignoles have much the same description but with more rose and violet spots, respectively.

briquet (bric ket'), a compressed block, such as that made of concrete for testing purposes.

brise-soleil [Fr.] (breeze so lay ee), literally, sun-break; an architectural shield, fixed or movable, on the exterior of a building to block the entrance of unwanted sun rays.

broach (brotch), to enlarge or ream a hole (usually in stone). 2. to dress a stone roughly. 3. a squinch. 4. one of the semipyramidal slopes at the corners of an octagonal spire springing from a square tower.

broach spire, a spire developed directly upon its tower walls, without interruption of setback or parapet.

broken pediment, one interrupted at the top by the return of its moldings on themselves, leaving a space usually filled by a vase form or other ornament on a centered pedestal (10*a*, *h*).

brolet'to [It.], a town hall or other municipal building.

bron'teum, in ancient Greek theaters, an underfloor space for the sound effect of thunder.

bronze, an alloy of copper and tin, frequently including other elements; widely used for sculpture castings and for the most durable metalwork.

bronz'ing, surface covering of a metallic powder carried in a liquid vehicle.

brown'stone, a sandstone of reddish brown color. Many so-called "brownstone fronts," however, were of imitation masonry in stucco.

B.t.u., British thermal unit, the amount of heat required to raise one pound of water one degree Fahrenheit at or near its greatest density.

bubinga (boo bing'ah) (*Guibourtia tessmanii*), also called African rosewood, a hard, heavy wood from West Africa, with pink or red stripes against a red-brown background; used chiefly for veneer.

Buckeye sandstone, a siliceous sandstone of Ohio that is available in several varieties which are uniform in texture and possess unusual enduring qualities: B. Gray, B. Buff, B. Golden Vein, B. Mahogany, B. Spiderweb.

buckle (buk'el), to curve from the normal line or face under strain.

buck'stay, an upright member, usually in cross-connected pairs, reinforcing a masonry furnace or flue. 2. any similar brace member.

bucranium (bew kra'neum), sculptured ox skull occurring on the friezes of the Roman orders of architecture.

Buffneato (buf ne ah'to), a marble of buff ground color, varying slightly in tone, with numerous tiny dark brown specks and fossils, evenly distributed. It is quarried near Trieste.

buhl (byool), a form of decoration developed by André-Charles Boule (1642–1732), in which woodwork was inlaid with metal or tortoise shell.

build (bild), to erect a structure.

building board, *see* compo board.

build'ing paper, paper used as interlining, as between sheathing and outside wall covering, or between rough and finish flooring.

built-up', term indicating the assembly of pieces or layers to complete a product.

built-up' roof'ing, an outer covering of a comparatively flat roof, consisting of several layers of impregnated felt, each layer mopped with hot tar or asphalt as laid, and the top layer finished with a protective covering of slag or fine gravel.

bulk′head, a structure built to prevent earth from sliding into an excavation; hence, the outside cellar entrance with its sloping cover. 2. a structure carried above floor or roof as a means of lighting, or to cover the head of an elevator shaft or the like.

bull-nose, convex rounding of a member, such as the front edge of a stair tread. 2. a rounded-end tile or brick.

bull's-eye, a circular window or louver, an œil-de-bœuf.

bungalow (bung′gal lo), in India, a one-story house, usually with thatched roof covering also the veranda; widely used term for one-story residential types.

bunk, a built-in bed.

burl, wood taken from a knotty part of a tree; usually a veneer having a characteristic curly pattern.

bush′hammer, a tool used by stone masons for dressing stones to a face surface; made of steel plates bolted together with channels between the cutting edges.

butt, or **butt hinge,** the common two-plate door hinge, with fixed or removable pivot pins.

butternut (*Juglans cinerea*), a pale brown, satiny wood with soft texture, resembling American walnut in grain; used chiefly for veneer.

but′tery, a storeroom for provisions; originally *bouteillerie,* a pantry.

butt joint, a meeting of two members squarely end to end.

but′ton, a small bar of wood or metal, turning on a central screw pivot, to fasten doors.

but′tonwood, *see* sycamore, American.

but′tress, an abutting pier which strengthens a wall, sometimes taking the thrust of an inner arch.

flying buttress, one that includes a rampant arch to carry the inner thrust to the pier (7*g*).

buz′zer, an electric signaling device resembling a small electric bell but with a buzzing sound instead of a ring.

BX, a cable form of insulated wire, the outer covering of which is a helical binding of interlocking, flexible steel strips. Also called armored cable.

byzant (buys′ant), **besant,** or **bezant,** a circular disc in series upon a molding; common in Norman architecture.

Byzantine architecture (biz an′teen), a style which had its beginnings about four centuries before Christ, and still persists, characterized chiefly by the use of domical construction with pendentives (7*b*) in brick and concrete, sheathed in marble and glass mosaics. It takes its name from Byzantium, founded about 750 B.C., which in 324 A.D. became the capital of the Roman Empire.

C

cabaña (kah bahn′yah), in its Spanish origin, a hut, cabin, or hovel; in recent use, a bathhouse.

cabil′do, chapter house of a cathedral or collegiate church.

cab′in, a shelter more finished than a shack but less than a cottage.

cab′inetwork, generic term for interior woodwork that is the product of the joiner or woodworking plant.

ca′ble, a bead set in the lower third of a flute. 2. heavy wire rope or group of parallel wires for a member in tension. 3. waterproof insulated electrical conductor.

cable molding, a ropelike molding, as found in Norman architecture (9*j*).

Caen stone (kahn stone), a fine-textured stone quarried near Caen, France; it is soft when quarried, permitting sharp carving, and hardens with exposure.

café (kaf fay′), a room or building for the sale and serving of refreshments.

cafeteria (kaffa tee′rea), a self-service restaurant.

cage, an elevator for temporary use during the construction of a building, usually incompletely enclosed.

cairn (kehrn), a memorial heap of stones.

caisson (kays′sahn), an air chamber without bottom, used in excavation through water or mud, and carrying down on its own top the beginning of a masonry foundation. 2. a sunken panel in a flat or vaulted ceiling (from the Italian *cassone*).

calathus (kalay′thus), the bell or core of the Corinthian capital (14*c*).

calcaire-grossière [Fr.] (kal sair gro see air), a fossiliferous limestone of the Paris basin, locally used for building.

calcimine (kal′sim mine), a cold-water paint of whiting, glue, coloring matter and water, used chiefly on plaster ceilings.

cal′cite, calcium carbonate in hexagonal crystals. Massive varieties are chalk, limestone, and marble.

caldarium (kal day′reum), the hot-bath section of a Roman bathing establishment.

calefactory (kally fak′tree), the heated sitting-room of a monastery.

calf's-tongue molding, one having a series of pointed, tongue-like members in line in relief against a plane or curved surface; sometimes radiating from a common center. It is found in archivolts of early medieval British architecture.

caliduct (kall′e dukt), a warm-air conduit used by the ancient Romans.

calk (kawk), to fill a joint with mastic, usually with a pressure gun.

calotte (kal lot′), interior of a small dome, so called from a skullcap worn by the Roman Catholic priest.

camarin (kamma rin′), a room in which privacy may be found—the sacristy or vestry of a church; the greenroom or actors' dressing-room of a theater; a closet.

cam′ber, a slight rising from the horizontal, to gain an actual or apparent effect of arching.

cambium (kam′bee um), the layer of cells between the bark and the wood of a tree.

came, a soft-metal division strip between adjacent pieces of glass in leaded- or stained-glass windows.

Campan marbles, a group name for a wide variety of variegated French marbles quarried in the Campan district, Hautes-Pyrénées. Some of the names are: Campan Griotte, Melangé, Rouge, Vert Truité, Vert, and Vert Vert. They range from a rich red ground with interlacings of very fine green veins, including large streaks and veins of white, to a light green ground broken by a lacework of fine dark-green veins.

campanile (kam pan ee′lee), a bell tower.

camp ceiling, a ceiling in which the center is horizontal while a border slopes with the roof rafters.

cam′po, an Italian measure of land, roughly an acre.

canalet′ta (*Cordia gerascanthus*), a hard, dense wood from tropical America having a tobacco or reddish brown color with brown or black streaks, affording attractive veneer.

canalis (kan ahl′iss), the space, usually concave, between the fillets of the Ionic volute (13).

canar′ywood (*Centrolobium paraense*), also called muiraquatiara; a wood from Brazil; heartwood yellow or orange, variegated, usually changing to red or brown; used for paneling and veneer.

cancelli (kan sel′ee), bars or thin balusters in a screen or railing; originally the railing dividing the semicircular court of a pagan basilica, and perhaps the origin of "chancel."

candelabrum (kandel ab′room), a shaft on a stable base, branching at the top to support lighting units.

can′dle beam, a beam so called because of its minor use to support candles for lighting an interior.

can′dlepower, a measure of illumination—the spermaceti candle burning two grains per minute.

cane, open weaving of cane or rattan, used for seats and backs of chairs and for screens and grilles.

canopy (kan′o pee), a sheltering member, as over a niche, a doorway, or a seat of honor.

cant, to set at a slant from horizontal or vertical.

cantharus (kan′tha rus), a laving basin set before ancient churches.

cantilever (kan′til leever), a form of construction in which a beam or series of beams is supported by a downward force behind a fulcrum.

canto'ria, choir gallery of a church.

cant strip, a beveled strip to ease roofing or flashing from horizontal to vertical surface, or to establish the proper angle for a first course of shingles or flat tile on a roof slope.

cap, the top member of a column or pilaster; capital.

cap'ital, the top member or group of members of a column, pier, shaft, or pilaster (12, 13, 14, 15, 16).

cap'itol, a building serving as legislative headquarters of a state.

capo'mo (*Brosimum alicastrum*), a South American wood resembling hard maple except that it lacks the bird's-eye grain; used for furniture, interior woodwork, and also veneer.

cap'stone, the crowning stone of a structure; differing from capital in that it is not a supporting member.

caracol [Fr.] (karra koll), a spiral staircase—*en caracol.*

carapa (keh rap'pa), *see* andiroba.

caravansary (kara van'sarree), a hostelry of the Orient, built around a court. Originally the caravansary offered shelter but not food for man or beast.

carcass, or **carcase** (kar'kass), the framework of uncompleted paneling or the like.

carceres (kar'seh rees), the stall doors of a Greek hippodrome or circus.

cardinales scapi (kar dinnal'ees skapee), in ancient Roman joinery, the stiles of doors.

carillon (kar'illahn), a set of bells tuned to musical intervals and arranged to be played as an instrument.

car'ol (plural, **caro'la**), a space enclosed with partitions, screens, or even a railing.

carolith'ic column, one with a foliated shaft.

car'penter, an artisan in wood.

car'port, shelter for the automobile in conjunction with a dwelling; usually roofed, but not fully enclosed, thus differentiated from the garage.

Carrara marble (kar rare'ah), a group name for marble quarried in the neighborhood of Carrara, Massa, and Seravezza, Italy. Best-known varieties are: Statuary White, Bianco P (Puro), Pavonazzo, English Vein, Veined Italian, and Bianco Chiaro.

carreau (kar ro'), a unit of glass or encaustic tile, usually square or diamond shaped.

carrel', a small room in a library, assigned for temporary, private use to student or researcher.

carrelage (kar'rellidge), an area of tile, terra cotta, or bricks in pattern.

carriage (kar'idge), the member into which the treads and risers of a wooden staircase are let for support.

car'riage porch, a shelter over an entrance, large enough to permit the passage of a carriage or motor car.

carton pierre [Fr.] (kar tonh pee air), a substance resembling *papier-mâché* and stucco, used to simulate carved stone.

cartoon′, a full-size drawing intended to facilitate the making of a fresco, mosaic, stained glass, or the like.

cartouche (kar toosh′), a panel, tablet or scroll, usually elaborately bordered as a decorative spot, its plane or convex field sometimes bearing an inscription or date; frequently the cartouche interrupts or is imposed upon a group of moldings, such as those marking the extrados of an arch (16*c*).

caryatid (plural, **caryatides**), (karry at′id, karry at′teh dees), a column taking the form of a sculptured female figure. The caryatides of the Erechtheum at Athens are the best-known examples.

casa [It.] (kah′sah), a house.

case′harden, to harden the surface of iron through a process of carbonization.

casein paint (kace′een), that in which a casein solution takes the place of the drying oils of common paints. For outdoor use, lime and cement supply the hiding property; for inside work, lime, powdered chalk, or kaolin. The paint is sold as a powder, to be mixed with water for use.

case′ment, a window, the sash or sashes of which are hinged on the jamb.

casing (kace′ing), door or window trim; also the finished millwork encasing a structural member.

casino (keh see′no), a building for public social gatherings, more frequently those for music and dancing; less commonly, a room for the same. 2. a building or a room for games of chance.

cassoon′, a sunken panel in ceiling or vault.

cast, a molded reproduction, usually in plaster of Paris, of a piece of sculpture. 2. past tense of the verb, used to describe metal which has been shaped by pouring in molten form into a mold—cast iron, cast bronze, etc.

cast in situ, formed in its designed resting place.

castel′la, in ancient Roman architecture, a distributing reservoir at the discharge end of an aqueduct.

cas′tellated, bearing turrets or battlements, like a fortified castle.

cast′ing, the end product of pouring molten metal into a temporary mold.

castle (kassl), originally a fortified house; more recently, the residence of royalty.

catacombs (kat′eh komes), subterranean vaults or excavations in rock, used for burial.

catch, a device for latching a light door or gate, or the like.

catch′basin, a walled pit, usually with perforated cover, to receive surface drainage and carry it into a connected underground stormwater sewer.

cat′enary, the curve assumed by a cord fastened at both ends and subjected only to the additional force of gravity.

cat′enated, bearing a line, incised or embossed to suggest the form of a chain.

cathe′dra, the bishop's throne in a cathedral.

cathe′dral, the mother church of a diocese, containing the bishop's throne (7*g*).

cath′erine wheel, a circular window, or circular panel of a larger window, the muntins or cames of which are radii.

cathe′tus, the vertical axis of the Ionic volute upon which is based the construction of the spiral.

cativo (ka tee′vo) (*Prioria copaifera*), a wood from tropical America, straight-grained, moderately strong, and easily tooled; heartwood brown, thick sapwood a dingy white; used chiefly for veneer, as it is not suited to exterior use.

cat's-head molding, a medieval molding using cat's-head grotesques (9*i*).

caulic′ulus, or **caulicolus** (plural, **caulic′uli,** or **caulicoli**), one of the upper acanthus stems just under the angle volutes of a Corinthian capital (14*c*).

caulis (kaul′iss), one of the lower circlet of acanthus stems forming the middle portion of a Corinthian capital (14*c*).

caulk, or **calk** (kawk), to fill cracks and crevices, chiefly along the intersection of wood or metal with masonry, using a non-hardening putty-like compound often applied from a pressure gun.

cavædium (kah vee′deum), in ancient architecture, an open court within a house, or as an entrance; an atrium.

cavea (kav′eea), the seating area of the ancient theater or amphitheater. Originally, the underground pens where the wild beasts were confined in preparation for the fights in the arena.

cavet′to, a concave molding, approximating a quarter-round (11*f*).

cav′ity wall, or **hol′low wall,** one built in two parallel, vertical withes with insulating space between, across which the two withes are held together with ties or bonding units (3*j*, *k*).

cavo-rilievo [It.] (kahvo rilly a′ vo), relief carving in which the high surfaces of the subject are in the plane of the border or surrounding surface. It is also called *intaglio-rilievato*.

cedar, African, *see* guarea.

Alaska yellow cedar (*Chamaecyparis nootkatensis*), a wood of the Pacific Northwest, moderately light, low in strength, highly resistant to decay, easily worked; used for interior finish and furniture.

aromatic red cedar (*Juniperus virginiana*), an aromatic wood available from Nova Scotia west to the Dakotas and from that line south to the Gulf of Mexico; used chiefly for plywood and for lining storage closets as a deterrent measure against moths.

Lebanon cedar (*Cedrus libani*), a wood from Europe, Asia, and Africa, yellowish brown when first cut but darkening with exposure to a rich lustrous brown with darker ring markings; used for exterior construction work and fencing.

Philippine cedar, *see* kalanta.

Port Orford white cedar (*Chamaecyparis lawsoniana*), a wood of northern California and southern Oregon; moderately light, of moderate strength, with a fine and uniform texture; used for Venetian blinds, interior finish, and furniture.

Spanish cedar (*Cedrela* spp.), woods from Central America marketed under a wide variety of names; they belong to the mahogany family but are lighter in weight and color; fragrant and formerly found in cigar boxes; also used in furniture and veneer.

spicy cedar (*Tylostemon mannii*), a wood from West Africa, with gray sapwood and reddish yellow to bright red heartwood; used for interior woodwork and furniture.

western red cedar (*Thuja plicata*), a widely used wood from the Pacific Northwest; used, because of its resistance to decay, for siding and shingles.

ceil (seel), to apply an interior sheathing.

ceil′ing, interior sheathing of an overhead surface.

celature (sel′a chur), the art of surfacing metals by cutting or embossing.

cella (sel′la), the inner enclosed room of an ancient temple.

cellar (sell′er), the excavated portion of a building, sometimes entirely below ground, sometimes partly below, when it is more properly called a basement story.

cellarino [It.] (chel lah ree′no), in a Roman Tuscan or Doric capital, the necking between astragal and echinus. 2. in the Greek Doric capital, the necking or collarino (12).

Celtic ornament (kel′tik), a geometrical pattern distinguishing early English monumental crosses.

celtis (sel′tiss) (*Celtis soyauxii*), a West African wood with sapwood and heartwood a light yellow, hard grained and fine textured; used for furniture, cabinetwork, and flooring.

celure (sel′yure), a canopy or its decoration.

cement′, a substance which, by hardening between two surfaces to which it adheres, binds them together.

hydraulic cement, cement having the property of taking its set under water.

Keene's cement, one made from gypsum and alum; used as a stucco, it attains a particularly hard surface, susceptible to polishing.

Portland cement, the commonly used building cement, made by calcining limestone with clayey substances; it sets under water.

pozzuolana cement, one made of pozzuolana and slaked lime, setting under water.

Rosendale cement, a light hydraulic cement.

cement block, a hollow building block, usually 8″ x 8″ x 16″, formed of cast cement.

cenotaph (sen′o taff), a monument to the memory of a person buried elsewhere.

cen′tering, the temporary support of masonry under construction, as under an arch or under poured concrete.

cen′terpiece, a plaster rosette or larger decoration for the center of a ceiling.

cen′tral heating, a system of heating a building, which depends upon one source, with distribution ducts or pipes.

centrolin′ear perspective, *see* linear perspective.

ceramics (sehr am′iks), the art of the baked clays.

cercis (kare′kiss), Greek term for the spectators' section of a theater; the Latin form is cuneus.

ceroma (sehr o′mah), in ancient architecture, a room in the gymnasia or baths where bathers or wrestlers were anointed with oil thickened with wax.

certosa [It.] (cher to′sah), a monastery of the order founded by St. Bruno in 1086 in the Chartreuse Valley of the French Alps.

cess′pool, a pit for the reception of sewage.

chain, engineer's, a measure used by engineers, equivalent to 100′.

Gunter's chain, a measure used by surveyors, equivalent to 66′.

chainblock, or **chainhoist,** a pulley hoist in which chain takes the place of rope.

chaînes, a term applied to quoins when the stones are square.

chair, a seat for one. 2. a support for reinforcing bars to maintain their designed location while concrete is poured around and over them.

chair rail, a plain or molded strip on wood or plaster wall as a protection against chair backs.

chaitya cave (chayt′ya), a rock-cut Buddhist temple in India, such as found at Karli and Ajunta.

chaj′ja, weather shade of a Hindu temple.

chalcidium (kal sid′eum), a term used by Vitruvius to denote a large building for the administering of justice.

chalet (shal lay′ or shal′lay), the house of the Swiss mountaineer.

chalk line (chawk), a marking line used by builders. A cord is rubbed with white or colored chalk, held taut between two ends of the line desired, then plucked in the middle to leave a straight line on the surface adjacent.

Chalukyan architecture (chal look′yan), that of Chalukya, a province of India, typified in star-shaped temples with stepped roofs, dating from the sixth century.

chamber (chaim′ber), a bedroom. 2. a room of state.

chambers, the private rooms of a judge, adjoining his courtroom.

cham′fer, to cut away the edge where two surfaces meet in an exterior angle, leaving a bevel at the junction.

cham′fer stop, the ending, usually decorative, of a chamfer where it approaches the end of its length and the beginning of an arris.

champlevé [Fr.] (shahmp levay), enameling on metal

areas of different colors separated by a thin edge of metal, somewhat similar to cloisonné.

Champville [Fr.] (shahmp veel), a marble quarried in southern France. It has a creamy ground of even and close texture, more or less tinged with yellow and sometimes rose, with occasional gray spots.

chan′cel, that portion of a church interior containing the altar and reserved for clergy and choir.

chan′cery, the group of rooms, or building, used for the business activities of an ambassador.

chandelier (shan deh leer′), a branching light source hanging from ceiling or roof.

chandry (shan′dree), a room in a palace for the storage of candles and other lights.

chan′nel, a rolled form of structural steel in varying sizes, each a straight web with equal right-angled flanges on both edges and on the same side of the web.

chan′try, strictly speaking, the endowment of priest, chapel, or altar for masses sung for a founder's soul. Architecturally it is taken to mean the founder's chapel of a church or monastery, often containing his tomb.

chaori (ka′oree), in India, the porch or hall element of the temple.

chap′el, a place of worship secondary to a church, sometimes a part of the latter, sometimes an independent structure.

Lady chapel, one dedicated to the Virgin Mary, and, where found, invariably part of a church or cathedral, situated behind the altar.

chapter house, the meeting place, and sometimes the residence, of the clergy serving a cathedral or other collegiate church. 2. the headquarters of a secret society.

chap′trel, in Gothic architecture, a capital of a pier or column from which springs an arch.

charrette [Fr. slang] (shar ret), the final drive to complete a design or set of drawings. Literally, *charrette* is a handcart, in which drawings are rushed to the judgment at the École des Beaux-Arts.

chartophylacium (charto fi lay′seum), in ancient architecture, a recess or a room for the preservation of valuable records or other writings.

chase, a rough channel formed in the inner face of a wall to receive piping, wiring, or ductwork and keep it behind the finished surface.

chassis (shassy), a frame on which a drawing or painting is to be stretched.

château [Fr.] (shah to), a country house of France; originally the French word for castle.

château d'eau [Fr.] (shah to do), the architectural front of a water reservoir.

chatri, in India, a pavilion.

chat-sawn, *see* shot-sawn.

check, a crack in wood, caused by uneven shrinkage.

check′er, checquer, or **chequer,** ornament of quadrangles containing right-angle lines in some form. Diaper is the term used when the contained lines are not straight.

check′er work, masonry of square-face stones not breaking joints.

check valve, a device which permits the flow of a liquid or vapor through piping in one direction only.

cheeks, or **cheek pieces,** any pair of upright facing members, as the cheeks of a window embrasure, or of a doorway, or of a flight of steps.

Chelmsford Gray, a light gray, medium-grain, muscovite-biotite granite of Massachusetts, used for heavy masonry and monumental building.

C. White, a very light-color granite of medium grain, its pinkish trend revealed in polished finish; quarried at West Chelmsford, Mass.

cheneau [Fr.] (shen o), a cresting (9*a*).

chenchen (*Antiaris africana*), a wood from West Africa, useful for its white to yellowish gray veneer, which has a good stripe.

cher′ry, African, *see* makore.

black cherry (*Prunus serotina*), a close-textured wood frequently used in cabinetwork, taking a high polish; heartwood light to dark reddish brown, sapwood nearly white.

ches′ter, Anglo-Saxon term for a fortified town built on the site of a Roman military post.

chest′nut (*Castanea dentata*), an American tree, formerly used for timber, now lacking in mature form because of the chestnut blight, a parasitic fungus.

chevaux [Fr.] (shev o), protective spikes along the top of a wall or fence.

chevet [Fr.] (shev vay), the eastern or altar end of a French Gothic cathedral or church.

chev′ron, a decorative pattern made up of two or more short bars meeting at an angle (9*f*).

chiaroscuro (kiah ro skoo′ro), pictorial effect resulting from the relationship of light and shade.

chickras′si (*Chukrasia tabularis*), a close-textured hardwood from India and Burma, of a golden mahogany color. Also called chittagong.

chimæra (ki mee′rah), a grotesque animal in sculpture, usually a fanciful combination of lion, goat, and serpent.

chime, five to twelve bells tuned to musical intervals. 2. in the plural, metal tubes tuned to musical intervals, sometimes accessory to an organ and sounded from the console.

chim′ney, a flue, approximately vertical, for conducting the smoke and gases of combustion from above a fire to the outside air.

chimney breast, a section of wall projected to afford space for a chimney behind it.

chimney piece, the ensemble of architectural and decorative treatment about and over the fireplace.

chimney pot, a short extension of a flue in round section above the chimney wall.

chimney stack, a group of flues contained within a common covering.

chimney throat, the narrow horizontal slot above a fireplace through which the gases of combustion pass to enter the smoke chamber and the flue.

Chinese architecture, an architecture, chiefly of timber and brick, that has remained without much change through many centuries, without distinction between sacred and secular work. The roof, with its upturned eaves, is the accented feature, often repeated in horizontal series, and supported by timber uprights independent of the curtain walls (16*e*).

chinikhana (chinny kahna), Hindustani term for a niche or other ornamental recess.

chink, to fill cracks or interstices, as between logs or stones of a wall.

chinoiserie (shin wah′zerree), decorative design characteristic of the Chinese.

chit′tagong, *see* chickrassi.

choir (kwire), the section of a church designed for the seating of the body of trained singers or the chanting of services.

choltry, an East Indian inn.

choragic monument (ko ra′ jik), a pedestal for the display of the bronze tripod which was the prize awarded the successful chorus in ancient Athens. The Choragic Monument of Lysicrates at Athens (334 B.C.) is one of the best-known examples.

choraula (ko ro′la), a room allotted to choir rehearsals in a church.

chord (kord), an essential member, approximately horizontal, of a truss.

chorometry (kor om′etree), the science of measuring land.

chrismatory (kris′meh toree), a recess near the font of a church, to contain the chrism or holy oil for anointing after baptism.

chrismographion (kris mo graf′eon), the oracle room in a Greek temple, between pronaos and naos or cella.

Chrismon (kriss′mon), a monogram of the first two letters of the Greek Christos, widely used in church symbolism.

chromacity (kro mass′itty), the characteristics of light specified by dominant wavelength and purity.

chrom′ium, a grayish white metal, resistant to corrosion and widely used as a plating.

chromium steel, or **chrome steel,** *see* steel.

chryselephantine (kris ella fan′ teen), of gold and ivory. Greek statues, often of clay or wood, were sometimes sheathed in thin plates of gold and ivory.

chuf′fy brick, one swollen by inner steam or air while in the kiln.

chulpa (tchool′pah), a prehistoric stone tower of Peru. Above a burial chamber were living quarters for the family of the deceased.

chunam (tchu′nam), a white plaster or stucco, used in India.

church, a building for Christian worship.

churrigueresque (choo reeger esk′), characteristic of the forms introduced into Spanish architecture by Churriguera, Ribera, and other designers early in the eighteenth century.

chute (shoot), a sloping trough or vertical passage.

chy′mol, literally, a twin; a hinge, the parts of which are inseparable. *See also* jimmer or gymmer.

ciborium (sibbo′reum), a baldachin or altar canopy. 2. a repository near the altar for the pyx.

cill, spelling of *sill* in England.

cimborio (sim bo′reo), Spanish term for the lantern or dome above the intersection of nave and transepts in a church.

cimelium (sim e′leum), a room in a church for the safekeeping of vestments and other treasures.

cincture (sing′choor), the fillet adjoining the apophyge at top and bottom of a classical column shaft (12).

cinder block (sin′der), a building block of cinder concrete.

cinder concrete, a concrete utilizing boiler cinders for the coarse aggregate, in the effort to achieve lightness of weight, and incidentally a nailing surface.

cinerarium (sinner a′reum), a recess for the permanent container of the ashes of cremation.

cinerator (sin′eray tor), a furnace in a crematory. *See also* incinerator.

cinquecento (sanka sahn′to), Italy's sixteenth century, the Renaissance.

cinquefoil (sank′eh foyl), a frame, usually for glass or panel, having five sides breaking out in arcs of a circle (9*h*).

cip′pus, a sepulchral monument, circular, square, or rectangular in plan and flat-topped; sometimes mistaken for an altar.

circuit (ser′kut), the closed loop of wire, or other conducting material, in which an electric current flows.

circuit breaker, an automatic switch which opens an electrical circuit when actuated by overload.

circulation (serkew lay′shun), in planning, the provision for proper means of access, intercommunication, and egress among the enclosed spaces. 2. in piping or ductwork, the movement of water, steam, or air through the system.

circum′feren′tial street, *see* ring road.

circumlition (ser kum lish′un), the coloring of ancient Greek figure sculpture.

circumscribe′, to draw a line around. 2. to restrict within a boundary.

circus (ser′kus), in ancient Rome, a large, open-top enclosure in which sport contests were held before an audience seated in tiers, these tiers being rounded at one end.

ciselure (size eh loor′), metal chasing.

cistern (sis′tern), a reservoir for liquids.

cit′adel, a stronghold; originally one protecting a city.

cité [Fr.] (see tay), a city, or a town, with its environs.

City Beautiful, a term somewhat scornfully applied to urban planning of an earlier day in which axial symmetry and architectural ostentation were favored at the expense of utilitarian and social considerations.

civ′ic center, in a community, that part in which are located the main public buildings.

clad′ding, English term for the surface material of a wall of which the main support is a frame.

claire-voie [Fr.] (klare vwah), an opening with grille in a garden wall.

clam′shell shovel, a powered excavating tool, the action of which is suggestive of its name.

clapboard (klab′bord), a board that is thin on one edge and thicker on the other, to facilitate overlapping horizontally to form a weatherproof, exterior wall surface. Early American clapboards were rived; later they were produced by woodworking machinery.

clas′sical, of, or based upon, the arts of ancient Greece and Rome.

clas′sicist, one who prefers classical art to that of other schools; one who bases his design upon classical forms.

clathri (klath′ree), bars of iron or wood used in ancient Rome to secure doors or windows.

clean′out, a screw-plugged opening in drain piping, through which obstructions may be rodded. 2. the door through which ashes are removed from an ash dump.

clear, applied to milled wood, without knots.

in the clear, describing measurement of a space unobstructed, as between floor and beam soffit rather than between floor and ceiling proper.

clear′ance, space to spare above actual need, as the height, greater than normal headroom, between a stair tread and the closed ceiling above it.

climatol′ogy, in architecture, the science of planning and building in accord with regional climatic variations.

clear′cole, a priming or sizing material used in Great Britain, white lead ground in water with glue.

cleat, a strip of wood fastened to a surface to serve as a batten, or as a support for another board, such as a shelf.

clere′story, an upward extension of enclosed daylighted space by carrying a setback, vertical, windowed wall through the roof slope, as over the columns between nave and aisles of a church (7*g*).

clerk of the works, one who supervises the construction of a building and keeps account of the materials used and, sometimes, of workmen's time.

cliff′ dwelling, prehistoric habitation of certain Indian tribes in southwestern U.S.A. and in northern Mexico, partly excavation, partly stone-walled on narrow shelves of the cliffs.

clinch, to bend over the protruding sharp end of a nail to prevent its being withdrawn.

clink′er, a brick overburned by reason of its nearness to the fire in a kiln.

clip′ped gable, a gable cut back at the peak in a hip-roof form (6*k*).

cloaca maxima (klow a′kah), the great sewer of Rome, built about 600 B.C. and used continuously since.

cloak′room, a room where outer garments may be hung, often in the care of an attendant.

clochette [Fr.] (klo shet), French term for a small, bell-shaped ornament in various forms.

cloisonné (kloy zon nay′), enamel ware in which pattern and color boundaries are achieved with divisions of flat wire.

cloister (kloys′ter), a paved and sheltered passageway, usually along the walls of an enclosed court, and thus open on one side. 2. the court and its passage.

cloister garth, a quadrangular area enclosed by a cloister.

close, an open space adjoining a building and bounded by fence, wall, or the building itself.

closed-string, descriptive of a stairway in which the edges of risers and treads are covered on the outside by a slanting member.

clos′er, a masonry unit of odd length, laid next to the end unit of a course, to meet dimension requirements. *See also* king closer and queen closer.

clos′et, space enclosed for storage purposes, yet not large enough to merit the term storeroom.

clos′ure, a freestanding length of low wall between neighboring columns of a range.

clothes chute, a duct, leading from an upper story, through which soiled clothes are dropped into a receptacle below.

clow′ring, surfacing a stone to rectangularity for ashlar.

clus′tered column, or **clustered pillar,** a group of shafts, with their bases and capitals, engaged as one support (15*g*).

coam′ing, curbing or parapet surrounding an opening in floor or roof.

coat, a single layer of surface covering, as of paint or plaster.

coat′room, a room where outer garments may be hung, often in the care of an attendant.

cob, earth and straw compacted as a wall filling.

cob′blestone, a stone naturally rounded, of a size suitable for rough paving.

cob′work, log house construction, as for retaining wall or breakwater.

cochleare (cock′leer), or **cogla,** a round stair tower.

cock, in plumbing, a valve and spout combined; a bibb; a faucet. 2. a weathercock.

cock′loft, or **cot′loft,** the unfinished space in a dwelling above the topmost ceiling.

cock's-head jimmer, a hinge in which part of the leaves represent a conventionalized cock's head (16*k*).

cocobo′lo (*Dalbergia retusa, D. granadillo,* or *D. hypoleuca*), hard and heavy woods from South and Central America; heartwood is very variable, striped orange and deep red, the latter often showing dark veins; yields a fine surface in lathe work.

code, or **building code,** legal restrictions of a given locality governing the building of various types of structure.

coefficient of expansion (ko effish′ent), a value denoting the rate at which a material expands with rising temperature.

cœnaculum (ken nak′yu lum), in ancient Roman architecture, an eating-room, sometimes in the second story.

cœnatio (ken nat′eo), a room in ancient Roman houses for supper or banqueting, in the first story or sometimes as an outside dependency.

cof′fee shop, an independent restaurant, or one supplementing the main dining-room of a hotel, offering a somewhat restricted menu.

cof′fer, a recessed panel in a flat or vaulted ceiling. 2. a recessed, ceiling source of artificial light—a troffer.

cof′ferdam, a temporary, watertight enclosure, carried below water line, to facilitate construction that will later be submerged.

cogla, *see* cochleare.

cogon (ko goan′), a Philippine coarse grass, infrequently used for thatching.

coigne, *see* quoin.

coilon (ko′illon), Greek term corresponding to the Latin cavea; the seating area of the ancient theater or amphitheater; originally, the underground pens for the wild animals awaiting fights in the arena.

cold cath′ode, an instant-starting variety of fluorescent lamps, using electrodes of cylindrical form; hot-cathode lamps use electrodes of coiled tungsten filaments.

Cold Spring Agate, a medium- to coarse-grain granite, reddish with broad, dark veining and a clouding of red, pearl gray, and a bluish shade, quarried at Odessa, Minn.

C. S. Carnelian, a porphyritic granite of medium grain and a general brownish red color, quarried at Milbank, S. D.

C. S. Diamond Pink, a coarse-grain granite, pinkish with mixed pearl gray and reddish colorings, quarried at St. Cloud, Minn.

C. S. Pearl Pink, a porphyritic granite of medium grain, quarried at Cold Spring, Minn.

C. S. Pearl White, a light pink granite, classed as white, of medium grain, quarried at Isle, Minn.

C. S. Rainbow, a medium- to coarse-grain pink granite with black and gray wavings, quarried at Morton, Minn.

C. S. Red, a medium-grain reddish granite with black and gray spottings, quarried at Odessa, Minn.

col′lar, a band or molding encircling a shaft. 2. collar beam.

col′lar beam, a horizontal tie between opposite rafters (7*h*).

collar brace, a member in medieval roof framing (7*h*).

collarino, or **cellarino** [It.] (kollar ee'no, or chellar ee'no), the necking of the Greek Doric, Roman Doric, and Tuscan capitals (12).

Colle'giate Gothic, Gothic architecture from which has been excluded any form or symbolism directly related to the church.

colombage [Fr.] (kollum bahzhe), Norman term for half-timber construction.

Colo'nial architecture, the architectural style, composed of various local characteristics, developed in the American colonial period. The term has been so loosely applied—stretched to include Early Republic, Georgian adaptations, and even the Greek Revival—that it has little present significance.

colonelli (kolon el'ee), Italian term for the posts employed in any truss framing.

colonnade', a row of columns with their entablatures. 2. a double row of such columns enclosing a walk.

colonnette', a small column of secondary use, such as that applied to the face of panel stiles.

Colorado Travertine, a marble with a color range from cream to pink and rose. Colorcreme and Colorosa are trade names.

color systems, efforts to arrange the colors of the spectrum in orderly graphic relationship, such as the systems of Munsell and Ostwald.

color temp'erature, a system of describing the chromacity of a completely radiating source.

colum'ba, in the medieval church, a dove-shaped receptacle for the sacrament.

columbarium (kollum ba' reum), a dovecote. 2. a small recess in a wall for the reception of timber ends. 3. a recess in a tomb wall to receive an urn with the ashes of cremation.

columbel'on, the court fountain of a basilica.

col'umn, a supporting pillar (11, 12, 13, 14, 15).

clustered column, a group of shafts, with their bases and capitals, engaged as one support.

engaged column, one of less than circular section set flatwise against a vertical surface.

twisted column, or wreathed column, one carved or molded to give the appearance of having a twisted shaft or intertwined twin shafts.

columnia'tion, the manner of grouping columns, particularly the various plans of the ancient Greek temples.

Colusa sandstone, a blue-gray stone of very even grain, quarried in Colusa County, Calif.

colymbethra (kollim beth'rah), a baptistery, or its font, in the Greek church.

colymbion (kol lim'bee on), a basin for holy water in the Greek church.

comb' grain, or **straight grain,** that face of wood in quarter-sawn boards or lumber which shows narrow, approximately parallel lines, such as are particularly clear in longleaf pine.

combing (kome′ing), in the shingle roof, a top course which projects somewhat above the ridge from the direction of prevailing winds (*7f*).

Comblanchien [Fr.] (kom blahnch anh), a compact, fine-grained, oölitic limestone of a rose putty color, having very fine fossils and some rust specks and glass veins. It is quarried in southern France.

com′fort sta′tion, a building, or part of a building, providing toilet facilities for the use of the public.

comfort zone, that range of effective temperatures in which 50% of persons feel comfortable—62–69° effective temperature.

commes′so, a geometrical mosaic practised in Italy during the Middle Ages, as in the pavement of the Baptistery at Florence.

com′mon room, or **com′mons,** a central, heated gathering-room in a chapter house, monastery, dormitory, or clubhouse.

commun′ity center, in urban planning, the chief location of provision for public, social, and sometimes recreational amenities.

compart′ment, a subdivision of enclosed space.

com′pass, a drafting instrument for describing circles of variable radii.

com′pass brick, one that is radially wedge shaped, for use in building cisterns and other radial walls.

competi′tion, a contest, usually by the submission of designs for a given problem, looking to the award of cash prizes or an architectural commission. Professional ethics restrict participation of architects to competitions which are to be judged, in the main, by architects.

compluvium (kom ploo′veum), an opening in the roof above the atrium of an ancient Roman house, for the admission of light and air. 2. an area in the center of such a house, so built as to receive the waters from the roof; a cistern.

com′po, stucco.

com′po board, insulating board, hard board, building board—loose terms for a sheet product of vegetable fibers mechanically or chemically formed into a pulp, rolled, and pressed; in some cases a binding material or chemicals have been added to provide resistance to moisture, fire, rodents, etc. These sheet products are widely used as sheathing, lath, insulation, and interior wall surfacing.

Compos′ite, the last of the five classical orders, a combination of Corinthian and Ionic devised by the Romans.

com′pound, an enclosure, by wall or fence, securing protection and privacy for a building and its dependencies, or for a group of similar buildings. 2. *see* clustered column.

compound arch, *see* arch (2*g*).

Com′preg, trade name for wood veneers impregnated with resin, dried, stacked, and cured under heat and pressure, making a hard, dense board.

compres′sor, a machine for compressing air or other gases, such as that used in some cooling systems.

concamerata sudatio (kon kahm erah′tah soo dah′teo), an apartment in ancient gymnasia or baths to which athletes retired to cleanse the sweat from their bodies.

concha (kon′chah), the half-dome of an apse. 2. the concave, ribless surface of a pendentive (7*b*).

conciergerie [Fr.] (kon see air zhe ree), French term for a porter's lodge.

concours [Fr.] (kong koor), a competition.

hors concours (or kong koor), literally, outside the competition; usually, ineligible for award. The abbreviation is H. C.

con′crete, a compound of cement, large and small aggregates, and water, deposited in temporary forms while in a fluid state. When set it attains hardness and strength not unlike stone.

reinforced concrete, concrete which has been poured into forms containing soft-steel bars or mesh disposed so as to add their tensile strength to the mass.

concrete mixer, a metal drum of several cubic yards capacity which can be revolved to mix the ingredients of concrete, sometimes while being transported on a motor-driven chassis.

condemn (kon dem′), to seize, by public authority and for public benefit, property of an individual, making due recompense. 2. to declare unfit for use.

condensa′tion, the conversion of moisture in air to water, as on the warm-room side of a cold wall.

conden′ser, an apparatus for storing, or intensifying, an electric charge. 2. an apparatus for reducing vapor to a liquid. 3. an apparatus for compressing air.

conduction (kon duk′shun), the passage of electricity, heat, or sound through material.

conductiv′ity, the property of permitting conduction.

conduit (kon′dwit), a continuous protecting sheath for electric wires. 2. an underground passage. 3. a pipe.

confessional (kon fesh′inal), a cabinet in which a priest can hear the confessions of a penitent, himself unseen.

congé (kon zhay), French term for apophyge (12).

con′gowood, *see* blackwood, African, and walnut, African.

conisterium (konniss tee′ reum), a room in the ancient gymnasia wherein the wrestlers, having been anointed with oil, were dusted to achieve better holds.

Connecticut brownstone, one of the first building stones to be widely used in America; fine grain, even texture, of a uniform, warm brown.

conserv′atory, a room which, in its abundance of glazed openings and provision for artificial heat, is suited to the growing of plant life. 2. an institution for the teaching of music.

consis′tory, a room or house for the use of an ecclesiastical court.

con′sole, a decorative bracket, usually taking the form of a cyma reversa strap. 2. the manuals of an organ, with their case.

construct′, to put together parts in building.

con′sulate, a building for the official business of a consul.

con′tact, the juncture of electrical conductors.

contact breaker, an electric switch actuated by overload.

conté crayon (kontay), a fairly hard French square-stick crayon; the dark reddish brown variety has long been a favorite for architectural sketching.

con′tour, the line of intersection between a horizontal plane at a given elevation and the land being surveyed. 2. the face of a molding or other outline of a solid.

con′tract, in architecture, a formal agreement between architect and owner, or between owner and builder or general contractor.

contraction (kon trak′shun), shrinkage in dimensions through lowering of temperature; applied usually to metals.

control′ desk, a location in library, hospital, or the like, from which an individual can oversee activities.

convection (kon vek′shun), the transfer of heat through flow of its carrier.

con′vent, a building for the use of a group of nuns.

cooinnew (koo′in yew), (*Gmelina leichardtii*), or white beech, an Australian tree, the wood of which is fine textured, termite resistant, and has low shrinkage; used for boats, furniture, and flooring.

coop′erative apart′ment house, one in which the individual apartments are held by different persons, usually stockholders in a corporation that holds title to the property.

copaiba (ko pi′bah) (*Copaifera* spp.) reddish brown, dark-streaked, lustrous woods from Central and South America; used chiefly for cabinetwork.

co′pal, a resin from several tropical trees, used in varnishes.

cope, to join two molded strips at an angle by fitting one over the other, instead of mitering.

cop′ing, the capping or top course of a wall, usually adapted to the protection of the wall from weather.

cop′per, one of the metallic elements—a reddish, extremely ductile metal in wide use for wire, flashing, eaves gutters, downspouts, etc.

Cop′tic, of the Copts, an ancient Egyptian race.

coquillage [Fr.] (ko kee lazh), shell-like decoration.

coquina (ko kee′nah), a soft building stone of Florida, composed largely of marine shells.

cor′alwood (*Adenanthera pavonina*), a yellowish wood of India and the Andamans, becoming coral color as it is cured; used in cabinetwork.

corbeil (kor′bel), a sculptured basket of fruit or flowers.

corbel (kor′bel), a bracket form, usually produced by extending successive courses of masonry or wood beyond the wall surface (16*o*).

corbel table, a range of corbels supporting a superstructure or upper moldings; commonly used beneath a spire or parapet or below the eaves line (16*o*).

cor′bie-stepped gable, *see* crow-stepped gable.

cor′don, a string course.

Cordova Pink, a coarse-grain, deep pink granite, mottled with black; quarried in Llano County, Texas.

core, the inner material of a veneered door, or the like. 2. a combination of utilities, sometimes including elevators, for the central stem of a building.

Corin′thian, one of the Greek orders, in which the column capitals show conventionalized acanthus leaves, the shaft being slender and sometimes fluted (14).

cork tile, flooring tile of compressed cork composition.

cork′wood, *see* balsa.

cor′ner bead, a strip of metal formed in a projecting angle of plaster wall to strengthen and protect it.

cor′nerstone, a conspicuous stone in the base of a building on which is usually carved the date of erection, and in a hollow of which are frequently preserved contemporary data.

cornice (kor′niss), the upper member of a classical entablature (12, 13, 14). 2. the projecting member at the top of a wall—a decorative development of the utilitarian coping marking the eaves of the roof.

coro, the choir space in a Spanish cathedral.

corolit′ic, bearing sculptured branches of foliage.

coro′na, the flat vertical member of a classical cornice between the cymatium above and the bed molding below; on its lower edge is formed the drip; corresponding to what is now commonly called fascia (11*j*).

corona lucis (kor o′nah loo′kis), a crown or circlet suspended from the roof or vaulting of a church to hold tapers, candles, or the like.

corpora′tion cock, the valve of a public water or gas main between it and the system being served.

cor′ridor, a passageway or hall serving a number of rooms.

corrugated (kor′you gated), formed into alternate ridges and valleys in parallel, giving greater rigidity to thin plates, usually of galvanized steel for roofing or side walls.

corrugated roofing, usually galvanized steel sheets 26″ wide, with 2½″ corrugations, laid with an end lap of 6″ and side lap of two corrugations.

cor′sa, Latin term given by Vitruvius to any plat band or square fascia with a height greater than its projection.

cortile (kor tee′leh), Italian term for a courtyard.

cost-plus, adjective describing a type of building contract in which the owner agrees to pay cost of materials and labor plus a fixed fee.

cot′loft, *see* cockloft.

cot′tage, a modest dwelling, frequently for summer use.

cot′tonwood (*Populus deltoides, P. trichocarpa hastata*), a light, weak wood which warps and splits easily and decays quickly in contact with the ground; used for boxes and crates and in veneer.

coulomb (kool ahm), the quantity of electricity carried in one second in a current of one ampere.

counter (kown′ter), a built-in table for a business establishment, the customer's side of which is usually closed to the floor, the other side usually shelved. 2. a fixed shelf or top member of a cupboard range for use as work space in kitchen, pantry, or the like.

counterfort [Fr.] (kown ter for), a wall buttress.

countersink (kown′ter sink), an added depression below a surface, as to receive the head of a nail, screw, or bolt. 2. the sinkage of any small area beneath the plane of the surface.

country seat (kun′tree), a pretentious country dwelling.

coupled columns (kup′ld), two columns which engage one another to serve as a single support.

coupling (kup′ling), in plumbing a sleeve-like element with hexagonal outside to be turned by a wrench and with right-hand and left-hand threads inside to couple the ends of two pipes.

course (korse), in masonry, a horizontal range of units the length and thickness of the wall.

court (kort), a building or a room where justice is administered. 2. a courtyard.

court′house, a building housing law courts.

court′room, in a courthouse, a principal room in which a judge presides.

court′yard, an outdoor space partly or wholly bordered by the building to which it belongs.

coussinet [Fr.] (koo seh nay), a stone at the top of a pier supporting the lowest stone of an arch.

cove, a concave molding. 2. the curved junction between a ceiling and side wall, above a cornice if there is one.

cove lighting, that in which the light sources are concealed from below by a cove, cornice, or horizontal recess, and direct their light upon a reflecting ceiling.

cover (kuv′er), that part of a course of tiles, slate, or shingles which is covered by the overlapping course.

cov′ing, the projection of upper façades beyond the lower, as common in Elizabethan architecture.

cowl, a revolving hood for the top of a flue, actuated by the wind to keep its open face to leeward.

c.p., abbreviation for candle-power.

Crab Orchard stone, a quartzite, easily lifted in layers, of variegated buffs and grays, quarried in Cumberland County, Tenn.

crab′wood, *see* andiroba.

cramp, a metal strap of U shape to hold two adjacent stones firmly together across a course joint, as on the top face of coping or stone steps.

cran′dall, a multi-pointed hammer for dressing the face of a stone.

crane, a power machine for hoisting and moving a load laterally. 2. a bracket-like pivoted fireplace accessory.

crapaudine (krappo deen′), pivoted on a vertical axis.

crawl, or **creep,** a fault in painted work, when freshly applied paint tends to overlap rather than keep to a plane surface.

crawl space, underfloor space where excavation has not been carried down to a full story height, but where access to pipes, ducts, etc., may be desirable.

craze, to develop minute surface cracks, as in pottery, stucco, or concrete.

crèche (kresh), a sculptured or posed representation of the Nativity.

cre′dence, a repository for the sacramental elements, located near the altar of a church.

creep, *see* crawl.

crematory, or **crematorium** (kree′ma toree, or kree ma to′reum), a building for the cremation of dead bodies.

Cremo, an Italian marble, often graded as: first quality, with cream ground and network of golden veins; second quality, creamy ground, golden veins, and also reddish and greenish spots with thicker veins.

cremorne bolt, a locking device for a French door, or the like, consisting of two long rods, the ends of which engage at sill and head; espagnolette.

cren′elated, describing a parapet in which the top is alternately and uniformly depressed; battlemented (8*b*).

crenelle′, or **crenel,** an embrasure which, alternating with the elevated portions of a wall, forms a battlement (8*b*).

cre′osoting, a method of preserving lumber by impregnating it with creosote under pressure.

crepido (kray pee′do), Latin term for the projecting members of a cornice or projecting ornament.

crepidoma (kray pee do′mah), the foundation base of an ancient columnless temple.

cres′cent, a building or row of buildings the façades of which follow the line of an arc in plan.

cres′set, a cuplike form of metal, open at top and with pierced or strap sides, to hold burning material, as a torch.

crest, or **crest′ing,** a decorative ridge for a roof, usually as a continuous series of finials.

crib′bing, the temporary lining of an excavation, to serve as shoring. 2. successive layers of logs or squared timbers, alternate layers at right angles, to hold an embankment.

crib′bled, descriptive of a perforated or dotted background on wood or metal.

crick′et, the watershed change in pitch of a roof slope, as behind a chimney (16*i*).

crimp, to bend metal sheets sharply, as in a lock joint of metal roofing. 2. to corrugate.

criosphinx (kry′o sfinks), a sphinx having the head of a ram instead of that of a man.

crip′ple rafter, a subordinate rafter for a hip or valley of a roof.

critique [Fr.] (krit eek), a critical analysis, as that of a patron to his pupil.

crock, earthenware. 2. tile sewer pipe.

crock′et, a projecting ornament common to Gothic architecture—the blunt terminal of conventionalized foliage, as frequently occurs along the edges of a spire (7*a*).

cromlech (krom′lek), a prehistoric sepulchral monument of large, unhewn stones; a dolmen.

croquis [Fr.] (kro kee), a sketch.

cross, a symbol taking various forms, some of which were known before recorded history (5).

ansata, *see* Egyptian (5*v*).

avellan, or **avellane,** a cross each of whose four arms resembles a filbert or nut of Avella (5*p*).

botonée, the budding cross (5*r*).

broadfoot, another variation of the pattée (5*i*).

Buddhist, *see* gammadion.

Calvary, a cross mounted on three steps, symbolizing Faith, Hope, and Charity (5*m*).

Celtic, Irish Cross or Cross of Iona (5*o*).

crosslet, also called the holly cross and the German cross (5*f*).

Egyptian, or ansata, the tau cross with a loop or handle at the top (5*v*).

formy, *see* pattée.

fourchée, the forked cross (5*s*).

gammadion, formed of four Greek capital gammas, back to back with voids between. Also called Buddhist cross (5*x*).

Greek, used by various ancient peoples, and as far back as a thousand years before the Christian era (5*e*).

Jerusalem, or potent, formed of four tau crosses (5*j*).

labarum, devised and used by Constantine (5*w*).

Latin, now the Christian symbol (5*c*).

Lorraine, a cross having two transoms or crossbars, the upper one shorter than the lower (5*n*).

Maltese, a cross formed of four arrowheads meeting at their points (5*g*).

moline, named for its resemblance to the crossed iron pivot of a millstone—a moline (5*u*).

nowy quadrant, a cross having each angle filled with a projection, the four making a square (5*h*).

papal, a cross with three transoms or crossbars (5*l*).

patriarchal, a cross with two transoms or crossbars (5*k*).

pattée, small at the center and widening toward the ends (5*d*).

pilgrims′, apparently a combination of the pilgrim's staff and the crosslet of Christianity (5*t*).

pommée, a cross whose arms terminate in knobs (5*q*).

potent, *see* Jerusalem.

St. Andrew's, *see* saltire.

St. Anthony's, *see* tau.

saltire, or **St. Andrew's,** the cross on which the saint was martyred (5*a*).

tau, or **St, Anthony's,** known to the Jews as the cross of the Old Testament, possibly adapted from a somewhat similar form used by the Egyptians (5*b*).

crossette′, croissette, or **crosset,** the side projection of an architrave at top, the double-mitered "ear" (*see also* ancon) (2*i*). 2. a side lug at the upper side of an arch stone, entering a corresponding space on the adjoining stone; joggle jointing (2*j*).

cross-gar′net, a T-shaped hinge, in a wide variety of decorative forms.

cross′ing, the intersection of nave and transepts in the cruciform plan.

cross section, a section of a body taken across its shorter dimension.

crotch veneer, veneer cut from the crotch of a tree, revealing unusual grain patterns.

crowde, croude, or **croft,** terms for the crypt of a church.

crow′foot, descriptive of the veining in stone that contains dark, uncemented material.

crown, of an arch, the top of the opening. 2. of a horizontal timber, the camber of a slightly warped length, always set as the top. 3. the slight camber of a sidewalk or road paving. 4. the upper part of a cornice, including the corona and the moldings above it. As a verb, to make higher in the middle, to camber, as in paving a road.

crown glass, glass blown into large, circular discs, afterwards out to the desired rectangular or other shape.

crow quill, a pen point of diminutive size.

crow-stepped, or **corbie-stepped,** gable, one whose rake is stepped rather than straight or curved.

crucible steel (kroos′ibbl), cast steel.

cru′cifix, a cross bearing the representation of Christ crucified.

cru′ciform, descriptive of the characteristic form of Gothic church plans—nave, apse, and transepts.

crypt (kript), the vaulted basement of a building, usually a church or cathedral, often with its own chapels and sometimes tombs.

cryp′to-port′icus, a gallery or portico having side walls with openings or windows rather than columns.

cubage (kew′bidg), the measurement of enclosed volume.

cubicle (kew′bikl), a diminutive room.

cubit (kew′bit), in ancient architecture, a unit of linear measure, usually considered about 18″.

cucumber tree, *see* magnolia.

cul-de-four [Fr.] (kul deh foor), a low, spherical vault on a circular or oval plan, as in an oven vault.

cul-de-lampe [Fr.), a convexly rounded or pyramidal lower termination of a newel post or the like.

cul-de-sac (plural, **culs-de-sac**) (kul′deh sak), a driveway or passage open at only one end.

cull, material rejected as below a stated grade, as in brick or lumber.

cul′men, in ancient Roman architecture, the ridge of a roof.

cul′vert, a structure affording passage for water beneath ground level, as for a small stream crossed by a roadway.

cuneiform (kew′nee iform), descriptive of ideographic characters used by the ancient Accadians, Babylonians, Assyrians, and others.

cuneus (kew′nee us), the spectators' section of a Roman theater.

cuniculus (kew nik′you lus), an ancient land drain.

cupboard (kub′bord), a shallow closet with shelves.

cupola (kew′po la), a terminal structure, square to round in plan, rising above a main roof.

curb (kerb), the change in level between sidewalk and street. 2. a low guard wall around an opening, as the curb of a well. The English spelling is *kerb.*

cure, in newly poured concrete, to avoid premature drying and consequent imperfect setting by keeping the surface moist.

curia (plural, **curiæ**) (kew′ree ah, kew′ree eye), a Roman council house.

curstable (kur′steh bl), a course of stones bearing moldings, to produce a string course.

cur′tail step, the bottom step in an open-string stair, extending in a half-round or volute following the volute of the handrail.

cur′tain wall, a wall supporting no more than its own weight, the roof or floor above being carried by the framework of the structure.

curves, or **French curves,** aids in drafting in the form of thin plastic or wood cut to the profiles of various irregular curves.

curvilin′ear gable, a gable in which the upper slopes have geometric curves.

curvom′eter, a measuring instrument registering units of length by running a small wheel along curved or irregular lines.

cush′ion, in plumbing, air pocketed beyond and above a faucet or valve, to obviate water hammer.

cushion capital, a capital common to Romanesque and early Medieval architecture, and, in another form, to Norman work (15*a*).

cusp, a terminal point marking the conjunction of arcs in Gothic tracery (8*g*).

cus′tom house, a building for receiving custom duties.

cut nail, one cut out of an iron sheet, as contrasted with the wire nail.

cut′out, a means of breaking an electric circuit, usually because of overload.

cyclone cellar, *see* storm cellar.

Cyclope′an, descriptive of ancient masonry structures in which huge blocks of stone are fitted closely together and without mortar. The name derives from the Cyclopes, a legendary race of Sicilian one-eyed giants.

cy′clostyle, the Greek term for a circle of columns and their entablature without an inner temple.

cyl′inder lock, one in which a set of interior tumblers prevents a cylinder from turning until the right key releases them.

cyma (si′mah), a molding having a reversed-curve profile; cyma recta (11*b*) has the convex half nearer the wall; cyma reversa (11*d*) has the concave half nearer the wall. *See also* ogee and talon (10, 12, 13).

cymatium (si ma′teum), Greek term for the upper molding of a cornice or capping (13).

cymbia (sim′bee ah), a fillet.

cy′mograph, an instrument for recording the profiles of moldings.

cy′press (*Taxodium distichum*), a wood found in the low swamplands in southeastern U.S.A. and in the Mississippi River valley. The heartwood is particularly resistant to decay, so that the wood is used for exterior woodwork and work in contact with the ground.

pecky cypress, cypress having disintegrated spots, caused by a fungus attack in the standing tree, which are thought to add interest to its texture and color.

cyzicenus (sizzy see′nus), in ancient architecture, a large hall decorated with sculpture.

D

dab, to dress the face of a stone by picking with a pointed tool.

da′do, a skirting, usually several feet in depth, above the baseboard of an interior wall. 2. of a classical pedestal, the flat space between base and crown moldings (12, 13). 3. a rebate or groove in woodwork.

Dædalus (ded′alus), a Greek mythological figure who personified the beginning of the arts of sculpture and architecture.

dag′oba, a Buddhist shrine of mound shape, containing sacred relics.

daho′ma (*Piptadenia africana*), a wood from West Africa; straw-colored sapwood and light to golden brown heartwood; a durable, moderately hard, termite-resistant wood.

dairi (di′ree), residence of the Japanese Mikado.

dairy (dare′ree), an apartment or a building for the preservation of milk and its manufacture into other products.

da′is, a platform raised above the floor level of a public room.

dak-bungalow, a travelers' rest house of East India.

dalan′, in Persian or Indian architecture, a veranda or other partly open shelter.

dallage [Fr.] (dal lazhe), a floor or pavement of marble, tile, or stone.

damaskeening (dammas keen′ing), the decoration of a metal surface by etching or by inlaying another metal in pattern.

dam′mar, a gum resin used as a base of certain varnishes.

damp course, a layer of water-impervious material insulating the wall or floor above it.

damp′er, a checking device to regulate the flow of air or gases in a pipe or duct, sometimes by admitting more air from outside the duct, as in a furnace damper.

dancette′, chevron-like molding, as in Norman architecture (9*f*).

d. & m., abbrev. for dressed and matched lumber.

dan′ta (*Cistanthera papaverifera*), a wood from West Africa with sapwood of pinkish yellow and heartwood reddish brown, lustrous, fine-textured, hard, and tough; its architectural use is in veneer.

dar, in Indian and Persian architecture, a gateway; usually compounded with a location name.

dar′by, a tool of plasterers and masons, used for smoothing a surface that is not to be troweled hard.

D.Arch., abbrev. for the degree Doctor of Architecture.

dark′room, a room from which actinic light is excluded, for photographic processing.

datum (day′tum), or **datum level,** a horizontal plane elevation (often in feet above sea level), used as a reference plane for other elevations in surveying and mapping.

daub, to coat roughly with mud or plaster.

David's shield, *see* Solomon's seal (5*z*).

dead'bolt, a lock bolt without a spring, that is, one not actuated automatically.

dead'ening, insulation against sound transmission.

dead'latch, a springless lock, actuated from the outside by a key, on the inside by a knob or handle.

dead load, a constant weight or pressure, used in computing strength of beams, or floors, or roof surfaces.

dead'man, buried cross timbers, or a bulk of concrete, to which are attached guy pieces of wood, or wire cable, to anchor an upright post nearby, as a fence end or a gatepost.

deal, English term for a commonly used pine. 2. a general term used in many parts of the world for board and plank sizes of softwoods.

white deal, *see* spruce, European.

dean'ery, a building for the office or residence of a dean.

debris (deb ree'), accumulated rubbish or waste matter resulting from the remodeling or building operation.

decadence (de kay'dense), the state or process of deterioration from a high point in a period of art.

decastyle (dek'a stile), indicative of a range of ten columns as a peristyle or as the front portico of a classical temple.

decibel (dess'uh bell), unit of loudness of sound. It is derived from the vocabulary of communication engineering, and is the equivalent of the loss in power in 1 mile of standard cable at 860 cycles.

deck, an unsheltered floor of wooden construction.

deck-on-hip, a flat roof capping a hip roof.

Dec'orated, a term applied to the medieval architecture in England prevailing during the reigns of the first three Edwards. It followed the Early English period.

decora'tion, ornamentation or embellishment, usually independent of construction, although elements of construction may be decorated.

dec'orator, an artist or artisan who, professionally or as a merchant, undertakes the furnishing and embellishment of interiors.

de'dans, a screened gallery for spectators at the end of a room designed for court tennis.

Deer Isle, a coarse, pinkish lavender-tinted, medium-gray granite of Maine.

deewan, *see* leewan.

deflec'tion, the amount by which a horizontal member bends at the center under stress.

deform'ed steel bars, reinforcing steel for concrete, twisted or roughened to secure better bond in tension or compression.

dehumidify (dee hyou mid'ifi), to reduce the moisture content of air.

delu′brum, holy of holies in an ancient temple.

demimetope (demmy met′o pee), a half metope or incomplete metope in a Doric frieze (12).

demolition (demmo lish′un), the systematic razing of a building.

den′sity, in urban planning, the number of persons dwelling upon an acre of land, sometimes upon a square mile.

dentic′ulated, or **denticular,** bearing dentils as enrichment (12).

den′til, one of a series of blocklike projections forming a molding, as in the Ionic entablature (13).

depen′dency, a minor building flanking a major one in a single composition; usually dependencies are in symmetrical pairs.

depot (dee′po), a railroad station. 2. a storage or collection center. 3. in France, a building for military storage.

dep′reter, pebble-dash stucco.

der′rick, a hoisting device, usually made up of a guyed mast, a boom hinged to it, and pulley ropes; a crane differs from it mainly in that the crane is power operated.

describe, to draw graphically with compass, as to describe an arc.

descrip′tive geometry, the study of lines and solids in space through their projections on two planes.

design (dee zine′), to express graphically a mental concept. 2. to bring into being a mental concept.

de′tail, a graphic representation of a part, usually at larger scale than the design to which it belongs. 2. a part of the whole.

devel′oped surface, a curved or angular surface graphically represented as flattened out upon a plane.

dew point, the temperature at which air becomes oversaturated with moisture and the moisture condenses.

diabase (dye′eh base), a granular igneous rock, dark gray to black, sometimes called dolerite.

diacon′icum, in ancient churches, a place roughly equivalent to the sacristy.

di′aglyph, sculpture sunk below the general surface.

diamic′ton, the ancient practice of wall building in which the faces were of ashlar with a filling of rubble.

Diamond Gray, a coarse-grain granite in gray with brown and black markings; quarried at Isle, Minn.

di′aper ornament, ornament repeated in a plane pattern.

di′astyle, classical term for buildings of wide intercolumniation.

diathyra (dee ah thy′rah), a vestibule leading to the doors of a Greek house.

diato′ni, the through-bonding stones in ancient Greek architecture.

diazo′ma, or **diazoma′ta,** in ancient classical work, the landings at various levels encircling an amphitheater.

dicasterium (di cass tee′reum), in ancient architecture, a tribunal or hall of justice.

dictyotheton (dik tee o the′ ton), Greek term for masonry laid up in meshlike courses. 2. open latticework.

die, the cube or dado of a pedestal (12, 13).

diglyph (di′glif), double-grooved, as triglyph is triple-grooved.

dimension (di men′shun), measurement between two given points.

dimension lumber or **stone,** these materials pre-cut to specified sizes.

dinette′, a diminutive dining-room.

di′ning-room, a room in which meals are served.

diora′ma, a representation of a scene or an event in which the third dimension is partly used, partly simulated.

di′orite, granular, crystallized igneous stone composed of feldspar and hornblende.

dip′teros, Greek term designating a building having a double peristyle.

dipylon (dip′ee lon), a pair of gates, side by side.

direct current, abbrev. d.c., an electric current which flows in one direction.

Directoire (dee rek twar), belonging to the period of the Directory in France (1795–1799).

discharg′ing arch, synonym for relieving arch. *See* arch, relieving (1*c*).

dispen′sary, that part of a hospital given over to dispensing medicines and the like, and, by extension, the department where outpatients are received.

distem′per, a paint which, at least before application, is soluble in water.

dis′tyle, Greek designation for two-columned.

ditch, a trench, as for burying underground pipe lines.

ditriglyph (di try′glif), a two-triglyph interval between columns in the Doric entablature.

divid′ers, a drafting instrument like a compass but with both ends bearing sharp points.

divining rod (di vine′ing), a forked branch, usually of hazel, by which it is claimed that the location of underground water can be ascertained.

'dobe, *see* adobe.

dodec′astyle, indicative of a range of twelve columns as a peristyle or as the front portico.

dog bars, vertical intermediate members in the lower part of a gate.

dog′leg stairs, those framed around a central newel and thus having no well.

dog′tooth molding, *see* tooth ornament (9*o*).

dog′trot, a covered passage, or wider space, joining two parts of a house, such as a covered porch between house and a wing; a breezeway.

dolmen (dole′men), a burial chamber of prehistoric times in Great Britain and France, of huge, unsurfaced stones standing aboveground.

dol′omite, a crystalline calcium magnesium carbonate, white to pale pink, resembling marble.

dome, a hemispherical roof form.

domes′tic architecture, that having to do with the house.

domicile (dom′issil), a place of fixed residence, a home.

dom′inant, in design, an element which dominates the composition.

don′jon, the major element of a medieval castle or fortress, containing the principal rooms; usually marked by its dominating tower.

door (dore), a hinged, pivoted, or sliding member, permitting passage through a wall.

door buck, a doorframe of rough material to which the finished doorframe is attached.

door check, an automatic door closer.

doorframe, the assembly of members into which a door fits when closed, consisting of jambs and head but not sill.

doorstop, a block or pin in floor or base, preventing a door from opening too far.

door′way, an opening for passage through a wall.

door′yard, fenced or walled space before a principal entrance.

Doric (dahr′ik), one of the classical orders of architecture (12).

dor′mer, a minor gable in a pitched roof, usually bearing a window or windows on its front vertical face.

dor′mitory, a residential building in an institution. 2. a common sleeping-room.

dos′sal, a hanging of rich fabric as a background for an altar.

dosseret′, a block used above the capital in Byzantine architecture—an inverted truncated pyramid form.

double-acting hinge, a hinge permitting a door to swing through 180° on its jamb, usually controlled by a spring tending to closure.

double-cone molding, a molding used in arches of Norman architecture.

double glazing, the use of two sheets of glass with rarefied-air space between, serving as insulation against passage of heat.

double-hung window, one having two balanced sashes, one sliding over the other vertically.

doucine [Fr.] (doo seen), French term for cyma recta (11*b*).

dovetail (duv′tale), a woodworking joint between boards or timbers (4*b*, *c*).

dovetail molding, a molding in which interlocked triangles are used (9*d*).

dow′el, a cylindrical pin used in woodworking joints (4*a*). 2. a reinforcing bar projecting above a base to strengthen the joint between the base and the object set upon it.

dow′er house, English term for the house occupied by a widow after the passing of her manor house to the eldest son.

down′spout, a rain leader or vertical pipe to conduct water from the eaves gutter.

drafts′man, or **draughtsman,** one who translates a design into drawings.

drain, a pipe or open trench for leading away water or waste.

drain′board, the surface adjacent to the rim of a kitchen sink, sloped or grooved to drain into the sink.

drain tile, clay pipe, usually with open joints, to lead moisture away from a footing or for use in a septic-plant disposal field.

draught (draft), old term for drawing.

Dravid′ian architecture, that of southern India in ancient times; it consisted largely of temples.

draw′er, a storage receptacle which reveals its open top by being drawn out horizontally.

draw′ing, graphic representation.

draw′ing board, a rectangular, smooth-surface slab, usually less than an inch thick and usually of soft wood, on which is fastened paper, linen, or other thin material on which a drawing is to be made.

draw′ing pen, a double-nibbed instrument for making ink lines of variable width when guided along an edge, as triangle or straightedge.

draw′ing-room, originally a room to which host and guests withdrew from the dining-room; a formal room for social intercourse in house or club.

dredge, to deepen a water channel or the bottom of a body of water.

dress, of stones, to cut to finished shape; of boards or timber, to plane smooth.

dress′er, a kitchen unit of furniture, movable or built in, with cupboards above and below an open counter space.

dress′ing-room, a room adjoining, and usually smaller than, a room for sleeping; usually having closet space for clothing.

dri′er, a varnish-like liquid that is added to paints or varnishes to hasten their drying; driers are usually metallic compositions, available also in solid form.

drill, to cut a cylindrical hole.

drink′ing foun′tain, a plumbing fixture for the dispensing of natural or cooled drinking water.

drip, the projection of a vertical surface beyond a lower one in a parallel plane, with undercut edge to drip rain water. 2. a condensation drain line in vapor heating systems or plumbing.

drip mold, a molding shaped for drip.

drip′stone, a label mold or hood mold.

drive′-in, descriptive of moving picture theaters where the spectator remains in his automobile; descriptive of banks, restaurants, and other buildings where the customer remains in his automobile while being served.

dro′mos, Greek term for race course. 2. a formal approach flanked by sculptured figures or colonnades.

drop′light, an electric light on a flexible cord.

drop sid′ing, exterior wall covering of horizontal boards rebated on the lower edge to overlap.

drove, a mason's blunt chisel for facing stone.

druids' altar, a dolmen.

drum, one of the cylindrical stone blocks of a column shaft. 2. the cylindrical wall supporting a dome, lantern, or cupola (7*b*). 3. a metal container for oil, tar, and the like.

dry-bulb temperature, the temperature of the air as recorded by the ordinary (as differentiated from the wet-bulb) thermometer.

dry′ing oil, an oil possessing to a marked degree the property of taking up oxygen from the air and changing to a relatively hard, tough, and elastic substance when exposed in a thin film to the air.

dry rot, decomposition of wood through fungus attack.

dry′-wall, descriptive of traditional construction in which prefabricated materials replace plaster for the inside wall covering. 2. outdoors, a masonry wall laid up without mortar.

dry well, a pit, usually filled with coarse stone, into which water or effluent is led for leaching.

dubbing out, in plastering, the rough formation of a cornice or other elaborate form before the finishing coat is run.

duct, a conduit or passageway for air. 2. an underground encased conduit, or group of them, for electric wiring.

ductil′ity, the property of being elongated when subjected to a tensile stress higher than the elastic limit; the converse of elasticity.

dumbwait′er, a small elevator for transporting dishes or other small objects between stories.

dungeon (dun′jun), an unlighted, or sparsely lighted, poorly ventilated chamber at the base of the central tower of a medieval castle; this tower, called donjon, gave the name to prisons generally.

Dunville stone, very fine-grain, light buff sandstone, soft when first quarried but hardening on exposure; susceptible to finest carving; much used in interior work.

duomo (du o′mo), literally a dome; by association, a cathedral.

du′plex apartment, one having rooms on two floors, with private stairway between.

Duralu′min, trade name for an alloy of aluminum used in construction, largely in rolled sheets.

dur′amen, the heartwood of an exogenous tree trunk.

dust′ing, the loosening of fine particles by abrasion, as on the surface of a cement floor.

Dutch bond, of brickwork, *see* bond.

Dutch door, one divided horizontally in two leaves which operate independently or, locked together, as one.

dwell′ing, a house for the family unit.

Dymax′ion, a word invented by R. Buckminster Fuller and defined by him as "mass-produced logic." The term has been known widely for its connection with his Dymaxion House, a design for a dwelling of hexagonal plan supported by a central mast and cables, close about which was a core of utilities.

dy′namo, a machine for transforming mechanical work into electric current.

E

ear, *see* crossette (2*i*).

Early English, a period of English ecclesiastical architecture extending from 1200 to 1300 A.D.

earth closet, a privy utilizing dry dust as an absorbent for the wastes.

east end, the chancel end of a Christian church, widely so called, irrespective of the orientation, because of the medieval tradition that a priest officiating at the altar should face east.

eaves, the edge of a roof that projects over an outside wall.

ebony (ebb′onee) (*Diospyros ebenum*), a fine-textured wood of Ceylon and India, heartwood jet black or, rarely, streaked.

American ebony (*Brya ebenus*), a wood from the West Indies; its yellow to dark-brown background is variegated or finely striped; it is exceedingly hard and takes a high polish.

black ebony (*Diospyros tomentosa*), a hard, heavy wood from India, the heartwood of which becomes black, often streaked with brown or purple, and can be highly polished.

calamander ebony (*Diospyros quaesita*), a wood from Ceylon, close-textured, hard, and of a hazel-brown color, mottled and striped with black; used in veneer and furniture.

Macassar ebony, *see* marblewood.

Mozambique ebony, *see* blackwood, African.

ecclesiastical architecture (ek leesy ass′tikl), that of the church in general.

ecclesiology (ekleez e oll′ogy), the science and art of building, decorating, and furnishing churches, including ecclesiastical antiquities.

echelle [Fr.] (eh shell), scale, as of a drawing.

echeum (ek e′um), a vase used in the ancient Greek theater for sound amplification.

echinus (ek i′nus), the circular molding immediately under the square abacus of a Doric capital, its profile approximating the quarter-round (12).

eclec′tic architecture, that based on, or imitative of, styles selected by personal preference.

École des Beaux-Arts (akole day boze ar), the French national school of fine arts in Paris.

ecphora (ek′fo rah), Greek term for the projection of a member or molding of a column beyond the face of the shaft, or sometimes from the axis.

edge grain, or **vertical grain,** descriptive of lumber in which the annual rings form an angle of 45° or more with the surface

edifice (ed′ifis), a building of dignity and importance.

effective temperature, an experimentally determined scale of temperature, independent of dry- or wet-bulb recordings, measuring bodily comfort or discomfort in all combinations of temperature and humidity.

efflores′cence, a disfiguring deposit of saline particles on the weather face of masonry, particularly brickwork, resulting from the presence of salts in the clay or mortar.

ef′fluent, the liquid discharged from a septic tank after bacterial action on sewage.

egg-and-dart, egg-and-tongue, or **egg-and-anchor,** a molding familiar in classical architecture, with the appearance of an engaged egg shape alternating with an engaged dart form (10*e*).

egg crate, a form of baffle diffuser used beneath fluorescent tubes for ceiling lighting.

e′gress, a path of exit.

Egyptian architecture, that of the most ancient civilization of which history gives us clear knowledge, carried on from at least 5000 B.C. to 100 A.D. It was an architecture based firmly on religion; it was created with little wood and little metal but with durable stone in the fertile valley of the Nile.

Egyptology (e jip toll′ogy), the science and art of Egyptian monuments, artifacts, inscriptions, and the like.

ejec′tor, in plumbing, a power pump for raising water or sewage to a drain at a higher elevation.

ek′ki (*Lophira alata* var. *procera*), a wood from West Africa with dark red to chocolate-brown heartwood, speckled; extremely hard, heavy, and coarse in texture; used for outdoor construction and flooring.

elæothesium (e leo theece′eum), in the Roman baths, a room in which the bather anointed himself after bathing.

elasticity (e lass tiss′ity), the property of matter which requires continued force to change its shape.

elbow (ell′bo), in piping, a fitting that effects change of direction in the line, usually of 90°

electric eye, *see* photoelectric eye.

electrolier (elek tro leer′), a luminaire supplied by electric current.

elec′troplating, applying a surface deposit of one metal on another, by electrolysis.

elevation (elleh va′shun), height above sea level or some other datum. 2. a graphic projection, at a given scale and upon a vertical plane, of an object, such as a building.

eleva′tor, a car and its equipment for vertical transportation.

Elgin Marbles, the collection of sculptured fragments brought to the British Museum in London by Lord Elgin; the collection consisted mainly of pieces of the metopes, frieze, tympana, and other parts of the Parthenon, the Nike Apteros, and the Choragic Monument of Lysicrates.

Elizabeth′an architecture, that of the era of Queen Elizabeth of England—the latter part of the sixteenth and beginning of the seventeenth century; a transition style with Gothic features and Renaissance detail.

ell, an extension of a building at right angles to its length.

ellipse (e lips′), the conic section resulting from cutting a cone obliquely through its curved surface. The adjective is *elliptical.*

elm, American (*Ulmus americana*), a moderately hard, heavy, and strong wood of the eastern U.S. It is used largely for core stock.

Carpathian burl elm (*Ulmus campestris*), a wood from France, England, and the Carpathian Mountains, resembling ash or oak burl and varying in color from almost brick red to light tan; used for veneer.

rock elm (*Ulmus thomasii*), a heavy, hard, and strong wood, prized for its bending qualities.

Elwood sandstone, a light buff and dark buff stone of western Pennsylvania.

Elysée (a lee zay), official residence in Paris of the President of the Republic of France.

em′bassy, official residence of an ambassador.

embat′tled, descriptive of a wall topped with an embrasured parapet (8*b*).

embel′lish, to add decoration.

emboss′, to ornament with pattern in relief, usually by a stamping process.

embrasure (em bra′zhoor), a beveled opening in a wall or parapet.

emeri, *see* ireme.

em′inent domain′, the right to expropriate or condemn private property for public use.

emissar′ium, a canal for the drainage of swamps, or a floodgate for the same.

empaistic (em pace′tik), the art of inlaying metal in metal, as practised by the ancients long before buhl.

Empire (ahm peer), design of the period of the first French Empire, largely initiated by the architects Charles Percier (1764–1838) and Pierre F. L. Fontaine (1762–1853).

emplec′tion, Greek and Roman masonry in which thick walls were faced on both sides with ashlar and filled with rubble.

enam′el, a paint which is characterized by an ability to form an especially smooth and glossy film.

en axe [Fr.] (ahn ax), French for on axis.

encar′pus, in classical architecture, a continuing festoon or swag (16*j*) of fruits and flowers, usually on a frieze.

encaus′tic tile, that having its surface or decoration in vitreous color.

enceinte wall (ahn see ahnt), an outer wall enclosing a group of buildings.

en′crinal marble, marble deriving decoration from fossils or shells.

end-grain, describing the face of a piece of timber exposed when the fibers are cut transversely.

enfilade [Fr.] (ahn feel ahd), the alignment of doors on an axis extending through a series of rooms.

engage′, to attach one element to a simpler and more extensive one so that the first element seems partly embedded, as an engaged column or baluster.

engineer′ing, the science through which the properties of matter and the sources of power are utilized for man's benefit.

English bond, *see* bond (3*d*).

English cross bond, *see* bond (3*g*).

English garden wall bond, *see* bond (3*f*).

English Renaissance, a period of architecture which Sir Banister Fletcher divides into two parts: Elizabethan (1558–1603) and Jacobean (1603–1625).

English roofing tile, a flat-top clay tile with interlocking side joints (6*e*).

enneastyle (en′neah style), in classical architecture, having nine columns.

entab′lature, in classical architecture, the horizontal group of members immediately above the column capitals; divided into three major parts, it consists of architrave, frieze, and cornice (12, 13, 14).

entail′, an early English term, derived from the French, for sculptured ornament or for any embellishment produced by carving or moldings. 2. to bequeath with restrictions.

en′tasis, the subtle curve by which the shaft of a column is diminished in section above the cylindrical lowest third (12).

en′terclose, a passage between two rooms in a house, or leading from a room to a hall.

entourage [Fr.] (ahn toor ahzhe), environment; the grounds immediately surrounding a building.

en′trance, the doorway, vestibule or lobby through which one enters a building.

entresol [Fr.] (ahn treh sohl), a mezzanine or half-story of a building between ground floor and the first story above it.

en′try, a short hall immediately inside an outer door.

en′velope, an imaginary assembly of planes to represent the maximum volume of a building with regard to zoning and other volume restrictions.

envoi [Fr.] (ahn vwah), a drawing made by a scholarship student to be sent to his masters.

eopyla (e op′illah), Greek term for a church with an apse at the eastern end.

eothola (e oath′olah), Greek term for a church with an apse at the western end.

ephebeion (effeh bee′yon), Greek term for a building for exercise and wrestling.

epi [Fr.] (a pee), a topmost point, as a spire.

epicranitis (epik ran′itiss), Greek term for the tiles forming the top member of a cornice.

ep′igraph, an inscription on a tomb, building, or sculpture.

epinaos (a pee na′os), the posticum or temple space in rear of the cella.

episcenium (eppy see′neum), the proscenium and fixed set of the ancient theater.

epistaton (a pee stah′tun) (plural, **epistata**), in Grecian archeology, the entablature, or sometimes all the masonry above the column capitals.

epistle side (eh pis′sl), of a church, the right-hand side as one faces the altar. The left-hand side is sometimes called the gospel side.

episto′mium, the spout of a water pipe, or its valve.

epistyle, or **epistylium** (ep′e stile, eppy sti′leum), in classical architecture, the architrave, or lowest of the three divisions of an entablature (12, 13, 14).

epitithedes (eppy tith′idees), Greek term for the crown or upper moldings of an entablature.

épure, French term for full-size detail.

Erechtheum (errek thee′um), the Temple of Athena Polias, on the Acropolis, Athens; famous example of the Ionic order.

erect′, to build. 2. in geometry, to draw a line at right angles to a specified base.

ergastulum (er gas′tchu lum), ancient Roman term for a slave prison.

eris′ma, a buttress or shoring to support a wall.

Es′calator, trade name of a system of treads, risers, and handrails actuated by machinery on a concealed loop, forming a moving stairway.

escoinson (es quan son), old French term for the inner edge of a window jamb. In Scotland it is "scuntion."

escutcheon (es kutch′un), the face plate of a keyhole, or one also backing the door handle. The term originally signified a shield on which arms were emblazoned.

esonarthex (e so nar′thex), the inner narthex in cases where there is also an outer narthex (exonarthex).

espagnolette bolt (es pah nyo let), a device for locking casements or French windows or doors, consisting of two long rods, recessed or flush with the inside face, engaged in sill and lintel by the turn of a handle at convenient height.

espalier [Fr.] (es pal yay), a lattice fixed against a wall, to which a fruit tree is fastened to induce a flattened shape.

esplanade (es plah nahd), a concourse or landscaped plateau with drives and walks.

esquisse [Fr.] (es keece), a preliminary sketch or plan; specifically, the nine-hour sketch made *en loge* at the beginning of a *projet.*

esquisse-esquisse [Fr.], a rough sketch; in the École des Beaux-Arts, the twelve-hour and twenty-four-hour sketches.

estaminet [Fr.] (es tah me nay), a public eating place where smoking is permitted.

esthet′ics, the science and philosophy of beauty.

es′timate, a valuation based on opinion, or upon incomplete data.

estrade′, a dais or raised platform.

estufa (es too′fah), an underground council chamber of a pueblo.

étage [Fr.] (a tahzhe), a story, or mere range of openings, of a building.

bel étage, the principal story.

etch′ing, lines cut into a metal surface, either by a cutting tool or by acid guided by a frisket of wax or other covering.

Etrus′can, of the arts or people of ancient Etruria in west central Italy, conquered by Rome in 283 B.C.

eucalyp′tus, trees native to Australia, having many species that have been widely planted outside Australia; only a few produce a commercial supply of lumber.

eurythmy (you rith′me), harmonious relationship among all the parts of a building.

eu′style, in classical architecture, descriptive of intercolumniation of 2¼ diameters, center to center.

évasé [Fr.] (a vah zay), widening outward or upward; flaring.

ewery (you′ree), a storage room in early English houses, perhaps the forerunner of the scullery.

ex′cavate, to dig earth below ground level.

exedra, or **exhedra** (eks′eh drah) (plural, **exedræ**), a form originating in classic architecture, generally open and semicircular in plan, with or without roof, providing a continuous seat; in later Renaissance architecture, frequently used to terminate a garden axis.

ex′it, a way of egress.

exonar′thex, an outer narthex.

expan′sion, enlargement of length or bulk by reason of temperature rise, or, less commonly, through absorption of water.

expan′sion bolt, one gripping a drilled hole in masonry or plaster by means of a socket that expands as the bolt end is screwed into it.

expan′sion tank, in a hot-water heating system, an open tank in which the expansion of the hot water can take place.

ex′pediter, one who checks and hastens the arrival of building materials or equipment to meet a progress schedule.

exten′sion, an addition to an existing structure.

exte′rior, outside, not fully enclosed.

ex′tra, work or material, or both, incorporated in a building and not included in the contract between owner and builder.

extrados (eks tra′doss), the upper face of an arch, on top of the voussoirs, even though these may be covered by supported masonry (1*b*).

extru′ded, formed by forcing plastic material or molten metal through a shaped opening.

eye, an opening at the top of a dome or cupola. 2. the center of the volute of an Ionic capital (13). 3. in hardware, the metal loop which engages a hook.

eye′brow, a dormer, usually of small size, the roof line over the upright face of which is an arch curve dying into a reverse curve to meet the horizontal at either end.

F

fab'ric, a structure, as the fabric of Amiens.
fabrica'tion, construction.
façade (fah sahd), a face of a building, usually the front.
face, to overlay one material with another, as to face a brick wall with marble. 2. (noun) the exposed side of a unit of masonry.
face brick, brick made or selected for color, texture, or other characteristic, to be used on the exposed surface of a wall, probably to be backed up with cheaper brick or other material.
facettes [Fr.] (fah set), the flat projections between the flutes of a column shaft (13, 14).
fac'tor of safety, the factor by which the expected weight or stress is multiplied to indicate the surplus of strength or resistance provided for safety's sake.
fac'tory, a building in which manufacturing is carried on.
F.A.I.A., Fellow of The American Institute of Architects.
faïence (fah yahns), enameled clay products, but not including the highest grades such as porcelain.
fail'ure, breaking point, as that of a material tested for compressive strength to failure.
fall, in water supply or drainage, the slope, usually given in inches per foot.
false work, temporary construction as an aid in building a structure meant to endure.
fan, a power-driven blower.
fane, a consecrated place, as a church; a sanctuary, a temple.
fan'light, an overdoor window, semi-elliptical or semicircular in shape, with radial muntins or leads (10*a*).
fan vaulting, a system of vaulting used in the Perpendicular period, in which a group of ribs spring from a slender shaft or from a corbel, and then diverge. Occasionally ribs also spring from a pendant at the center of the vaulting (8*a*).
farm'house, the residential unit on a farm.
fasces (fas'sees), a bundle of rods bound by a thong and showing a projecting ax blade near one end, a symbol of power often used in Roman architecture.
fascia (fay'shah), a horizontal band of vertical face, usually in combination with moldings, as in the lowest member of a classical cornice (12).
fastig'ium, the apex of a pediment, a top roof ridge.
fatigue (fa teeg'), in structural members, a weakening of elasticity.
fau'ces, in a Roman house, the passage from the peristyle to the atrium.
faucet (faw'set), a terminal valved outlet in a pipe line bearing a liquid.
fault, a dislocation of strata which may interfere with natural underground drainage.

fa′vas, one piece in a paving of hexagonal units; a unit of sectilia.

feather edge (feth′er), a sharp arris formed by beveling a board or the like.

felt, as insulation, compacted fibers of various materials in flexible sheet form. 2. as roofing, tar-impregnated paper, commercially supplied in rolls.

fem′erell, a ventilating shaft through a roof.

fe′mor, shank, or **orlo,** a plane space between the channels of a triglyph in the Doric frieze. The Greek term is meros (12).

fence, an enclosing framework for land, bearing pickets, boards, rails, or other means of barring passage.

fen′estell, or **fenestel′la,** a niche for the piscina and occasionally the credence, on the left side of the altar as one faces it.

fenestra′tion, the disposition of windows in a façade.

fer′etory, a church's repository for sacred relics.

fero′her, a symbolic winged disc, observed in Mesopotamian monuments (16*b*).

ferro-concrete, concrete construction reinforced by steel bars, mesh, or the like. The more widely used term is reinforced concrete.

festoon′, a sculptured swag or garland in a catenary curve between two points (16*j*).

feuage (few′age), a tax on chimneys; fumage.

fi′berboard, a sheet material made of compressed wood fibers held with a binding substance; hardboard, building board.

fi′ber conduit, tubing of molded fiber for insulating purposes.

Fi′berglas, trade name for products of glass fibers; of a wool-like consistency for insulation; longer fibers are used for weaving fabrics that are incombustible.

fictile (fik′til), of clay, capable of being molded.

field tile, *see* drain tile.

fig′uring, the process of adding dimensions to working drawings. 2. the process of estimating quantities and costs from working drawings and specifications.

fill, or **backfill,** replacement of excavated earth.

fil′ler, a pigmented composition in liquid or paste form, used for filling the pores or irregularities in surfaces of open-grained woods, preparatory to application of other finishes.

fil′let, a narrow, flat band serving as a molding or as a division between larger moldings (13).

finial (fin′e al), a terminal form at the top of spire, gable, gatepost, pinnacle, or other point of relative height.

fin′ish, exterior or interior millwork. 2. the final treatment of a surface, as eggshell finish on paint, brushed-brass finish, etc.

finish floor, the exposed top member of a flooring assembly.

finish hardware, hardware that is within sight, given a special finish.

Fink truss, *see* truss (4*r*).

fir, Douglas (*Pseudotsuga taxifolia*), also called "Oregon pine," although neither a fir nor a pine; found abundantly in the northwest U.S.A.; a wood of strength and density approximately equal to those of southern yellow pine; widely used for flooring, sheathing, and timber.

white fir (*Abies concolor*), a wood cut mainly in Idaho and California; both heartwood and sapwood a reddish tinge of white; a wood of many architectural uses. *See also* spruce, European.

fire′back, a plate of cast or wrought iron, usually ornamented, placed vertically at the back of a fireplace just above hearth level, to protect the masonry from excess heat.

fire′brick, brick made of a clay containing no fusible material.

fire clay, a clay that will withstand intense heat, used in brick for fire chambers.

fire door, a metal-sheathed door, often held from sliding shut by a fusible link.

fire escape, a fixed or movable supplementary means of egress from a building.

fire hydrant, an outdoor water-supply outlet with wrench-actuated valve and a connection for fire hose.

fire′place, an opening on a hearth, served by a chimney flue, where an open fire may be laid.

fire′proof, protected against fire; relatively incombustible.

fire-resist′ant, descriptive of building material which resists destruction by fire for a definite duration of time.

fire screen, a movable barrier against excess heat or flying sparks, set before a fireplace.

fire stop, a retardant to flue action between wall or floor timbers.

fire tower, a stairway enclosed with fire-resistant construction, usually entered from the various floors of a building through fire doors.

fire wall, a wall resistant to the spread of fire.

fish′plate, a plate or plank fastened to the sides of two beams or rails placed end to end, to effect a splice; flitchplate.

fix′ture, an article of equipment in a building, usually the part that is last added, making a system operative, as lighting fixtures, plumbing fixtures.

flag′ging, paving of flagstones or other flat stones.

flak′ing, a fault in painting; the peeling off of the coating.

flambeau (flam′bo), a torch or torchlike lighting fixture.

Flamboy′ant, the term applied to a period of Medieval architecture in France, in which the mullions and tracery terminate in waved lines of contrary flexure in flamelike forms. It extended through the fifteenth and half of the sixteenth century.

flange, a projecting edge, as the flange of a heavy pipe, by which it is bolted to another flanged pipe, forming a flanged joint; or the projecting edge of a steel beam or a truss.

flan′ning, the interior splay of a window jamb.

flare, the widening of a tubular form, funnel-like.

flash, to make a joint weathertight, usually with sheet copper but also with composition flashing, such as the joint between a chimney and a roof, or the joint between wall and windowhead. The noun is *flashing* (16*i*).

flat, to finish paint without gloss. 2. an apartment on one floor level.

flat arch, *see* arch (1*a*).

flat roof, a roof having only sufficient slope for drainage.

flat′ting agent, a material added to paints, varnishes, and other coating materials to reduce the gloss of the dried film.

flèche [Fr.] (flesh), a slender spire, usually over the intersection of nave and transept axes.

Flem′ish bond, *see* bond (3*b*).

Flemish gardenwall bond, *see* bond (3*i*).

fleur-de-lis [Fr.] (fler deh lee), a conventionalized iris form, often used as a finial; the royal insignia of France.

fleuron (fleron), the anthemion, the honeysuckle motif (11*i*).

flexible conduit, *see* BX.

flight of steps, a continuous series of steps from floor to landing.

flint wall, one built in the English custom, its outer shell of flints with their rough faces.

flitch, a bundle of veneer sheets in sequence as they were sliced from the log. 2. a log made ready for cutting into veneer.

flitch beam, or **flitched girder,** a steel web bolted between two timbers.

flitchplate, a reinforcing and connecting member bolted or riveted over the butt joint of two plates in the same plane, effecting a splice; fishplate.

float, a mason's tool, a flat board with handle on one side, used for spreading and smoothing plaster or cement. 2. a float valve.

float valve, in plumbing, a valve actuated by a floating ball on a lever, as in a flush tank.

floodlighting, the bathing of an exterior in light by night, using carefully positioned and unobtrusive lights with reflectors.

floor (flore), the usually horizontal bottom surface of an enclosed space; also, less frequently, an outdoor paving.

floor plan, the plan, or horizontal section, of a building.

floor plug, in electricity, an outlet flush with the floor, into which may be connected extension circuits.

flor′iated, bearing carved flowers or leaves, as the Corinthian capital (14).

flue, a passage for air or gases of combustion.

flue lining, round or rectangular tubular unit lengths made of clay products, around which chimneys of masonry are built.

fluores′cent lighting, electric lighting in which the lamp is usually tubular and coated on its inner surface with a substance which glows under the excitation of a gas-conducted current in the presence of mercury.

flush, descriptive of adjoining surfaces in the same plane. 2. to activate a toilet, or to fill and empty any receptacle.

flush bolt, a fastening bolt which is flush with the surface of its door or window.

flush handle, one which folds into a receptacle so that it does not project beyond the face of the door.

flush joint, in masonry, when the joint mortar is pressed by the trowel flush with the surface.

flush tank, the nearby reservoir from which a toilet is flushed with water.

flush valve, *see* float valve.

flut′ing, or **flutes,** parallel grooving as an embellishment (12, 13, 14).

fly, or **flies,** the space in a theater, above and behind the proscenium arch, in which scenery is hung.

fly′ing but′tress, a buttress including a rampant arch (7*g*).

foil, a small arc in tracery (9*b*, *e*, *h*).

fold′ing doors, the assembly of two or more hinged leaves which, when straightened in a line, can close the opening.

fol′iated, using small arcs or foils in tracery.

folia′tion, the use of foils.

font, a basin for the water of baptism, or for holy water.

foot, linear unit of measure; 12 inches.

footcandle, unit of illumination; that of a surface 1′ square on which is uniformly distributed a flux of 1 lumen.

foot′ing, the spread foundation base of a wall or pier.

footlambert, or **apparent footcandle,** unit of brightness; that emitted or reflected from any surface emitting or reflecting 1 lumen per square foot.

foot′light, one of a series of lights along the front edge of a stage, lighting the stage but sheltered from the audience.

foot′pace, a resting space in the form of a platform set lengthwise in a straight flight of stairs. Sometimes loosely used as synonym for half-pace, which see.

foot scra′per, an edged metal strip, usually decorative in its supports, set by an outside doorway to scrape mud from the soles of shoes.

foot′stall, the pedestal of a column (12, 13).

foot′stone, springer, or **kneeler,** a stone built into the lower end of a gable to support its coping.

forging (forj′ing), a metal product shaped by hammering while softened by heat.

form, a temporary mold, such as that into which concrete is poured.

for′meret, the arch rib lying next to the wall in groined vaulting, shorter than the others.

Formica, trade name for a plastic material, usually in sheet form.

fo′rum, a public square for assembly.

foss, a moat, a barrier of water.

founda′tion, the nethermost member of a structure, the part in or on the supporting earth.

foundry (fown′dree), a place where metal casting is done.

fountain (fown′tin), jetted water and its receptacle. 2. an abbreviation for a dispensary, such as a soda fountain.

foyer (foy yay), a subordinate space between an entrance and the main interior to which it leads, in a theater, hotel, or apartment.

fract′able, a gable coping when broken into steps or curves.

frake, *see* limba.

frame, the skeleton structure of a building. 2. (adjective) wooden construction.

Francis I style, denoting work of the early Renaissance in France, during part of the sixteenth century.

Franklin stove, a stove substitute for a fireplace, invented by Benjamin Franklin.

frater house, the refectory or common room of a monastery.

frater′nity house, a building erected for the residential and meeting place of a student association known as a fraternity.

freehand drawing, that with the unaided hand, as contrasted with drawing with instruments.

free-standing, independent of an adjacent wall or other background, as a free-standing column.

free′stone, stone that is adapted to squaring up for use as a building stone.

French Creek granite, a fine-grain, hard, dark-colored granite of Pennsylvania; when polished the surface is almost black, the hammered faces light.

French curve, a drafting aid in template form, enabling the draftsman to draw various curves or arcs thereof by guiding his pencil or drawing pen along an edge.

French door, *see* French window.

French Grand Antique, a marble composed of large and small black-and-white fragments, producing sharp contrasts.

French polish, a finish for wood secured by repeated rubbing with shellac or a varnish gum dissolved in an abundance of alcohol.

French roofing tile, a flat, corrugated tile about 9″ x 16″, with interlocking flush side joints (6*c*).

French truss, same as Fink truss; *see* truss (4*r*).

French window, a doorway equipped with two glazed doors hinged at the jambs.

Freon, trade name for a group of refrigerants used in air-conditioning systems.

fres′co, mural painting in which the color is applied on, and becomes part of, wet plaster.

fresh-air inlet, an opening for the introduction of fresh air into a ventilating system. 2. in plumbing, an outside vent for a house drain trap.

fret, ornament, usually in band form, which we have from ancient Greece; a geometrically meandering strap pattern (11*a*).

F.R.I.B.A., Fellow of the Royal Institute of British Architects.

fric′tion latch, or **friction catch,** a spring-actuated device, mortised in the edge, for holding a small door closed, but allowing it to be opened by merely pulling its knob or handle.

frieze (freez), a band member in the vertical plane, sometimes decorated with sculpture relief, occurring just under a cornice (12, 13, 14).

frigidarium (frij id air'eum), in ancient Rome, a cooling-room or cold-bath room in a public bath.

frith'stool, a stone seat near the altar of a church, sacred refuge for one who claimed the privilege of sanctuary.

front, the more important face of a building, or that containing its main entrance.

fron'tal, the hangings or decorative panels in front of an altar; antependium.

fron'tispiece, in architectural drawing, a composition of several related elements resulting from an exercise in undergraduate design and rendering.

fronton [Fr.] (fronh tonh), a pediment, particularly the pediment form used over door or window.

frus'tum (plural, **frusta**), a drum of a column or pier, or a stump that remains after demolition or after ages of weathering.

fudge, to depart from correct drawing for the sake of appearance.

fugitive (fyou'jitiv) of colors, those liable to early fading.

fumage (fyou'midj), a tax on chimneys; feuage.

fume (fyoum), to treat finish woodwork with the fumes of ammonia to secure certain colors.

fumigation (fyou meh gay' shun), disinfecting with gas for the destruction of germs, animal, or insect life.

functionalism (fung'shinnal ism), the principle of establishing form and structure on the basis of the most economical satisfaction of physical needs.

furnace (fur'niss), the fire-containing apparatus for central heating by warm air.

fur'nishing, the equipment of an interior with furniture, floor covering, hangings, and other removable articles.

furniture (fur'ne choor), equipment for inhabited interiors and outlying spaces—chairs, tables, beds, desks, cabinets, and the like.

fur'ring, the separation of an inner wall surface from the main wall behind it, to secure air space between them or to modify the inner perimeter.

fusarole [It.] (fyou'sah roleh), a member, the section of which is a semicircle, carved into beadlike forms, as under the echinus of certain columns in the Doric and Ionic orders.

fuse (fyouz), a replaceable fusible link in the wiring for an electric circuit to break the circuit by melting in the event of overload.

fusible link, a link that is broken by the melting of a short length of low-melting-point metal in an electric circuit, thus releasing a fire door, sprinkler valve, or the like.

fylfot (fill'fot), early name for the swastika, as used as a religious symbol in India and China before 500 A.D.

G

gab′bro, family name for igneous granular stone composed chiefly of pyroxene, augite or diallage, and plagioclase.

ga′ble, the upper part of a terminal wall under the ridge of a pitched roof. 2. the end or wing of a building so gabled.

ga′blet, a miniature gabled top, as over a buttress (7*g*).

gaboon′, *see* okoume.

gadroon, *see* godroon.

gage, *see* gauge.

gain (gane), in wood, a mortise.

gal′ilee, a porch usually built near the west end of abbey churches.

gal′lery, the space provided by inserting an intermediate floor over part of an enclosed space, this floor projecting from one or more of the enclosing walls and being terminated by a balustrade or parapet. 2. a roofed passageway above grade projecting from an exterior wall. 3. a connecting room in a formal interior. 4. a museum or a room thereof.

gal′lery apart′ment house, one of two or more stories with open galleries at each story giving sole access to the apartments within.

gal′leting, a form of masonry jointing embellished by embedding on the surface small chips of flint and the like; same as garreting.

gal′vanized iron or **steel,** these materials coated by immersion in molten zinc. The word is improperly used, for galvanizing means electroplating.

gamboge (gam bozhe′), a gum resin used as a yellow pigment.

gam′brel, a form of roof in which the angle of pitch is abruptly changed between ridge and eaves.

gamma′dion, *see* cross (5*x*).

gang, connecting hall between rooms of the Dutch dwelling.

gång, entry of the Swedish dwelling.

gang-sawn, adjective descriptive of a moderately smooth granular surface of building stone that results from the gang sawing alone.

gano′sis, the dulling of polished surface on marble.

gan′try, a traveling-crane structure, as for work on the walls or ceiling of a lofty interior.

garage (gah razh′), a building or room for the storage of automobiles.

gar′den apart′ment, a multiple dwelling of two or three stories in height, usually in a suburban residential community, with at least a minimum of landscaping on the site.

gar′den city, one in which the single-family detached house and open spaces are predominant.

gar′derobe, a storeroom for clothing or other articles. 2. a bedchamber. 3. a privy.

gare [Fr.] (gahr), a railroad station.

gar'goyle, a grotesque sculptural projection from a roof scupper, to drop rain water clear of the walls; characteristic of Gothic church architecture.

gar'land, sculptured ornament, usually in relief, in the form of a swag or festoon of flowers and fruits (16*j*).

gar'ret, unfinished space under a pitched roof. 2. a room in a dwelling immediately under the roof. If the garret had a ceiling, the space above it was sometimes called the cockloft or cotloft.

gar'reting, the insertion of small splinters of stone in the mortar joints before the mortar has firmly set; same as galleting.

garth, an enclosed yard in connection with a building.

gas main, the community supply line of gas for heating, illuminating, and cooking.

gas meter, a measuring and recording device for gas used from the main by an individual building.

gatch, in the Orient, decorative work in modeled plaster.

gate, a barrier, hinged or hung, usually of open structure.

gate'house, a servants' lodge close by an important entrance gateway.

gate'post, a post to which a gate is hinged or against which it latches.

gate tower, entrance to a walled city.

gate valve, a valve for piping, utilizing the guillotine gate action.

gauge, or **gage,** to rub brick for contrast in color and texture to adjacent brickwork, as in colonial Virginia. 2. to add lime putty to cement mortar. 3. to slow the setting of plaster by adding a substance such as glue. 4. to hasten the setting of plaster by the addition of plaster of Paris. 5. (noun) the measure of thickness, of sheet metal; or of wire, the diameter.

gauging (gaje'ing), the process of selecting for color and rubbing the exposed surface of brick for a special place, as in jamb, lintel, or arched head of an opening.

gazebo (ga ze'bo), a belvedere. 2. a spherical mirror on a pedestal, used as a garden ornament.

geison (guy'son), in classical architecture, the total projection of the entablature beyond the plane of the wall or face of column shafts, or that of the tympanum of a pediment.

generator (jen'erator), a machine that converts mechanical energy into electrical energy.

Genessee Valley bluestone, a dark gray stone of New York State used for trim, flagging, and steps.

gentese (jen teese'), cusps in the arch of a doorway, such as are found in Early English architecture.

Georgia marble, a group name for sparkling, crystalline varieties with white or light gray grounds, although some—such as Mezzotint and Creole—have heavy black clouding as a distinguishing characteristic.

Georgia also produces Etowah Pink, a large-grained marble ranging from old rose to deep pink, with greenish black and greenish gray veinings.

Georgian architecture, a term roughly denoting the architecture of England under the reigns of Anne and the four Georges, 1702–1830.

German silver, an alloy of nickel, copper, and zinc.

gesso (jes′so), also called **gesso duro,** a hard plaster or stucco, common in Italy for sculptural decoration.

ghanat, *see* quanat.

ghat (gawt), Hindu term for a monumental stairway or landing place on a river bank.

giglio [It.] (gee′leo), a decorative form, resembling the fleur-de-lis, and especially associated with Florence, Italy.

gin (jin), originally spelled gyn, a tripod with windlass, for use in construction.

girandole (zhir′ahn dole), a wall bracket with branching arms for holding candles or electric lights, usually with a circular convex mirror against the wall.

girder (gur′dur), a horizontal beam, usually supporting secondary beams, such as floor joists.

girt (gurt), a horizontal member between columns or bents, acting as a stiffener. 2. old term for the heavy timber used in the location of our present plate, supporting rafter ends. 3. a beam of an outside wall to receive the ends of floor joists; it also supports the summer when the summer does not rest on a post.

glare, brightness in the field of view which causes either visual disability or a sensation of discomfort.

glass (window glass), fused silica with alkaline bases, formerly blown in cylindrical form, cut, flattened, and annealed; now drawn up with a metal bar from a tank of the molten glass, and flattened between asbestos rollers into a continuous sheet.

actinic glass, glass designed to filter out the actinic rays from daylight.

bullet-proof glass, a lamination of thin sheets cemented together under heat and pressure, usually three layers of glass and two of the colorless binding material. Shatter-proof glass is similar but with fewer and thinner laminations.

cathedral glass, sheet glass with a lightly hammered surface, used in ecclesiastical work and also in other locations where an obscure glass is wanted.

ground glass, glass made obscure by grinding the surface.

obscure glass, that made translucent by one of various means.

plate glass, glass from the same molten mixture as is used for window glass; it is flowed on an iron plate, rolled to proper thickness, annealed, and polished.

quartz glass, pure quartz transmitting the ultraviolet rays of daylight which are beneficial to health.

shatter-proof glass, *see* bullet-proof glass.

stained glass, a combination of pigmented glass and that which is painted and fired, arranged in a design of leading.

structural glass, cast glass in squares or rectangles, 1″ to 2″ thick, sometimes laid up between concrete ribs, frequently as tile. Larger units are made in hollow or vacuum blocks. The wide use of the product is in colored and polished sheets for interior wall surfacing.

wire glass, ¼″ glass in which wire mesh is embedded to prevent shattering.

glass block, structural hollow units of glass, with plain or variously textured surface; it is laid up with mortar joints.

glass tile, transparent or translucent units to afford light through a roofing surface.

glass wool, material composed of flexible glass fibers, used as insulation and also for fireproof fabrics.

glaze, to install glass panes. 2. to add a glossy surface, as on tile or brick. 3. (noun) a very thin coating of a paint product, usually a semitransparent coating tinted with Van Dyke brown, burnt sienna, or a similar pigment; applied on a previously painted surface to produce a decorative effect.

gla′zier, one who installs glass panes.

glebe, the land, and by extension the residence, of the holder of an ecclesiastical benefice from the Church of England.

globe valve, one in which a circular disc shuts off the flow of a liquid, moving in a plane parallel to the connected piping.

gloss, of painted surfaces, a highly polished finish, such as that given by certain enamels without afterpolish.

glue, a cementing substance.

casein glue, made from casein and borax.

flake glue, made from animal substances.

marine glue, waterproof glue made with a shellac or caoutchouc base and oil solvent.

waterproof glues, made from synthetic resins.

glyph (glif), in Greek architecture, a vertical V-cut groove, as in a triglyph, which is a panel containing two glyphs and two half glyphs, the latter as beveled edges (12).

Glulam, trade name for glued and laminated wood structural timbers, such as arches or trusses for spanning church interiors or other assembly halls.

glyptic (glip′tik), carved or incised.

glyptotheca (glip toe the′kah), Greek term for a building or room for the preservation of works of sculpture.

gneiss (nice), crystalline rock with a tendency to cleave in slabs.

gnomen (no′mon), that part of a sundial which casts the shadow upon the dial plate.

gocciolatoio [It.] (got′seo lah toy′yo), Italian term for corona (11*j*).

godown′, a Chinese or East Indian storehouse.

godroon′, or **gadroon,** continuous ornamental band forms in considerable variety, chiefly found in silverware and usually showing repetitive convex ovals.

gola, or **gula** (go′lah, goo′lah), Italian term for cyma (11*b*).

gold′leaf, sheet gold of exceeding fineness, used for gilding exterior or interior surfaces.

goncalo alves (*Astronium fraxinifolium* or *A. graviolens*), a wood chiefly from Brazil, of straw color, streaked with dark reddish brown; hard and close-textured, taking a high polish; used for flooring, wainscoting, furniture, and veneer.

goose′neck, a vertical pipe having a half loop to a downward outlet, and the whole on a swivel joint, as in a kitchen sink. 2. a ramp of the handrail on a stair.

gopura (go′poora), a pyramidal gateway tower entrance to a temple, characteristic of the Dravidian architecture of southern India.

gorgerin (gore′jerin), or **gorge,** the necking of a column or pilaster (11*j*).

gorgoneion (gor go ni′on), in classical architecture, a sculptured or painted head of Medusa, as in antefixæ.

gospel side, of a church, the left-hand side as one faces the altar.

Gothic architecture, the medieval architecture of the thirteenth, fourteenth, and fifteenth centuries in Europe, mainly an architecture of balanced thrusts in stone masonry, a structure of visible sinews, with curtain walls of pointed arches and stone tracery.

Gothic Revival, a period extending roughly from 1750 to 1900, when interest in medieval work was stimulated by the publications of the Pugins, father and son, of John Britton, and of Horace Walpole and others.

gouache (gwash), a medium of painting, using opaque colors suspended in water to which gum is sometimes added.

gouge (gowj), a chisel with arc edge.

gouge work, incised woodwork for which the gouge is the principal tool, as in trim and mantels of the so-called Dutch Colonial architecture of New Jersey and Pennsylvania.

grade, the existing or established level of the ground about a building. 2. to bring to a desired level or contour the ground about a building, or the surface of a road or path.

gradetto (grah det′to), a fillet molding, an annulet (11*j*).

gra′dient, angle of inclination, as of a road.

gradin [Fr.] (greh danh), or **gradine** (grad een), a step; a seat raised above another, as in an amphitheater. **2.** a shelf at the rear of and above the mensa of an altar.

gradino (gra dee′no), a decoration on the face of a gradin.

graffito, or **sgraffito** (graf fee′ to), plaster surfaces made decorative by scoring a pattern upon them while soft, often revealing the color of an undercoat.

grain, or **grain′ing,** an outmoded practice of imitating the grain of woods with paint. *See also* comb grain and edge grain. 2. composition and texture, particularly as of stones.

Grand Prix de Rome [Fr.] (granh pree deh Rome), an architectural scholarship for study in Rome, awarded through competition at the École des Beaux-Arts; it is the most advanced student competition, open only to French students.

grand′stand, sheltered seating for the spectators of racing, games, and the like.

grange, the group of buildings of a farm.

gran′ite, crystalline igneous rock of rather coarse grain and great compressive strength.

gran′o-, used in combination to mean granitic, or of great hardness.

gran′olith, a concrete used for paving, the coarse aggregate being pulverized granite.

graph (graff), a diagram presenting a system of related facts.

grate, an iron framework of parallel or crossed bars for holding fuel above a space for draft.

gratic′ulate, to superimpose a system of squares in line upon a design or drawing, with the purpose of enlargement to a like system of larger squares.

grat′ing, a grill; a framework of bars over an opening, or set as a strainer across a flow of liquid.

grav′el, weather-worn stones or pebbles, usually found mixed with sand.

Gray Canyon, a fine-grain Ohio sandstone of light blue-gray, even in texture and resistant to fire.

grease trap, a plumbing trap with greatly enlarged body in which kitchen waste is given a chance to cool, solidifying the grease for periodic removal.

Great Monad, or **ovum mundi,** the Chinese symbol representing the mystic union of the two fundamental principles, the material or feminine and the spiritual or masculine (5*aa*).

Greek architecture, an architecture chiefly of marble, with its beginnings in the Minoan and Mycenæan periods and culminating in the Acropolis at Athens under Pericles, when from B.C. 444–429 Greek art and culture reached an apogee which has since influenced much of the world (11, 12).

Greek Revival, a period of English architecture extending from soon after 1750 to 1850, marked by interest in Greek antiquities, the publication of Stuart and Revett's *Antiquities of Athens*, and the bringing to London of the Elgin Marbles. It affected design in America at the beginning of the nineteenth century and continued throughout the century.

green, freshly applied, not hard —applied to concrete, plaster, and sometimes to paint.

green′belt, a boundary, or division, of a community, consisting mainly of a belt of trees.

Green County sandstone, a light gray Pennsylvania stone, massive-bedded, of even grain, soft, and easily worked when freshly quarried.

green′heart (*Ocotea*[*-Nectandra*] *rodioei*), a tough and durable wood from the Guianas, its color pale yellow-green to black; used for marine construction and veneer.

green′house, a shelter, largely of glass and heated artificially, for the more rapid development of plant life.

green′room, a waiting-room for the cast in a theater.

grees, early English term for steps or a staircase.

grey′wood, Indian silver (*Terminalia bialata*), a tree native to the Andaman Islands, producing two different kinds of wood, one a yellow straw color and the other a smoky yellow with rich dark streaks; it is moderately hard and heavy and works well; used extensively in England for decorative woodwork and veneer.

grid, a mat of crossed reinforcing bars for incorporation in a concrete footing; a grillage. 2. the plan, section, or elevation of the 4″-module spacing, over which a working drawing is made.

grid′iron, a term borrowed to describe the rectangular plotting of city streets.

griffe, an ornamental form, somewhat like a claw, extending from the torus of a column base and lying on the four corners of the plinth.

grif′fin, a winged lion, familiar in the sculpture of Greece and Persia (11*j*).

grillage (grill′idj), a foundation mat of beams crossed and perhaps recrossed, often embedded in concrete.

grille (gril), a frame of bars, slender balusters, or other openwork, usually decorative, to serve as a screen.

griotte (gree ott′), a marble of the Pyrenees, dark green or red and purple in color.

grisaille (griz ale′), surface painting in several tones of gray, suggesting bas-relief. 2. uncolored and non-transparent glass elements in leaded windows, sometimes with occasional color (*en grisaille*) (griz aye).

groin, the line of intersection of two vaulted surfaces.

groin arch, a rib form accenting the intersection of two vaulted surfaces (7*g*).

grotesque (gro tesk′), a decorative detail, usually sculptural, expressing an extravagantly whimsical idea.

grotto (graht′o), a recess or cave.

ground, synonym for grade, as at ground level. 2. a connection with earth for an electric wire. 3. a strip, usually of wood, to which thickness plastering or cement is worked.

ground floor, a floor approximately at grade.

ground joint, a closely fitted joint in masonry, usually without mortar. 2. a closely fitted joint between metal surfaces in piping or valves.

ground rent, the rent paid for the use of ground by the owner of a building upon it.

ground′sill, grund′sill, or **grun′sel,** the bottom horizontal frame member now called the sill in buildings of wood-frame construction.

group′ed columns, two or more columns having an integral base and integral abacus.

grout, concrete with small aggregates and heavy liquid consistency, capable of being poured to fill small interstices.

grub, to remove trees, shrubs, and the like, with their roots.

guapinol (gwah pee′nol) (*Hymenaea courbaril*), or West Indian locust, a cabinet wood from South and Central America, somewhat resembling both cherry and mahogany; used for veneer, construction, and furniture.

guard (gard), a protective railing or enclosure about moving parts of machinery, or about an excavation or materials near a building project.

guare′a (*Guarea cedrata*), a wood from West Africa, sold under many names, such as "pink mahogany" and "African cedar"; sapwood pinkish white, heartwood pink to light mahogany with a veined or curly appearance; aromatic scent when freshly sawn; used for furniture, flooring, and interior woodwork, also veneer.

Guastavino (gwas tah vee′no), a method of constructing the inner shell of a dome or vault with two or more layers of rectangular tiles; so called for the name of the inventor.

gud′geon, the stationary leaf of a hinge.

guglia [It.] (goog′lee ah), a structural form, generally upright and slender, when not easily classified as pyramid, obelisk, pinnacle, or some other well-known form.

guijo (gwee′ho) (*Shorea guiso*), a reddish wood from the Philippines, hard and heavy, used quarter-sawn for its attractive figure in furniture and cabinetwork.

guildhall (gild′haul), the headquarters building of a guild. The Guildhall is the corporation headquarters of the City of London.

guilloche (gill oash), an ornamental motif in band form consisting of intertwined strips of curved form (11*h*).

gula [It.] (goo′lah), synonym for ogee (12).

gum, black (*Nyssa sylvatica*), also known as sour gum, black tupelo, and pepperidge; quarter-sliced it exhibits a ribbon stripe and is used for veneer.

blue gum (*Eucalyptus globulus*), an Australian wood, pale straw yellow when freshly cut, turning on exposure to a pale brown or red background with darker reddish brown broken stripes and sometimes a curly figure, for veneer.

red gum (*Liquidambar styraciflua*), sweet gum, a wood from the moist lands of the lower Ohio and Mississippi basins, the southern coasts of the U.S.A., and Mexico and Central America; reddish brown heartwood and pinkish white sapwood.

red river gum, *see* yarrah.

water tupelo gum (*Nyssa aquatica*), a wood of the southeastern U.S.A. and the Gulf States with white sapwood and pale, brownish gray heartwood.

Gun′ite, trade name for a concrete of grout consistency applied to its reinforcement through a hose, using compressed air.

gur′jun (*Dipterocarpus* spp.), woods from Burma, India, and the Andaman Islands, reddish brown or yellowish tan with a coarse texture and stripe figure; used chiefly for flooring.

gus′set, a triangular piece stiffening an angular meeting of two or more members in a framework.

gut′ta (plural **guttæ**), a drop-like, truncated cone form, pendant from mutules and regulæ of the Doric entablature; supposedly reminiscent of wooden pegs (11*j*).

gut′ter, a channel for water, at a roof edge or at ground level.

guy (gye), a rope or wire which, with others, prevents a slender vertical member of structure from side sway.

gymmer (jimm′er), *see* jimmer.

gymnasium (jim nay′ze um), a building or room for indoor athletics.

gyneceum (guy neh kee′um), the women's section of a Greek dwelling.

gyneconitis (guy neh ko nee′tiss), the section of the Greek church reserved for women.

gypsum (jip′sum), hydrous calcium sulphate, an important element of plaster and plasterboard.

H

hab′itable, fit for occupancy.

hab′itacle, early English term for a dwelling or habitation. 2. a niche for a statue.

hachure (hash′your), hatching on a drawing.

hacienda (hah see en′dah), South American term for a productive estate in the country.

hack′ing, in stone masonry, the introduction of two courses in place of one, usually done because of a lack of the larger stones.

hagiasterium (hay zhe as tee′ reum), that section of the early Latin Christian church in which the clergy officiated.

hagioscope (hay′zhe o skope), an oblique slit in an interior wall of a medieval church, to afford a view of the altar. Also called *squint*.

haha (hah′hah), a drop in grade level to serve as a barrier to grazing stock, preventing their too close approach to lawns about the house.

hal′du (*Adina cordifolia*), a wood of India, Burma, and Ceylon; bright yellow, darkening with exposure; very fine, even texture and straight or interlocked grain; used for turnery, construction, boxes, and veneer.

half-and-half solder (sod′der), an alloy of equal parts of tin and lead.

half-pace, a landing interrupting a stair where a turn of 180° is made. 2. a raised section of flooring, as in some bay windows.

half-round′, a molding of semicircular section, such as the torus (12).

half-story, a mezzanine or, less frequently, an attic.

half-timber, descriptive of sixteenth- and seventeenth-century buildings, particularly in England and France, where the interstices in the framework of heavy timbers were filled with brick or plaster.

Halicarnassus (halley car nass′ us), *see* mausoleum.

hall (hawl), a building of importance for public use. 2. the main living-room of a large house in England. 3. a corridor. 4. an entry.

Hallowell granite, a light gray of fine texture, of Maine, used for monumental work, buildings, and bridges.

hall′way, a corridor. 2. an entry.

hallyngs (hawl′eens), the hangings of the early English hall.

halpace (hal′pas), a raised floor, as in a bay window or before a fireplace; also a dais or even a stair landing; half-pace.

halve (hav), to splice or cross two lengths of wood or other material by halving the thickness of each for a lap joint (4*o*).

ham′mer beam, a short beam projecting from an interior wall and, as a cantilever, supporting one end of an arch timber (7*h*).

ham′mer brace, the member bracing a hammer beam against the pendant post (7*h*).

ham′mer-head key, a joint of wood or stone, in which a squared dumbbell key is cut in across the face of the joint.

hance, the half-arch joining a lintel to a jamb. 2. haunch.

handicraft (han′dee kraft), a craft that depends for its success largely upon the skill of manual labor.

hand′rail, the member at hand height of a railing, as along stairs, or at the edge of a porch or balcony.

hangar (hang′ur), a building for the shelter of aircraft.

hanger (hang′ur), a pendant support. 2. a stirrup (4*e*).

hang′ing stile, or **hinge stile,** the jamb of door or window opening upon which is hinged the door or casement.

hang′ings, curtains, draperies, tapestries, and the like.

hard board, *see* compo board.

hard′pan, firmly compacted clay and sand or gravel.

hard′ware, metal fittings permanently incorporated in a building as adjuncts to doors, windows, drawers, etc. *See also* finish hardware.

hard′wood, wood of the broad-leaved trees—oak, maple, ash, walnut—as contrasted with softwoods of the needle-leaved trees, such as pine, spruce, hemlock, etc.

hare′wood, English (*Acer pseudoplatanus*), called sycamore in England; a wood that is dyed to many colors; used for furniture and veneer.

San Domingo harewood (*Zanthoxylum* spp. , a wood from San Domingo and the West Indies resembling San Domingo satinwood; yellow in color with a satiny luster; used for veneer.

har′mus, Greek term for a tile covering the joint between two common tiles.

hasp, the arm with a slot which, fitting over a staple, permits the use of a padlock.

hatch, or **hatch′way,** an opening in floor or roof, with removable cover, for the passage of packing cases, furniture, and the like.

hatch′ing, parallel shading lines on a sectional drawing. *See also* hachure.

Hathor′ic column, in Egyptian architecture, a column the capital of which bears a sculptural representation of Hathor, goddess of love.

haunch (hawnch), that buttressing part of an arch extending from the spring to the crown, including as much of the wall as is contained between a vertical line through the impost at the extrados and a horizontal line through the crown (1*b*).

Hauteville (oat veel), a compact, calcareous marble with fine-grained, fossiliferous calcite crystals filling a monotone warm buff ground color.

haw, mansion or dwelling, as used in *Domesday Book*.

H-beam, a rolled-steel shape similar to the I-beam but having longer flanges—an over-all square in section.

head (hed), the height, and therefore the measurable pressure, of a fluid above a given point. 2. the top of a door frame or window frame.

head′er, a cross member in a series of beams, to support one end of the tail beams it interrupts. 2. in masonry, a stone, brick, or tile presenting its end in the front surface.

head′room, unobstructed height between a floor or a step and the ceiling or beam that is overhead; it should be at least 6′.

head′stone, a stone set at the head of a grave. 2. a principal stone in masonry, as a cornerstone or keystone.

head′way, of stairs, the unobstructed distance from a landing or the face of a step to the ceiling above.

hearth (harth), that part of a fireplace on which the fire is laid, including the projection of this surface beyond the fire chamber.

hearth′stone, originally the single large stone used for the hearth; now used figuratively for the fireside.

heartwood (hart′wud), the mature wood at or about the center of a timber tree.

heat (heet), a form of energy which is an internal motion of molecules, imparting a change in temperature or the performance of work. The unit measurement of heat is the British thermal unit (B.t.u.), the amount of heat required to raise one pound of water one degree Fahrenheit.

heat pump, a device for transferring heat, based on the property possessed by water and many other liquids of evaporating when heat is added and condensing when heat is taken away.

hecatompedon (hekka tom′pedon), Greek term for a temple of one-hundred-foot front length—the length of the Parthenon in Attic feet.

hedge (hej), a barrier of shrubs or small trees, often clipped and usually interlaced.

heel, of a rafter, the end that rests on the wall plate.

height (hite), distance on a perpendicular line between two points.

helicline (hel′eh kline), a helical ramp.

heliocaminus (heely o kam′ inus), in ancient Roman houses, a sunroom.

helm roof, a steeply pitched roof in which four faces rest diagonally between gables and converge at the top (6*f*).

hem, the slightly raised border rim of an Ionic capital volute (13).

hemicycle (hem′mee si kl), a semicircular structure open toward the center.

hemiglyph (hem′mee glif), the half-channel which forms a chamfer on each vertical edge of a triglyph (12).

hemitri′glyph, a half-triglyph.

hem′lock, Eastern (*Tsuga canadensis*), a wood from the Lake States and eastern mountain country of the U.S.A.; used chiefly for framing, sheathing, roofing, and subflooring; more brittle and liable to splinter than spruce.

Western hemlock (*Tsuga heterophylla*), a wood chiefly

from the Pacific Coast and western Canada, straight-grained, fine-textured; used largely for framing.

Henri Deux (anh ree dyuh), the period of Henri II, King of France (1547–1559).

Henri Quatre (anh ree katr), the period of Henri IV, King of France (1589–1610).

hep′tastyle, descriptive of the Greek temple having seven columns across the front.

Her′culite, trade name for a specially tempered, thick plate glass, usually used for doors without enframement.

Her′ma (plural, **Hermæ**), a stone pillar, usually quadrangular in plan and tapering downward, supporting a bust of Hermes. Used widely by the ancient Romans to mark land boundaries, or as outdoor decoration.

her′ringbone, descriptive of masonry or tile work in which the units are laid slantwise (3*l*).

herse, a portcullis. 2. a frame for a pall over a coffin or an effigy above a tomb.

hewn, of wood, roughly dressed by ax or adze; of stone, cut to form by mallet and chisel.

hexapro′style, in classical architecture, having a main front of six columns, and no columns at sides.

hex′astyle, descriptive of the Greek temple having six columns across the front, rear, or both.

H-hinge, the flat, surface hinge of which the uprights are fastened respectively to door and to jamb, the horizontal piece supplying the pivot. A variation is the so-called HL-hinge.

hick′ey, a tool used for bending pipe, metal conduit, or reinforcing steel.

hick′ory (*Carya laciniosa, C. tomentosa, C. glabra, C. ovata*), wood found plentifully in the eastern United States and available commercially as white (sapwood) and red (heartwood), both of which are tough, hard, and strong.

hieracosphinx (hi′er ay′ko sfinx′), sculptured lion with hawk's head.

hieroglyphics (hi ro glif′iks), picture writing of primitive peoples.

hieron (here′on), the whole of the sacred enclosure surrounding a temple and its dependencies.

high altar, the principal altar of a church or cathedral.

high-early-strength, descriptive of a variety of Portland cement which attains more quickly the strength that ordinary cement and its concrete acquire in setting.

hi′ling, early English term for roof.

hinge, a device for joining a movable piece to another movable piece or to one which is fixed, as the hinge of a door.

hinge loop, a pair of pointed, loop-end irons, the loops engaged to form a rude hinge such as was used chiefly for chest lids.

hinge stile, *see* hanging stile.

hip, of a roof, the line of intersection of two roof planes, the eaves lines of which are not parallel (7*f*).

hip knob, a finial.

hip′podrome, in classical architecture, a race course bordered by seats in tiers.

hip rafter, a rafter used to form the hip of a roof.

hip roll, the half-cylindrical surface, usually of metal, for finishing the hip of a roof.

Hispano-Moresque (hiss pan′ no mo resk′), descriptive of Moorish art in Spain.

hoarding (hord′ing), an enclosure of rough boards for a building operation.

hob, a shelf at the side of the fire chamber in a fireplace, on which pots may be kept warm.

hoist, a device for lifting articles of some weight or bulk.

hol′low tile, cavity tile in block form used in walls or partitions.

hol′low wall, a wall built in two withes with space between for checking the passage of water, or for insulation; a cavity wall (3*j*, *k*).

hol′ly (*Ilex opaca*), a white wood of extremely close texture, used largely for inlay.

homestall, homestead.

honeycombing (hun′nee co ming), a common fault in concrete: voids caused by incomplete filling of the form.

hon′eysuckle ornament, the anthemion of Greek art (11*i*).

hon′ing, the process of giving stone a very smooth finish by rubbing; it is usually found only in interior work.

hood, an overhead shelter, as of a doorway, a chimney, a kitchen range (in which case the hood is an inverted funnel leading into a ventilating flue).

hood mold, a drip molding over door or window.

hook, a member that is bent at right angles at one end to engage an eye or slot as a fastener.

hook strip, a horizontal band of wood to which coat hooks are attached, as in closets.

hop′per, type name for an early form of water closet having a funnel-shaped bowl over a trap in the waste line.

hop′per head, a rain-water head.

hori′zon, in perspective drawing, the intersection of the picture plane by a plane at right angles passing through the station point.

horn′blende, a mineral containing iron, silicate of magnesium, calcium, and aluminum; black or greenish black in color.

horologium (ho ro lo′jeum), a clock. 2. a building to shelter a timepiece.

hors concours [Fr.] (or kong koor), *see* concours.

horse, a support for temporary use, as a sawhorse, a trestle.

horse′power, unit of the rate of work—33,000 pounds lifted one foot in one minute; applied to a boiler, the rating indicates the amount and pressure of steam that will drive an engine to perform at that rate; applied to an electric motor, a horsepower requires 745,941 watts.

horse′shoe arch, an arch continuing beyond a semicircle, as used in Saracenic architecture (1*g*).

hose′cock, *see* sillcock.

hos′pice, a building for the lodging and entertainment of travelers; an inn.

hospital (hos′pitl), a building for the care of the sick.

hospital′ium, in ancient Roman architecture, a guest chamber.

hos′tel, an inn.

hos′trie, an inn.

hot-air heating, a system of heating by which air warmed above a fire chamber is distributed through ducts.

hot cath′ode, the variety of fluorescent lamps using coiled tungsten filaments; there are both instant-starting and preheating types.

hotel′, a building for the lodging and feeding of transients.

hôtel [Fr.] (aw tel), a residence in town or city, particularly the residence of an official. 2. a public building.

hôtel Dieu [Fr.], a hospital.

Hôtel de Ville [Fr.] (aw tel deh veeyeh), the town hall or city hall.

hot′house, a greenhouse.

hot-water heating, a system of heating utilizing hot water circulated through pipes, coils, and radiators.

house (howce), a building for human habitation.

house drain, in plumbing, the main, lower, horizontal pipe or pipes which connect with the sewer.

hous′ing, dwelling units in quantity. 2. a sinking in one member to engage a projection from another (4*f*).

hous′ing author′ity, a group of elected or appointed individuals in whom a municipality vests the responsibility and power of directing its public housing.

hov′eling, the extension of the windward and opposite sides of a chimney top to support a flat or arched cover.

Howe truss, *see* truss (4*p*, *q*).

hue (hew), the main quality factor in color; one factor of three, the others being saturation and brightness. Saturation is the percentage of hue in a color; brightness is the quantitative aspect of the mental image.

humidifier (hew mid′ih fier), a device for moistening air to a desired degree.

humidistat (hew mid′istat), an instrument for showing the degree of humidification in the surrounding air and for controlling the addition of moisture.

Hummelstown brownstone, a dense and massive sandstone, quarried in Dauphin County, Pa., varying from reddish to purplish brown.

hut, a small and rough habitation.

hutch, early English term for a chest or locker in which sacred vessels were kept.

hyalog′raphy, engraving on glass.

hy′drant, a valved outlet on a water main, usually with connections for fire hose.

hy′drated lime, carbon hydroxide or slaked lime that has been reduced to dry powder. Adding water and sand will make it into plaster or mortar.

hydraulic (hi draw′lik), involving the use of a liquid as a force.

hydraulic cement, *see* cement.

hydraulic lime, a lime having the property of hardening under water.

hygrometer (hi grom′eter), an instrument for measuring the degree of moisture suspended in the air.

hypæthral (hi pee′thral), Greek term descriptive of a roofless temple or other building.

hyperthyrum (hi pur thi′rum), Greek term for a doorway lintel or its moldings.

hyphen (hi′fen), the connecting link between a main building and an outlying wing, such as is found in the South Atlantic states, in the Georgian mansions of the eighteenth century.

hypocaust, or **hypocaustum** (hi′po kawst, hi po kaws′tum), in ancient Roman architecture, an underground furnace for heating rooms or baths by warm-air flues in floor or walls.

hypogeum (hi po gee′um), a subterranean structure hewn out of the rock, such as abound along the Nile. 2. the portion of a building below grade.

hypophyge (hi pof′ijee), synonym for apophyge (12).

hypostyle (hi′po stile), shelter supported by columns; in Egyptian architecture the two middle rows of columns were often carried higher to effect a clerestory.

hypotrachelium (hi po trak ee′leum), the narrow channel, sometimes doubled or trebled, marking the junction of capital and shaft in the Doric column (11*j*).

I

I-beam, a beam of rolled steel, having in cross section the shape of an I with somewhat exaggerated top and bottom horizontal strokes.

ibira′ro (*Pterogyne nitens*), a wood from Argentina, light pinkish brown, deepening on exposure, with occasional black stripes; it is hard, heavy, strong, and durable, suggesting mahogany; used for cabinetwork and veneer.

ichnograph (ik′no graf), a ground plan.

ichnolite (ik′no lite), a stone bearing the impression of a foot.

i′con, a sacred picture, as used in countries where the Greek Church prevails.

iconography (i kahn og′raffee), that branch of knowledge dealing with graphic representation.

iconostasis (i kon os′tasis), in the Greek Church, a screen corresponding to the altar rail in other churches.

ideograph (id′eo graf), a graphic representation of an object or idea without naming it.

idiabo, *see* ireme.

ig′loo, the house of the Eskimo, usually of compacted snow or ice.

IHS, in church symbolism, a corruption of the Greek ΙΗΣ, shortened from ΙΗΣΟΥΣ, Jesus.

iliahi (eely ah′hee) (*Santalum freycinetianum*), a tree of Polynesia, known in commerce as the yellow sandalwood.

illumination (il loomin a′ shun), the amount of light brought to bear upon a surface.

imbow (im bo′), to arch over.

im′brex (plural, **im′brices**), in classical architecture, a half-round roofing tile.

imbricated (im′brih kay ted), overlapping and breaking joints, as tiles, slate, or shingles on a roof, and as in some ornament.

imbu′ia (*Phoebe porosa*), a wood from Brazil, frequently misnamed Brazilian walnut; it has a rich brown color and is finely figured in veneer cuttings.

impage′, Vitruvius' name for the rail of a door.

Imperial Mahogany, a medium-grain granite, pinkish with black and gray spottings; quarried near Minneapolis, Minn.

impluvium (im ploo′veum), same as compluvium.

im′post, the cap of a pier or pilaster supporting the spring of an arch (1*b*).

Im′preg, trade name for wood veneers impregnated with resin, dried, stacked, and cured under low pressure.

in an′tis, signifying a temple form in which side walls project to provide a closed end for the front colonnade.

Incan (ink′ahn), descriptive of the architecture of the pre-

Columbian inhabitants of Peru and its neighboring countries.

incandes′cent light, or **electric filament lamp,** a light source consisting of a glass bulb containing a filament that may be kept incandescent by the transmission of an electric current.

incer′tum, wall masonry of rough stones and without horizontal course lines.

inch, unit of linear measure, the twelfth part of a foot.

incinerator (in sin′erator), a furnace for consuming waste by fire. 2. a furnace for cremation; a cinerator.

incised (in size′d), cut in, graven beneath the surface.

incline′, a sloping way.

inden′ture, a deed of mutual covenants.

In′dia ink, lampblack in water with gelatin; made in stick form in China, Japan, and India.

Indian architecture, an architecture extending from 250 B.C. to 1750 A.D., characterized by its Buddhist, Jaina, and Hindu temples, built of massive granite and lavishly embellished by sculptured ornament inspired by religion and mythology. 2. the primitive structures of the American Indian.

Indiana limestone, oölitic limestone produced by a group of quarries in the state and sold under the following variety names:

Rustic Buff, a grade of fairly uniform color but of coarser texture than Select or Standard; ranging from finest grain to coarse, shelly, honeycomb formation.

Select Buff, a fine-grain buff of uniform texture and color.

Select Buff Statuary Stock, a very fine-grain, uniform buff, produced in limited quantities and used chiefly for sculpture and interior carving.

Select Gray, a fine-grain gray of uniform texture and color.

Special Hard Buff, a dense, hard, and somewhat crystalline variety.

Special Hard Gray, like the Special Hard Buff except for color.

Standard Buff, the fine-grain buff variety that constitutes the major part of the buff output.

Standard Gray, the fine-grain gray widely used for general building purposes.

Variegated, a variety in which both buff and gray are sometimes present, in varying proportions.

in′dicator valve, one which indicates by sign an open or shut position.

in′direct lighting, a system of artificial lighting in which light from the sources is directed at ceiling or wall to be reflected for general illumination.

Indo-Ar′yan architecture, a style of northern India developed previous to that of the Jains in the tenth and eleventh centuries.

Indo-Saracen′ic architecture, Mohammedan architecture.

induction (in duk′shun), the production of magnetism or an electric current in a conductor by the close proximity of another conductor that is magnetized or is bearing an electric current.

infirmary (in fur′maree), a room or building in which patients are received for, or given, treatment.

ingle (ing′l), a fireplace.

in′glenook, a fireplace recess or corner, usually provided with built-in seats.

in′gress, entrance.

initial set (in ish′l), of freshly placed concrete, the early, incomplete solidification of the mass.

in′lay, surface decoration achieved by the insertion of lines or patterns of contrasting material.

inn, a small hotel or tavern.

INRI, in church symbolism, *Iesus Nazarenus Rex Iudæorum*, Jesus of Nazareth, King of the Jews.

inscrip′tion, lettering in durable form on a building, tombstone, or memorial tablet.

insola′tion, exposure to direct sunlight; penetration of sunlight; extent to which sunlight enters an interior space, such as a classroom.

install′, to place in position for use.

in′strument board, a panel of recording instruments, switches, and the like, usually the electric-control center of a building; but the term is also used in an engine room, laboratory, theater, and other operational centers.

in′sula [It.], a city block; the space bounded by four streets.

in′sulating board, *see* compo board.

insula′tion, a protecting barrier of low conductivity against heat, sound, or electricity.

intaglio (in tah′leo), surface decoration by slightly depressed plane of line or pattern.

intar′sia, or **tarsia,** surface decoration of wood by the use of inlay in contrasting colors.

in′tercolumnia′tion, distance between columns, measured between bottoms of shafts, just above the apophyge. In classical architecture the more commonly used spacings were designated by name: pycnostyle, 1½ diameters; systyle, 2; eustyle, 2¼; diastyle, 3; areostyle, 4 or 5.

in′tercom, intercommunicating telephone system not using a central switchboard.

intercool′er, a tank in which compressed air is cooled before being subjected to further compression.

in′terdome, the space between the inner and outer shells of a dome.

interfer′ence, conflict between waves of light or of sound.

inte′rior, the inside of a room or of a building.

in′terlacing arch, or, more properly, **interlacing archivolt,** one of a series in which interlacing is simulated (2*h*).

intermu′ral, or **intramural,** between the outer walls, as of a walled city.

interna′tional candle, unit of luminous intensity, so called by reason of an international agreement.

interrupt′ed arch, broken pediment of arch form.

intersec′tion, of a cruciform plan, the crossing.

interstitium, or **intersticium** (inter sti′teum, inter sti′keum), the crossing in a building of cruciform plan.

intertri′glyph, the space separating triglyphs in the Doric frieze; the metope (12).

intonaco (in to′nako), the plaster ground for fresco.

intrados (in tra′dos), the curved surface bounded by the parallel lower edges of an arch—its soffit.

intramural (intra mew′ral), within the walls.

invert′ed arch, as described in the term; used to distribute weight over a foundation.

invert elevation, abbreviation, I.E., the lower inside point of a pipe or sewer, at a given location and in reference to a bench mark.

Ionic (i on′ik), the Greek order which followed the Doric and preceded the Corinthian, its capital known by its volutes (13).

ipé (*Tabebuia* spp.), woods from Brazil, used there for outside, rough construction work and piles; in veneer cutting the woods are a lustrous brown with a slight greenish tinge, some highly figured.

i′pil (*Intsia bijuga*), a hardwood of the Philippines, valuable for its brown, strong, highly durable timber.

ire′me, or **emeri** (*Terminalia ivorensis*), also called idiabo; a wood from West Africa, used chiefly for veneer; pale yellow to light brown in color.

iro′ko (*Chlorophora excelsa*), one of the most useful woods of West Africa; of light yellow-brown color, becoming darker with exposure to air; rather cross-grained and does not readily split; used for construction, railway ties, and veneer.

iron, a metallic element of which the following varieties are of chief interest to the architect:

cast iron, a blast-furnace product high in compressive strength and low in tensile strength. Its chief use is in parts that are readily and thus cheaply formed by cast ing with occasional machining

malleable iron, cast iron that has been put through an annealing process that gives it some ductility and some resistance to shock through bending or twisting. It cannot be rolled or forged.

wrought iron, pig iron that is puddled and rolled, never melted or cast; it is less dense and homogeneous, usually containing less than 0.12% carbon and from 1% to 2% slag. After puddling it is squeezed, hammered, and rolled into muck bars; and these bars are piled together, heated, and rolled into plates, rounds, squares, etc., known as merchant bars.

isacoustic (i sah koos′tik), equal in acoustic correction.

ISM, in church symbolism, *Iesus Salvator Mundi*, Jesus, Saviour of the World.

isocephalism (iso sef′alism), in Greek bas-reliefs, the custom of designing the heads of all figures along one horizontal line.

isod′omum, masonry in which the courses are of equal height, the stones of equal length, with joints breaking in the middle above and below a stone.

isomet′ric, a form of orthogonal perspective in which all three of the main dimensions are at the same inclination to the plane of projection.

Is′trian Nua′ge, an Italian marble of brownish cream or light brown ground color, with clouds of darker shade scattered through the mass. Very small, hairlike veins of yellow, barely perceptible, are also characteristic. The name is merely another way of saying "dark Botticino."

i′vorywood (*Balfourodendron riedelianum*), white to pale yellow-brown wood from South America, sometimes with a slight greenish tinge; it is hard, heavy, tough, and strong, but not durable; used for cabinetwork and lathe work.

IX, in church symbolism, *Iesous Christos.*

J

jacal (hah kal′), a mud-plastered pole or wicker construction found in Mexico and among the Indians of southwestern U.S.A.

jack, a device for lifting heavy weights, utilizing leverage, the screw, or hydraulic pressure.

jack arch, same as Welsh arch (1*p*).

jack′et, a covering of insulation, usually applied to exposed heating pipes.

jack rafter, any one of the shorter rafters used from plate to the angle rafter of a hip roof.

Jacobean (jacko bee′an), designating the period of the early seventeenth century in England.

Jacobean architecture, literally, that of the reign of James I, but generally understood to be that of the Stuarts' reign, including the brief period of the Commonwealth; roughly, the seventeenth century.

jail (jale), a building for the confinement of prisoners.

Jain architecture, a style developed in India during the tenth and eleventh centuries by the Jains, who were followers of a contemporary of Buddha.

jalee (jah′lee), the decorated, pierced marble or stone of India, such as is found notably in the Taj Mahal.

jalousie (zhal loo see′), a collapsible window or door blind of movable slats, somewhat like a Venetian blind.

jaman (jay′man) (*Eugenia jambolana*), a wood from India and Burma, reddish to brownish gray in color with some darker streaks; it is moderately hard, heavy, strong, and fairly durable; used for decorative paneling and for doors.

jamb (jam), the side of a window or door opening, against which the sash or the door abuts.

japan′, a resin varnish used chiefly as a drier in paints.

Japanese architecture, one derived mainly from China, but of smaller scale and extreme fineness of decoration. The module of the 3′ x 6′ floor mat governs the planning, with interior partitions largely of sliding paper-cover screens. It is an architecture mainly of wood, in the joinery and carving of which is shown great skill. Its history has been written only since 712 A.D., but extends back at least six or seven centuries before Christ. Japan began to show the influences of Western civilization as recently as 1875.

jardin [Fr.] (zhar danh), a garden.

jarrah (jahr′ah) (*Eucalyptus marginata*), a timber tree of southwestern Australia, its brick-red to mahogany-colored wood strongly resistant to decay, in air or under water; its sometimes curly grain makes it useful also for veneer.

jaspé (jas′pay), surface mottling in colors, as in jaspé linoleum.

jawab (ja wahb′), a building duplicating or matching another architecturally.

jequiti′ba (*Cariniana* spp.), sometimes called Brazilian or Colombian mahogany; a South American wood used chiefly for cabinetwork and paneling.

jer′kinhead, a roof form in which the top of a gable is cut off by a secondary slope forming a hip (6*k*).

jer′ry builder, one who produces flimsy construction.

jesse (jes′see), a branched candlestick form as used in religious symbolism, recalling the geneological tree of Jesse.

jest′ing beam, a beam introduced into a structure for ornamental purposes only.

jet, a projecting source, usually valved, of liquid or gas. 2. a sprue or gate for the introduction of molten metal in the casting process.

jet d'eau [Fr.] (zhay doe), a jet of water, a fountain.

jet′ty, an overhanging part of a building

jew′el, a boss of glass in a leaded window.

jig, a framework in one plane to facilitate the assembly of duplicate pieces of construction.

jig saw, a thin, narrow saw blade operated mechanically up and down to achieve sawing along curved lines.

jimmer, a hinge of which the two leaves are inseparable, usually further described, as, for example, cock's-head jimmer (16*k*).

job (jahb), the whole of a work of construction, or some individual part of it; a piece of work.

jog, an offset; a change of direction in a surface.

jog′gle, in masonry, the joining of two adjacent units by mutually indenting or rebating them (2*j*). A joggle joint corresponds to the carpenter's rebate (4*h*).

join′er, one skilled in joinery.

join′ery, the more intricate branches of carpentry.

joint, in masonry, the interstice between units. 2. (verb) to break joints, in masonry, to avoid continuous joints between units in successive courses.

joint′er, a woodworking tool for truing the edges of boards that are to be closely joined.

joist (joyst), a horizontal member in the framing of a floor or ceiling.

Jonesboro, a pinkish gray biotite granite of Maine, with a medium-coarse grain.

jubé [Fr.] (joo bay), a screen, usually with gallery, dividing nave and choir in Gothic ecclesiastical work.

ju′das, an inspection panel in an entrance door.

jut, to project beyond a given surface.

K

kabiki (kah bee'kee) (*Mimusops elengi*), a tree of the Philippine Islands, the reddish brown, hard, heavy wood of which is used in building.

kalan'ta (*Toona calantas*), sometimes called Philippine cedar; a red to reddish brown, light, soft wood with a strong cedar odor; used for furniture and cabinetwork.

kalmansa'nai (*Neonauclea* spp.), a wood from the Philippines, yellow to bright rose red, fading when cut; used for veneer.

kalsa, Hindu term for the pinnacle on a dome.

kal'somine, *see* calcimine.

kalun'ti (*Shorea mindanensis* [= *S. polita*]), a light yellow or light grayish wood from the Philippines, used chiefly for cabinetwork and furniture, but difficult to saw.

kam'era, an interior subdivision of a Russian prison.

kamertje, small storeroom in the Dutch dwelling.

kamidana (kah mee dah'nah), a shelf in a Shinto house, the location of a sacred image.

kammara, bedroom in the Swedish dwelling.

kammer, bedroom of the Dutch dwelling.

kang, a built-in divan in Chinese houses, made of brick and tile and heated by enclosed fire.

kat'mon (*Dillenia philippinensis*), a hardwood from the Philippines with light to dark reddish brown color; used chiefly for veneer.

kauri (kow'ree) (*Agathis* spp.), conifers with light brown or pinkish color, of Queensland and New Zealand, the long, straight-grained wood of which is useful for timber.

keblah, or **kibleh,** the point in a mosque designating the direction in which lies Mecca.

keel arch, the inflected or ogee arch (1*h*).

keel molding, a molding having a section resembling the keel of a ship, two ogee curves meeting in an arris.

Keene's cement, a hard plaster, made by recalcining plaster of Paris with other substances; invented about 1840.

keep, that part of a medieval castle given over to its chief defense.

keep'er, the receiving member of a lock bolt or latch.

kelo'bra (*Enterolobium cyclocarpum*), a wood from Central and South America having a brown background with a slight greenish or reddish tinge, and a coarse texture, which in crotch cutting is prized for veneer.

Kentucky bluestone, a light bluish gray sandstone, hard and durable.

kerb, British equivalent of *curb.*

kerf, the slot made by a saw.

keru'ing (*Dipterocarpus* spp.), woods of many species from the Malay Peninsula and North Borneo; dull, purplish red or reddish brown or tan with a striped figure; used for veneer.

key, the removable operating member of a lock. 2. a wedge cross-reinforcing a miter joint or locking a tenon (4*i*). 3. a wedge-shaped floor board. 4. a roughened surface that receives glued veneer. 5. the plaster or mortar extruded behind lath which, when hard, serves to hold the plaster in place. 6. a sinkage in tile or terra cotta to engage mortar.

master key, a key made to operate two or more different locks.

key′stone, the wedge-shaped top member of an arch (1*b*, 14*d*).

key switch, an electric switch operated by a removable key rather than by a button or tumbler.

key valve, a valve operated by a removable key rather than by a fixed handle.

khan (kahn), in Turkey, a caravansary.

khasi (kah′see), a form of Persian and Indian wall decoration, using tiles of varied colors.

khaya (ka′yah) (*Khaya* spp.), a wood of many localities in Africa, the color ranging from light pink through bright red to red-brown; hard, works well, and is usually figured, producing a good veneer.

kibleh, *see* keblah.

kickplate, protection against foot damage to the bottom vertical face of a door, usually in the form of an applied metal plate.

kill, to cover knots or other resinous parts of wood with shellac to prevent the resin from "bleeding" through later coats of paint.

kill′esse, a gutter, groove, or channel.

kiln-dried (kill-), said of lumber which has been freed of excess moisture by heating in a kiln.

kil′owatt, abbrev. kw; 1000 watts; the kilowatt-hour is the unit by which electrical energy is usually sold.

king bolt, a tie rod replacing the king post of a truss.

king closer, a portion of a brick greater than a half-length, to complete a dimensional course.

king post, the central vertical member of a triangular truss (4*j*).

king′wood (*Dalbergia cearensis*), a wood from Brazil with alternate fine, regular striping, violet-brown and blackish; used principally for veneer.

Kingwood stone, trade name for a hard West Virginia quartzite, medium to coarse in grain and varying from antique yellow and light buff to a rather purplish buff; ground mass is white quartz, and color is caused by innumerable brown spots of completely oxidized iron; used for heavy masonry.

kiosk (kee ahsk′), a small pavilion, such as a garden shelter, newsstand, or public toilet.

kirk, in Scotland, a church.

kistvaen (kist′vine), a primitive sarcophagus.

kitch′en, a room for the preparation and cooking of food.

kitchenette′, a small kitchen, often as an alcove from the room in which meals are served.

kiva (kee′vah), the ceremonial chamber of the pueblo, usually entered by a ladder from the top.

knee (nee), a convex length of handrail; the reverse of a ramp, which is concave. 2. a timber following its natural bent, usually employed as a brace.

knob (nahb), a projecting handle, usually round or oval, operating a latch. *See also* knot.

knob-and-tube wiring, an early system of electrical wiring, without conduits, in which the insulated wires were supported on porcelain knobs and through porcelain tubes in traversing timbers.

knocker (nock′ur), a hinged striker on a door, usually of metal.

knot, or **knob** (not, nob), a cluster of leaves or flowers, as a terminal of a label or the boss at the intersection of vaulting ribs (8*c*). 2. variation in grain of a wood surface where interrupted by a branch of the tree.

knull′ing, nulling, knurling, or **milling,** as on the edge of most coins. 2. a molding, slightly convex, having the character of milling on a larger scale.

koa (*Acacia koa*), a wood highly prized for veneer, also valued as timber; abundant in the Hawaiian Islands; rich red, golden brown, or brown with black lines in old trees; walnut-like uniform texture and lustrous sheen.

kôk′ko (*Albizzia lebbeck*), a wood from the Andaman Islands, India, Burma, and Ceylon, its background grayish brown to golden in color, marked with black lines; used for veneer.

komis′tra, the pit or dance floor of a Greek theater.

konak (ko nahk′), an official residence, or other large residence, in Turkey.

korina, *see* limba.

kosmeterion (kos meh tee′ reon), a robing-room for religious processions in ancient Greece.

kraal (krahl), a compound of native huts in Africa.

krem′lin, the official center of a Russian town or city.

kur′gan, a primitive tomb in Russia.

kurhaus [Ger.] (koor′howce), a central pavilion in a health resort.

kursaal [Ger.] (koor′zahl), the central gathering-room of a kurhaus.

kyanise (ki′an ize), to make wood decay-resistant by impregnation with mercuric chloride.

L

lab′arum, the imperial standard of Constantine, bearing the Chrismon (5*w*).

la′bel mold, a drip mold over a wall opening; a hood mold.

la′bel stop, an ornamental terminal of a drip mold; a knot or knob.

lab′oratory, a room or a building for research and other scientific activities.

la′borer, a workman qualified only for unskilled work.

la′brum, a stone bath of ancient Rome.

labyrinth (lab′irrinth), a maze of tortuous passages, covered or uncovered.

lac (lak), a resinous exudation of an East Indian insect, used as a base of shellacs, varnishes, and lacquers.

lace′wood (*Cardwellia sublimis*), also called silky oak; a tree that grows throughout southeastern Queensland and down into New South Wales; the wood is pink with a silver sheen, and, quarter-sliced, is used for veneer.

lac′ing, a course of brick in a wall of rubble. 2. a bonding course between brick courses of an arch.

laconicum (lah conn′ekum), a steam-bath chamber of ancient Rome.

lacquer (lak′kur), a coating for wood or metal, formerly made by dissolving shellac in alcohol, with or without the addition of coloring matter; more recently, of cellulose esters or ethers in a volatile vehicle.

lactarium (lak tay′reum), a dairy house.

lacuna (lah kyou′nah), a depression in a finished surface, such as for inlay. 2. a sunken panel in a soffit or ceiling.

La′dy chapel, one dedicated to worship of the Virgin Mother.

lag′ging, temporary support for the masonry of an arch or vault.

lag screw, a wood screw of medium to large size having a square bolt head.

laitance (lay tahnce), a frothy, gelatinous deposit occurring on the top surface of cement or concrete, caused by an excess of water in the mixture.

lake dwelling, primitive dwelling of those who built upon piles over the water.

Lally column, trade name for cylindrical steel filled with concrete and used as a supporting member.

lam′bert, unit of brightness; the average brightness of any surface emitting or reflecting one lumen per square centimeter.

lamb's-tongue (lams tung), a molding combining a small ovolo and a fillet, as in wood muntins; the fillet was originally a long pointed section.

Lamel′la roof, a combination of arch and short-timber network, patented in 1925 by a German engineer; used for roof framing of large enclosures.

lam′inated, made up of thin layers, as plywood or laminated structural members; the latter maintain the direction of grain in successive layers.

lanai (lah nah′ee), the Hawaiian veranda or terrace.

lan′cet, the sharply pointed Gothic arch. It is commonly formed by a radius equal to the span of the opening and struck from both sides on the springing line; the springing line may be far above the impost line (1*i*).

land′ing, the horizontal plane at the top of a stairway, or a platform interrupting the flight.

land′scape arch′itect, one skilled in the utilization and adaptation of land to man's use.

land use, in urban planning, a division of available land into categories such as residential, industrial, commercial, recreational, public, etc.

Languedoc (lang′we dok), a compact marble of brilliant red blotched with white, quarried in the Montagne Noire and elsewhere in the Pyrenees.

lan′tern, a superstructure on a roof, a dome, or a tower, glazed at the sides and sometimes without its own floor.

lap, to overlap one surface with another, as in shingling. 2. the actual length of such overlap.

lap weld, to weld overlapping edges.

lararium (lah ray′reum), in ancient architecture, the apartment in which the lares or household gods were sheltered.

larch, European (*Larix decidua* [= *L. europæa*]), a tree found throughout northern Europe, which in England is an important softwood, exceedingly durable under all conditions.

western larch (*Larix occidentalis*), a native of Montana, Idaho, Washington, Oregon, and southeastern Canada, the wood of which splits easily, is heavy, strong, and stiff; it is frequently logged with Douglas fir and sold as larch fir.

lar′der, British equivalent of pantry; originally, a room in which meat was hung.

lar′dose, corruption of the French *l'arrière dos*, used to designate the screen behind the high altar of Durham Cathedral.

larmier [Fr.] (lar me a), the corona, or, by extension, any drip member (11*j*).

lat, in Buddhist architecture, a detached column for the support of a lamp or some object of religious significance.

latch, a catch for a door, usually a pivoted arm, the outer end of which engages a slot.

lath, riblike support of wood or metal upon which plaster is spread.

latrine (lah treen′), a privy, such as those used in military camps and temporary dwellings.

latrobe′, a stove heater set against a chimney breast and heating its surroundings by direct radiation, heating one or more rooms above by warm air.

lat'ten, an early English alloy, resembling brass.

lattice (lat'iss), an openwork grille or shield of interlacing strips.

lattice truss, a truss the upper and lower members of which are joined by lattice-like struts.

lauan, red (low'an) (*Shorea negrosensis*), also spelled lauaan; a wood from the Philippines shading in color from light red to dark reddish brown, coarse texture; quarter-sawn it has a conspicuous ribbon stripe; used for furniture, cabinetwork, and veneer.

white lauan (*Pentacme contorta*), also spelled lauaan; a tree of the Philippines, the wood of which is light to grayish brown to light reddish brown; it is fairly heavy and coarse in texture; used for furniture and cabinetwork.

yellow lauan, *see* manggasinoro.

laundry (lawn'dree), a room, or a commercial building, wherein clothes are washed and ironed.

laundry chute, *see* clothes chute.

laundry tray, or **laundry tub,** a deep sinklike plumbing fixture in which clothing may be washed.

lau'rel, *see* myrtle burl and tepesuchil.

lavabo (lah vay'bo), a small lavatory for the washing of the hands by the priest in the sacrament of the Eucharist; not to be confused with the piscina, which see.

lav'atory, a built-in washbasin; by extension, a washroom.

lay'er, in masonry, a course.

lay'out, a schematic plan.

lazaret'to, a ward or building for the quarantine of diseased persons.

leaching cesspool, a cesspool built so as to permit waste liquids to percolate through its walls into the surrounding soil.

lead (led), a metallic element, soft and heavy, with many uses in building.

lead and oil, popular name for white lead (carbonate of lead) as a pigment in linseed oil, forming a paint widely used before the present improved techniques of paint making.

lead'ed glass, glass set in lead cames; that the glass is painted is often implied.

leader (leed'ur), rain leader, a downspout.

leaf (leef), one part of a double or multiple door.

leaf-and-dart, a repetitive band design alternating a dart with a conventionalized leaf.

lean-to (leen'too), a subordinate building, the ridge of its single-slope roof supported by the major structure (6*j*).

lease (leese), a contract securing the tenure of real property for a specified time.

lectern (lek'turn), an ecclesiastical reading desk.

lectorium (lek toe'reum), that part of a church in which the epistle is read.

ledge batten, the top or bottom batten securing the vertical boards of a batten door.

ledge'ment, a string course or horizontal molding; ledgement table indicates any of the projections of a plinth in Gothic architecture except the lowest, or earth table.

ledger (led′jer), a slab of stone used horizontally to cover a tomb.

ledg′er board, the top covering board of a fence. 2. a board let into the face of studding to support on its upper edge the floor joists; a ribbon.

leewan, a raised portion of the floor, in Mohammedan countries, upon which one may recline; furnished with cushions, it becomes a deewan.

Les′bian rule, a thin strip of lead which is used to record temporarily the profile of moldings.

leschi (les′key), in ancient Greece, a public forum, usually sheltered.

lessee′, one to whom a lease is granted.

les′sor, one who grants a lease.

let in, verbal description of a housing joint (4*f*).

let′ter chute, *see* mail chute.

let′terwood, *see* snakewood.

lev′el, surveyor's level, an instrument for measuring heights of land or other objects above a plane of reference. 2. an instrument used by carpenters or masons for establishing horizontality or verticality in a member.

levercel (lev′ur sell), early English term for door hood, or sometimes an open shed.

le′wan, an open-side room in Oriental houses, opening upon an inner court. *See also* leewan.

lew′is, or **Lewis anchor** (ang′ ker), a metal wedge clamp, secured in a recess, for lifting building stones.

Lewis holes, sinkages in stones on surfaces that will be hidden in building, for engaging Lewis anchors in hoisting and placing the stones.

li′brary, a room or a building in which books are kept for reference.

lich gate, *see* lych gate.

lien (leen), a legalized claim on certain property as security for a debt.

lierne (lee urn′), French term for a subordinate rib in vaulting (8*h*).

lierne vaulting, vaulting in which lierne ribs are freely employed (8*h*).

life class, a group engaged in making drawings, paintings, or sculpture from living models.

lift, an elevator; a sidewalk lift is an elevator rising through iron doors in a sidewalk. 2. a metal aid in lifting a sash or door.

light (lite), a pane of glass. 2. the amount of illumination, generally daylight, captured in a room or an interior. Borrowed light is that which is received through or over a partition from an outside lighted space.

light′house, a tower-like building to hold and serve a guiding light with its individual characteristics, usually on a coast.

light′ing, provision for either artificial or natural light, usually indoors.

light′ning rod, an electric conductor projecting above a tower or roof ridge and leading to a ground, to divert lightning.

lignumvitæ (lig′num vi′tee) (*Guaiacum* spp.), very heavy woods of great strength, with white or yellowish sapwood and olive to dark brown heartwood, originating in the coastal regions of Central America and the West Indies. They are used for propeller-shaft bearings of ships and other machinery, pulley sheaths, caster wheels, and mallet heads.

lim′ba (*Terminalia superba*), a West African wood also known as afara, frake, offram, and "korina," varying in color from pale cream to brown; used chiefly for furniture and veneer.

lime, calcium oxide; with water added it becomes a paste—lime putty, a common element of plaster and mortar.

lime′stone, calcium carbonate in non-crystalline form, a widely used building stone. *See also* oölite.

lime′wood, *see* basswood.

lin′den, *see* basswood.

lin′ear perspective, graphic representation in two kinds, in both of which it is assumed that the line of sight is perpendicular to the plane of projection: centrolinear, or station-point, perspective (conic projection) in which the spectator is assumed to be at a local fixed distance from the object; orthogonal perspective (cylindrical projection) in which the spectator is assumed to be at an infinite distance from the object. *See also* anisometric, monodimetric, and isometric.

line drawing, a drawing of lines, dots, and solid masses, as distinguished from tonal variations of a wash drawing. Such a line drawing is capable of reproduction for printing, by the line process of photoengraving.

lin′enfold, or **linen scroll,** a theme of surface decoration in wood carving, widely used in the late fifteenth and the sixteenth centuries (8*d*).

linoleum (linn o′leum), a finish floor covering made of linseed oil, ground cork, etc., oxidized upon a fabric base.

lin′seed oil, one of the most commonly used paint oils, processed from flaxseed.

lin′tel, the horizontal member of the most common structural form—a beam resting its two ends upon separate posts.

lip joint, in terra cotta, a joint similar to a carpenter's rebate.

lisena [It.], in Romanesque architecture, a pilaster.

lis′tel, or **list,** a border fillet molding.

Lithonia granite, a blue-gray, fine-grain granite of Georgia.

lith′opone, zinc sulphate and sulphate of baryta, used as a white paint pigment.

liv′ing-room, the main communal room of a dwelling.

load (lode), dead load, total downward pressure of all fixed elements of the structure; live load, downward pressure that might be added to the structure temporarily.

lob′by, an anteroom. 2. a large vestibule. 3. the main-floor circulation center of a hotel.

lobe, of Gothic tracery, a foil (9*b*, *e*, *h*).

lock, a mechanical means of fastening a door, drawer, or the like.

lock′er, a small cupboard; a receptacle in which personal clothing and other property may be locked; it is frequently of metal and is vented, in a range, as in schools, factories, etc.

lock′ rail, the rail of a door into which the lock is set.

lock′up, a building or room for temporary imprisonment.

loculus (lok′yu lus), in ancient tombs, a recess or compartment for an urn or a body.

lo′cus colum′bæ, *see* peristerium.

lo′cust, black (*Robinia pseudoacacia*), a tree of North America, the hard, heavy wood of which is particularly resistant to decay underground.

West Indian locust, *see* guapinol.

loc′utory, or **locuto′rium,** reception room for visitors to a monastery or convent.

lodge, a hut; a cabin. 2. a meeting place of certain fraternal organizations. 3. gate lodge, or porter's lodge, a small building attending the entrance to the grounds of a large residence or an institution.

loft, originally the unfinished story just under the roof of a commercial building or warehouse; now, any undivided floor of a commercial building, the subdivision and equipment of which is left to the tenant. 2. the unfinished space under the rafters of a large building, as a barn, church, or schoolhouse.

log′arithm, the exponent indicating the power to which a base number (10 in the decimal system) must be raised to produce a given number.

logarith′mic spiral, a spiral which intersects all of its radiants at the same angle (2*k*).

log cabin, a primitive dwelling, the walls of which are of logs laid horizontally and notched for a similar series meeting them at a corner.

loge [Fr.] (lozhe), a small room or stall in which a student is enclosed to work alone—*en loge*. 2. a stall or a location in some theaters.

logeum (lo gee′um), that part of an ancient theater reserved for the chorus and others not taking a more active part in the performance.

loggia (lozh′yah), a passage or gallery, colonnaded on one or both sides.

log house, a shelter built of logs notched at ends to fit snugly together and sometimes chinked with mud or plaster.

logiste [Fr.] (lozh eest), a student admitted to a loge for a competition; specifically, one competing for the Prix de Rome.

Lom′bard architecture, a style developed in northern Italy between the sixth and thirteenth centuries.

long house, a council house of North American Indians.

Longmeadow sandstone, a stone of fine and even grain, in dark reddish brown, quarried at East Longmeadow, Mass.

lonja [Sp.] (lawn'hah), an exchange, a bourse.

look'out, a cantilevered beam or a bracket for the support of overhanging construction.

loop'hole, a slotlike aperture in a wall, originally used for small-arms action in defense; a crenelle (8*b*).

Loredo Chiaro (low ra'do she arro), an Italian marble of light coffee ground color, with irregular fragments of reddish brown distributed through the mass and with many glasslike veins.

lot, a measured portion of land, usually a building site.

lo'tus, a flower of the Nile valley, conventionalized in Egyptian architecture and sculpture (15*d*).

loudspeak'er, the production end of an electrical sound-amplifying system.

Louis Quatorze (loo ee katorz), the style of architecture and decoration developed under Louis XIV in France, 1643–1715.

Louis Quinze (kahz), the style of architecture and decoration developed under Louis XV, 1715–1774.

Louis Seize (sayz), the style of architecture and decoration developed under Louis XVI, 1774–1793.

lounge (lownj), a lounging-room, usually in a clubhouse or hotel.

louver, or **louvre** (loo'ver), one of a series of horizontal slats, tilted to exclude rain and snow but to pass air. 2. a ventilating panel.

lovo'a, *see* tigerwood.

loz'enge, a diamond-shaped parallelogram.

lucarne (lyou kahrn'), (plural, **lucarna**), a small window in a dormer or spire; if in a spire it is often capped by a gablet and finial.

Lucite, trade name for a plastic material available in transparent sheets and other forms.

lucul'lite, a black, fine-textured marble, named for Lucullus, a consul of ancient Rome.

lug, a small projecting member of a larger body, to engage an adjoining unit or to serve as an aid in handling. 2. the part of a sill for window or door opening that extends horizontally beyond the opening into the masonry.

Lumachelle (looma shell'), a shell marble of dark grayish brown ground interspersed with pearl-lined shells. The best-known product comes from the Tyrol.

lumbayao, or **lumbayau** (lum bay'o) (*Tarrietia javanica*), a wood from the Philippine Islands frequently sold as Philippine mahogany; differentiated from mahogany by a decided purplish brown tinge; used for furniture and cabinetwork.

lum'ber, wood in dimensioned form after being sawn from the log.

lu'men, unit of luminous flux, the flux through a unit solid angle from one international candle.

lu'men-hour, unit of lighting; lighting at a rate of one lumen for one hour.

luminaire′, a lighting unit or fixture, complete and also detachable.

Lunel Uni (loo nel′yunee), one of the many varieties of "Notre Dame" marbles quarried in northern France. Lunel Uni Clair is brownish gray with occasional small fossils and is streaked with very fine grayish white calcite veins. Lunel Uni Foncé has like characteristics but larger and more numerous fossils on a much darker brown.

lunette (loo net′), a small round or arched-top window in a vaulted or coved ceiling or roof.

lu′thern, a window above the cornice of a classical building, rising vertically in line with the outside wall; these were square, arched, bull's-eye, semicircular, etc.

lyceum (li′see um), a building for an institution of learning.

lych gate (litch gate), a sheltering gatehouse near a church or burial ground, under which a bier may be rested.

lychnites (lik ni′tees), another name for Parian marble.

ly′sis, Greek term for a plinth or step occurring above the cornice of the podium of ancient temples.

M

macad′am, a common method of paving with crushed stone, named for John L. Macadam (1756–1836), a Scottish engineer.

macaya (mah ki′yah) (*Andira inermis*), also called moca or mocha; a wood from Central and South America and the West Indies which is considered one of Mexico's potentially valuable species; coarse-textured, hard, strong, and durable, it is described as yellowish, reddish, or brown, sometimes very dark; light-colored specimens suggest hard pine, others palm wood, and some are compared to English oak; used for interior woodwork and furniture.

macellum (mak ell′um), in ancient Rome, a produce market.

machicolation (mah chiko la′ shun), the corbeling out of the top of a defense wall to gain openings downward.

machined (mah sheend), descriptive of a metal surface which has been finished on lathe or planer.

machinist (mah sheen′ist), one skilled in the working of metals by machine tools.

made land, land brought to a higher level by earth fill, sometimes brought out of water.

madrone′ burl (*Arbutus menziesii*), a wood from the Pacific Coast, U.S.A., heavy, tough, and, in color, a light reddish brown with occasional spots of deep red; used chiefly for veneer.

magazine (mag′ga zeen), a room or building designed for storage, especially the storage of explosives.

magen-Dawid, star of David; also called Solomon's seal (5*z*).

magister (maj′ister), in medieval times, a master craftsman.

mag′nesite, a material usually combining calcined magnesium oxide and magnesium chloride, applied in plastic state for flooring, integral bases, and wainscots on wood with metal lath, or on concrete.

magnesium (mag nee′shum), a silver-white metal, used in alloys of light weight.

magno′lia, Southern evergreen (*Magnolia grandiflora*) and cucumber tree (*Magnolia acuminata*), trees of the southeastern U.S.A. frequently marketed with the lower grades of yellow poplar; used for furniture, siding, millwork.

mahog′any (*Swietenia* spp.), widely regarded as the premier cabinet wood of the world, based on its use through centuries. Attractive appearance of its very pale to very dark reddish brown color, ease of working, strength, and low shrinkage are outstanding properties. Commercially, three species are important: *mahagoni* of the West Indies; *humilis* of the west coast of

Mexico and Central America; and *macrophylla* of Central and South America. The last-named species produces the bulk of mahogany in the world's markets.

African mahogany, misleading term for the red khaya. *See* khaya, red.

Brazilian mahogany, *see* jequitiba.

Colombian mahogany, *see* jequitiba.

Philippine mahogany, *see* lumbayao and seraya.

pink mahogany, *see* guarea.

rose mahogany, *see* rosamay.

mail chute, a chute leading from above into a mail box.

main (mane), a major supply pipe for liquids or gases. 2. a major conductor of electric current.

mairie [Fr.] (may ree), in France, the offices of the chief official of a city.

maison Dieu (mazonh dyuh), early French term for a hospital.

makor'e (*Mimusops heckelii*), also called African cherry and baku; a tree native to the Gold Coast and Nigeria, the wood of which is pink to pinkish or red-brown, somewhat resembling khaya but with dark red growth lines similar to cherry; used principally for veneer.

maksoo'rah, a screen or partition in a mosque.

mal'leable iron, *see* iron.

Malone, Potsdam, or **Adirondack sandstone,** a dense, strong, very hard quartzite of New York State, composed wholly of quartz grains with siliceous cementing material and varying in color from a rather light pink to a reddish brown.

Maltese cross (mawl tees'), *see* cross (5*g*).

mal'tha, a mineral pitch used in ancient times as a mortar or stucco.

malugai (mah'lu gi) (*Pometia pinnata*), a wood from the Philippines, light red to reddish brown in color, hard, and heavy; used for construction, cabinetwork, handles, furniture, and where a strong, tough wood is required for bending.

man'doral, *see* vesica (2*l*).

manège (mahn ezhe), the exercising court of a riding school.

manganese' steel, *see* steel.

manger (mane'jer), a feed box or trough in a stable.

manggasinoro (manga see' noro) (*Shorea philippinensis*), or yellow lauan, a wood from the Philippines, yellowish white to pale brown, moderately hard and heavy, of medium fine texture; used for furniture and interior work.

man'hole, an access chamber for underground piping, wiring, or the like, or the cover of same at grade. 2. an access hole, with cover, for a boiler or tank.

man'ifold, a section of pipe into which branches are led.

man'or, a tract of land granted by the king.

man'or house, the residence of the lord or proprietor of a manor.

man'sard roof, a roof having a slope in two planes, the lower of which is usually much the steeper. Named for François Mansard, a French architect (1598–1666) (6*g*).

manse (mance), the official residence of a clergyman.

mansion (man′shun), a dwelling of some size and pretension.

manso′nia (*Mansonia altissima*), also called ofun; a wood from the west coast of Africa, frequently used as a substitute for American walnut where long length is required; used also for veneer.

man′tel, or **mantelpiece,** the shelf and facing embellishment of a fireplace opening.

man′teltree, a beam across the opening of a fireplace.

manual (man′you ul), the keyboard of an organ, and its cabinetwork.

ma′ple, hard or **sugar** (*Acer saccharum*), a wood occurring from Newfoundland and Quebec to southern Manitoba and south to Georgia and Oklahoma; of dense texture, strong, and durable; used for flooring particularly and for cabinetwork.

M.Ar., or **M.Arch.,** abbreviation for the degree Master of Architecture.

marble (mar′bl), calcium carbonate with other components which give it color, pattern, and texture suitable for a desirable building stone.

marbleizing (mar′bl izing), simulating the appearance of marble by painting.

mar′blewood (*Diospyros discolor*), an East Indian tree also known as Macassar ebony; its roseate gray-and-black wood is prized for cabinetwork and veneer.

marmoraceous, or **marmoreal** (mar more a′shus, mar more′ eal), marble-like.

mar′nut (*Machaerium* spp.), woods from Brazil, of rich violet-brown streaked with lighter and darker markings of golden yellow; used for cabinetwork, doors, and veneer.

marouflage (mah roo flahz), the backing of a painting with another canvas or a wood panel, or the structural support of a mural.

marquetry (mar′ket ree), mosaic of varicolored woods, sometimes interspersed with other materials, as mother-of-pearl.

marquise (mar keez′), a shelter projection over an entrance, frequently ornamental and of metal, with or without glazing. By extension, an outdoor shelter, sometimes of tent character. The word is sometimes debased to "marquee."

martel′lo tower, a defense tower originating in sixteenth-century Italy.

martyrium (mar teer′eum), a shrine or sepulcher containing the relics of a martyr.

Maryland Verde Antique, a serpentine that ranks high as a beautiful green marble. It is a mottled light and dark grass-green with interlocking veins of lighter green.

ma′sawood (*Platymiscium* spp.), woods occurring from Mexico to the Brazilian Amazon, of a rich red or reddish brown color with light and darker veins; used chiefly for veneer.

mascaron (mas′kah ron), a human head grotesque, often used as an architectural ornament. *See also* mask.

mashrebeeyah (mah shree bee′ yah), a latticed window.

mask, or **mascaron,** a sculptured face, usually in bas-relief, used as a decorative spot.

ma′son, a workman skilled in constructing masonry.

Ma′sonite, trade name for a compo board.

ma′sonry, that branch of construction dealing with plastering, concrete construction, and the laying up of stone, brick, tile, and other such units with mortar.

massier [Fr.] (mah see a), the student head of a school or atelier.

mastaba (mas′tah bah), a built-in seat or bench. 2. a mortuary structure above an ancient Egyptian burial place.

mas′ter, title of the master builder in the Middle Ages.

mas′ter key, a key made to operate two or more locks requiring different keys.

mas′ter plan, a plan, usually of a community or city, made to guide or restrict future development.

mas′ter switch, an electric switch controlling the operation of two or more subordinate circuits.

mastic (mas′tik), a form of cement or calking compound that retains a measure of elasticity.

mat, a grid of reinforcement for foundation concrete.

mat sinkage, a depression in a floor near an entrance so that a doormat placed therein will be approximately at floor level.

match′ed boards, boards tongued and grooved on opposite edges to effect a close joint with their neighbors (4*n*).

mausole′um, a memorial structure in connection with a tomb.

Ma′yan architecture, the work of a people or peoples of Yucatan, appearing in history about 600 B.C., who built magnificent cities of stone in the early years of the Christian era.

McDermott sandstone, an even-bedded sandstone with a medium fine grain, in buff and blue colors; easy to work and carve.

meander (mee an′dur), the Greek fret (11*a*).

mechanic (mek an′ik), one skilled in some branch of handicraft.

mechanician (mekka nish′un), one skilled in the nature and use of machinery.

medaille [Fr.] (med eye), a medal.

medallion (med al′yun), a circular or oval bas-relief used in decoration.

medianæ (me de an′ee), the columns in the middle of a classical portico where the intercolumniation was enlarged.

medieval (meddy ee′vul), of the Middle Ages, that period extending from the decay of Rome to the Renaissance.

Medie′val architecture, *see* Gothic architecture.

medres′seh, a college of Moslem law, often a mosque so used.
meet′inghouse, a house of public worship in one of the nonliturgical faiths.
meet′ing rail, a horizontal member of upper or lower double-hung window sash at their junction.
meeting stile, the stile of a door on which the lock is set; in a double door, the stiles which meet when the doors are closed.
meg′alith, a stone of great size, as in prehistoric remains such as Stonehenge in England.
meg′aron, in an ancient Greek house, the room which was the main gathering place.
meh′rab, *see* mihrab.
mem′ber, a component part.
membret′to [It.], a minor wing of a building; an alette.
memo′rial, a commemorative monument, or even an inscribed tablet.
M.Eng., abbreviation of the degree Master of Engineering.
menhir (men′her), a prehistoric monument, usually a single tall stone, sometimes marking a grave, sometimes perhaps commemorating a battle.
men′sa, the top horizontal member or surface of an altar.
mention [Fr.] (mahsee onh), a mark of merit given drawings in a competition or school problem.
meranti, *see* seraya.
mer′chant bars, *see* iron, wrought.
mer′cury-va′por light, an electric light source of tubular form depending on mercury vapor made luminous by the passage of electricity across a gap.
merlon (mur′lun), the solid alternate in an embattled parapet (8*b*).
me′ros, the plane face between the channels of a triglyph; femor, orlo, shank (12).
mesau′la, Greek term for a minor interior court.
meson (may′son), in Mexico, a crude inn.
mess′mate, *see* yuba.
meta (plural, **metæ**) (ma′tah, ma′tie), in ancient Rome, a limiting mark, as a column or columns in the circus, around which the chariots turned.
met′atome, or **metoche,** the interval between dentils (13, 14).
me′ter, unit of linear measure in the metric system used in France and elsewhere; equivalent to 39.37 inches. 2. an apparatus for measuring the flow of liquid, gas, or electrical current.
metes and bounds (meets, bownds), a means of describing the location of parcels of land by defining boundaries in terms of directions and distances from one or more specified points of reference.
metoche (met′o kee), the space between dentils in the Ionic order (14). The word is also used by Vitruvius to denote the space between triglyphs.
metope (met′o pee), the plain or sculptured stone between adjacent triglyphs in the Doric frieze. In very ancient examples of the Doric order this space was open (11*j*).

mews (myoos), a courtyard or subordinate street upon which face stables and the like.

Mexican architecture, a term too broad to be useful, for it includes the most primitive forms of shelter; the stone architecture of the Mayas, built at the beginning of the Christian era; the ceremonial grandeur of the Toltecs; the carved mosaic stonework of the Zapotecs; the luxurious terraced cities of the warlike Aztecs; and the varied splendors of the Spanish conquistadors who arrived in 1519.

mezzanine (met′zah neen), a story of lesser height and area interposed between floor and ceiling of a high story; an entresol.

mezzo-rilievo [It.] (met′so rilly ā′vo), a degree of sculpture relief between the slightly projecting bas-relief and the extreme projection of alto-rilievo.

mia-mia (me ah me ah), a hut of circular plan, the walls of which are of trees sloped or bent inward; peculiar to Australia and neighboring islands.

mi′ca, family name for a class of silicates affording thin, tough laminations of variable translucency; formerly used widely for electrical insulation.

Micar′ta, trade name for a plastic material made of resin-soaked layers of paper or cloth fused together under heat and pressure. Used in sheet form for table tops and similar durable and decorative needs, and in many other forms for insulation, gears, etc.

mi′croclimatol′ogy, in architecture, the science of planning and building in accord with climatic characteristics of the individual building site.

Mid′dle Ages, the period extending from the fall of Rome, 476 A.D., until about 1500 A.D.

miedan (mee′dan), in Persia, an open square surrounded by shops; a bazaar.

mihrab, or **mehrab** (mir rob′), a niche or other feature of a Mohammedan mosque, indicating the direction in which lies Mecca.

mild steel, that containing from 0.2% to 0.5% carbon, having more nearly than ordinary steel the properties of wrought iron.

Milford pink granite, a pink of medium to coarse grain, mottled with black mica spottings, quarried in Massachusetts; it is used for monumental and general building work.

miliary pillar, on Roman highways, a stone indicating a distance of 1000 paces.

mill, originally a building in which grain is ground; by extension, a factory, especially a woodworking establishment.

milled, having a serrated surface useful in circular metal forms that are to be turned by hand.

Millstone, a buff, blue, and pink granite of Connecticut.

millwork, woodworking-mill product assembled at the mill.

mim′bar, that part of a Mohammedan mosque in which the pulpit is located.

minar (mih nar′), in Moslem architecture, a tower.

minaret (mihnar et′), specifically, a tower of a mosque from which the muezzin calls to prayer; an alkorane. 2. more loosely, a slender tower, usually among others.

minch house, a place of shelter and rest, usually a small inn.

min′dra, the cella of a Hindu temple.

mineral wool, a fibrous material made from mineral slag and used for insulation.

Minnesota Black, an igneous rock of the gabbro or "black granite" class, of medium grain, quarried at Ely, Minn.

Minnesota Mankato, a fine- to coarse-grained, compact, semicrystalline, dolomitic limestone, sometimes cellular in texture, and ranging from buff to cream, yellow, and gray. There are also pink and pink-buff varieties.

min′ster, the church of a monastery.

min′ute, or **part,** one-thirtieth of Palladio's module of the classic orders. Vignola divided the module into 12 parts in the Tuscan and Doric orders, 18 parts in the Ionic, Corinthian, and Composite orders. 2. in measurement of angles, one-sixtieth of a degree.

mirador (mirra thor′), in Spanish architecture, a window, loggia, or balcony located to command a view.

mischio (me′skyo), in Italian architecture, a form of mosaic marble flooring.

miserere (miz uh reh′re), an ecclesiastical stall seat that is hinged so that when raised it offers support for one standing.

misericorde (meez ur e kord′), in monastic architecture, a refectory for the preparation and serving of flesh meat.

mission (mish′un), the church of a congregation that has not attained the status of a parish. 2. specifically, the mission buildings built by the Franciscans in Mexico and southern California.

mission roofing tile, a clay tile 14″ to 18″ long, curved to the arc of a circle, slightly tapered lengthwise, laid alternately with the convex side up, flanked by units with the concave side up (6*i*).

Missouri marble, crystalline limestone from the lower carboniferous strata, generally gray with a slight bluish tint and consisting of irregular grains of calcite and shells bound in a mass of calcite. Suture joints occur parallel to the bedding and about 2″ to 20″ apart. Ozark Gray is quarried at Carthage, Napoleon Gray at Phoenix. At Marlo a different range of monotone and decorative marbles are produced under the trade names of Adorado, Eldorado, Graydorado, Hondorado, Indorado, and Sheldorado.

Missouri Red granite, of medium to coarse grain and a rich red color.

mi′ter, the junction of two members at an angle, the junction line of which bisects the angle (4*b*).

mi′ter arch, French name for a pediment form used in early Greek, Celtic, and Norman work (1*o*).

mjölkbod, dairy room of the Swedish dwelling.

moat (mote), a trench surrounding a defense wall.

moca, or **mocha** (mo′kah), *see* macaya.

mod′el (mahd′el), a representation in three dimensions at a small scale.

Mod′ernism, a school of thought in design which stresses contemporary needs and technics as against following forms of the past.

modillion (mo dil′yun), a bracket form used in series under a corona (14).

mod′ular coordina′tion, a dimensional system affording more efficient assembly of buildings from standard building products by correlating the dimensions of a structure and the unit sizes of the materials going into it, through reference to a 4″ cubical module.

module (mod′yule), an arbitrary unit of measure. Vignola used as module half the diameter of the column, and divided the module into 12 parts in the Tuscan and Doric (12) orders, 18 parts in the Ionic (13), Corinthian (14), and Composite orders. Modular coordination uses a 4″ module.

modulus (mod′you luss), unit of measure used in describing the strength of materials.

modulus of elasticity, the ratio of the unit of stress to the unit of deformation resulting from tension applied to one end of a bar of which the other end is fixed.

modulus of rupture, the stress at which a specimen of material breaks in the testing.

mo′ellon, the inner filling of a masonry wall—spalls, broken stones, and grout.

Mohammedan architecture, *see* Saracenic architecture.

Mohs' scale, a gage of hardness among minerals.

moisture barrier, *see* vapor barrier.

mold′ing, or, rarely, **mold,** formerly **moulding,** a deviation from a plane surface, involving rectangular or curved profiles, or both, with the purpose of effecting a transition or of obtaining a decorative play of light and shade.

mole (Italian, **molo**), a sea wall, dam, or quay.

mo′ment, or **bending moment,** the measure of the tendency of a force to produce rotation about a given point.

monastery (mon′as tair ee), the communal dwelling place of a religious order of monks.

Monel metal, trade name for an alloy of nickel and copper having high resistance to corrosion.

mon′itor, a continuous section of roof raised to admit light on a vertical plane (6*l*).

monkey puzzle, *see* araucaria.

monodimetric, a form of orthogonal perspective in which two of the three main dimensions are at the same inclination, the third at a different inclination, to the plane of projection.

mon'olith, a single block of stone or concrete in or for a structure.

monop'teron, or **monopteros,** in classical architecture, a temple of circular plan and colonnaded perimeter.

mon'ostyle, of a single column, as a shaft monument.

monotri'glyph, the intercolumniation in the Doric order which spans one triglyph and two metopes in the entablature.

mon'strance, a receptacle in which the consecrated wafer is displayed to the worshippers, in the Roman Catholic Mass. 2. a receptacle for the display of holy relics.

montant [Fr.] (monh tanh), any vertical member of a framework, as a stile.

mon'ument, a structure the chief purpose of which is commemorative. 2. a boundary stone set by land surveyors, locating a property line or corner.

monumen'tal, enduring and impressive in character and appearance.

Moor'ish, or **Moresque,** in the architectural or decorative manner of the Moors; Saracenic (16*h*).

mop'board, or **baseboard,** a skirting board, usually with moldings, extending along an interior wall or partition primarily as a protection against defacement of the wall surface at floor level.

morastuga, or **tvärumstuga,** a three-room dwelling of Sweden, common in Mora, province of Dalecarlia.

Moresque (more esk'), *see* Moorish (16*h*).

morgue (morg), a room or building for the temporary reception of corpses.

morn'ing-room, in English architecture, a sitting-room with morning sunlight, used chiefly by ladies.

mor'tar, a mixture of sand, water, lime, and cement, sometimes including moisture-repellent substances, used to bind together the units of masonry.

mortgage (mor'gage), a pledging of property by the debtor (mortgagor) to the creditor (mortgagee) as security for a money debt to be paid in a specified time.

mortise (mor'tiss), a cut-out receptacle in one member to receive the tenon of another to which it is to be joined (4*g*). 2. a cut-out receptacle or depression to receive a lock mechanism, a hinge leaf, or the like.

mortise lock, a lock designed to be let into a mortise extending edgewise into the stile of a door or the like, and occasionally even deeper into the rail.

mortuary chapel (mor'tchoo ary), a chapel for the temporary reception of and services for funeral parties.

mosaic (mo za'ik), inlaid tessellated surface.

mosaique [Fr.] (mo zi ik), mosaic. 2. in rendered plans, the embellishment of individual floor spaces.

mosque (mosk), a place of worship for the Mohammedans.

motel′, a roadside inn or group of small cottages, but usually both, for the transient use of the motorist.

motif [Fr.] (mo teef), motive; an element in a composition.

moucharaby (moo shar′abbee), French term for a latticed oriel or a machicolated balcony in Moslem architecture; same as mushrebeeyeh.

Mouchette (moo shet′), a French limestone, a variation of Comblanchien. Of buff ground with some tendency to rose and gold veins and with characteristic fossilistic and glass speckles.

mould or **mold,** to form into a desired shape by having a plastic substance harden in a matrix.

moul′ding, *see* molding.

Mt. Airy granite, trade name for a medium-grain, even-textured, light gray to nearly white biotite granite quarried at Mt. Airy, N. C. There is also a White Mt. Airy, very light gray with predominant colors of black and white and a few faint pink quartz crystals scattered through it; the stone is of medium grain.

mounting, the process of attaching a thin sheet—drawing, photograph, or the like—to a stiffer background.

Mt. Waldo, a light to medium gray granite of Maine.

movin′gui, *see* ayan.

mow (mau), upper level of a barn in which hay is stored.

Mudejar (moo da′har), descriptive of early Spanish Renaissance architecture showing Moorish influence.

mud′sill, the horizontal wall timber at the base of a wood-frame structure.

mud′ wall, a wall made of tamped mud, sometimes stuccoed.

muiraquatiara, *see* canarywood.

muisetanden [Dutch], literally, mouse teeth; the introduction into the brickwork, at edge of a gable, of brick set at right angles to the slope. In Virginia the practice is called tumbling (3*m*).

mullion (mull′yun), an upright division member between windows or doors of a close series, first used in Early English (7*d*).

muniment house, a place in a cathedral, church, college, or the like for the safekeeping of charter, seal, etc.

Munsell system, a widely used system for the designation and nomenclature of surface colors, developed by Albert F. Munsell of Boston, Mass., and published as the *Munsell Book of Color* by Munsell Color Company, Baltimore, Md.

mun′tin, a bar member supporting and separating panes of glass in a sash or door. The word seems to have once been *montant.* In England, the term is glazing bar. 2. in England, the vertical members of a paneled door between stiles.

mural (mew′ral), of a wall. 2. a wall decoration.

mus′covite, white or potash mica.

museum (mew ze′um), a building for the preservation and

public inspection of rare and instructive objects.

mushrebee′yeh, Arabic term for a lattice-enclosed balcony. *See* moucharaby.

mutule (mew′chule), a member of the Doric cornice, supporting the corona; it is derived from the rafter ends of wooden construction (11*j*).

Mycen′æan architecture, that of a civilization recorded principally in Greece, Asia Minor, and Sicily before the Hellenes, probably about fourteen centuries B.C.

myrtle burl (mur′tl) (*Umbellularia californica*), also called California laurel or baytree; a wood of the west coast, hard, strong, golden brown and yellowish green in color, sometimes with dark purple blotches; used for veneer.

N

N.A., abbreviation for National Academician.

nail (nale), a slender metal shaft with point and head, for fastening woodwork and the like together.

naos (na′ahs), in classical architecture, the inner chamber of a temple.

nargusta, *see* aromilla.

nar′ra (*Pterocarpus indicus*), also called sena and angsena; a wood from the Dutch East Indies and the Philippines, in a red variety and a yellow variety; moderately hard and heavy, of limited strength, fairly easy to work, takes a good polish; it is a popular cabinet wood in the Philippines.

nar′thex, the entrance vestibule of a church; sometimes the rear end of the nave behind a screen.

natato′rium, a building or room sheltering a swimming pool.

nattes (nat′tez), basket weave surface decoration.

natural bed, the horizontal base of a stone as it was formed in the quarry.

nave, that portion of a church interior on the main axis, and not including the transepts, for the occupation of the lay worshipper.

neat (neet), used without the addition of other materials, as "neat cement."

nebule (neb′yool), a form of ornament characteristic of Norman architecture—in band or corbel table—the lower edge of which is undulating.

neck, of a capital, the space, in the Doric order, between the astragal on the shaft and the annulet of the cap. The Ionic order rarely has a neck of the capital; hypotrachilium (11*j*).

neck′ing, or **neck molding,** a molding circling the shaft of a column near its top (12).

necrop′olis, a place of graves and tombs.

nee′dle, a shoring member inserted through a wall at intervals and resting on outside and inside supports.

nee′dle bath, a shower bath in which water jets strike the user horizontally.

neo-clas′sic, any revival of classical architectural forms.

Neo-Gothic, a revival of Gothic forms, such as occurred both in England and the United States in the nineteenth century.

Neo-Greek, a revival of Greek forms; néo-greque in France, where a revival developed in the first half of the nineteenth century.

ne′on lights, elements of illumination depending upon electrical discharge in tubes of neon gas.

neorama (nee o rah′mah), a panoramic elevation of an interior, originally of a Greek temple.

nephrite (nef′rite), a hard, jade-like mineral used in prehistoric ornaments and utensils, and more recently in Asia for fine carving.

Nero-Antico (nero antee′ko), a black marble of ancient Greece.

nervure (ner′vyoor), a side or secondary rib of a groined vault.

new′el, a post terminating the handrail of a stairway at top, bottom, or on a landing. Originally, the central pillar of a spiral staircase.

niche (nitch), a recess in a wall, usually the location of sculpture.

nick′el, a mineral used widely, as is chromium, for electroplating upon other metals, as in plumbing fixtures.

nickel steel, *see* steel.

niello (nee ell′o), decorative engraving on metal surfaces, the incised lines filled with a black alloy.

nigged ashlar (nig′d), stone faced with pick or pointed hammer instead of a chisel.

night latch, a spring lock, knob-operated inside, key-operated outside.

nip′ple, or **thimble,** a short piece of pipe, male-threaded for connecting two lengths of pipe or hose.

Nis′sen hut, a semicylindrical structure of corrugated steel, adapted to military use, taking its name from the designer, a British engineer.

nog′ging, filling of brick, clay, or other solid material, between the closely spaced studding of a frame wall.

non-conductor, any material that does not readily conduct electrical current, used as insulation.

nook, a recess in, or extension beyond, a room, without separation from the main body unless it be a slight change of level.

noraghe (no rah′gay), a prehistoric structure of Sardinia, circular or elliptical in plan, used probably for defense but possibly as temple or tomb.

Nor′man architecture, the development of Romanesque in Normandy, and in England for a century after the Conquest.

North River bluestone, a New York stone used for trim, curbing, and paving.

nosing (no′zing), the rounded front edge of a stair tread.

nouveau [Fr.] (noo vo), a beginner in an atelier.

novelty siding, a term formerly used as descriptive of siding with a lower edge intended to be decorative.

noz′zle, an outlet at the end of piping, open as for a fountain jet, or valved as in a hose nozzle.

nun′nery, the communal dwelling place of a religious order of females.

nurs′ery, a room, or a department, for the shelter and care of children.

nut, a square or multi-sided block of metal, tapped with a through thread, for engaging the end of a screw bolt.

nymphæum (nim fee′um), in classical Roman architecture, a room, or a niche, featuring water, flowers, and sculpture. 2. the architecturally decorative outlet of a reservoir or an aqueduct.

O

oak (*Quercus* spp.), hard, heavy, strong woods used for heavy framing and prized for furniture, interior trim, and flooring. There are two principal groups, white and red.

brown oak, *see* tartan, royal.

English brown oak (*Quercus robur* and *Q. sessiliflora*), one of the finest woods in use for furniture, interior woodwork, and veneer; its color varies from light tan to a deep, leathery brown with black spots, similar to tortoise shell.

silky oak, *see* lacewood.

Tasmanian oak, *see* yuba.

tulip oak, *see* tartan, royal.

oast house, a building in which hops are kiln-dried.

ob′elisk, a shaft of square section and pyramidal tip, frequently tapering, usually commemorative.

obscure′ glass, sheet glass that has been made translucent instead of transparent.

obser′vatory, an upper room or lantern. 2. a building, usually with glazed and rotating dome, for astronomical observations.

obsid′ian, a hard, dark-colored, glassy, volcanic rock.

obsolescence (ob so less′ence), the deterioration of a building, not so much physically as in failing to meet progressive change in needs and usage.

o.c., on centers, an abbreviation frequently used in dimensioning working drawings, designating dimensions from the center of one member to the center of the next.

occus (ahk′kuss), in ancient Rome, the banqueting-room in a dwelling.

oc′tastyle, in classical architecture, having eight columns across the main façade.

oc′ulus, the circular opening occasionally formed at the top of a dome.

odeon, or **odeum** (o dee′un, o dee′um), in ancient Greece, a theater with a roof.

œcus (e′kuss), in the Greek house, a room for the use of the mistress and her sewing women; also used for banquets.

œil-de-bœuf [Fr.] (euh duh beuf), a "bull's-eye" window, circular or oval.

office (ahf′is), a room or building in which business can be carried on, or a profession practised.

off′ram, *see* limba.

off′set, a shift in the plane of a wall, resulting in a ledge or a shallow, right-angled break.

o′fun, *see* mansonia.

ogee (o jee′), a profile section or a molding with a reverse-curve face, concave above and convex below (12). *See also* cyma reversa (11*d*) and talon (10*f*, *g*).

ogee arch, a pointed arch, the sides of which are each formed with a reverse curve, slightly convex at the top. Also called keel arch (1*h*).

ogive (o′jive), a diagonal rib of simple vaulting intersection. 2. French term for pointed arch. The adjective is *ogival.*

Oglesby Blue granite, a fine-grain biotite granite of Georgia, with an azure blue color, taking a high polish.

ohm, unit of electrical resistance: pressure (volts) divided by current (amperes) equals ohms.

oillette, a small loophole, usually circular, as contrasted with a crenelle.

oil paint, a paint that contains drying oil or oil varnish as the basic vehicle.

okoume (o′koo mee) (*Aucoumea klaineana*), also called gaboon; a wood from the African west coast, light reddish brown with dark, broken stripes and a lustrous sheen; moderately soft and light in weight, yet strong; used chiefly for veneer.

olive, Italian (*Olea europæa*), a wood of yellowish brown color, streaked with darker markings of various shades; used largely for inlay, working smoothly to the tool.

ol′ive hinge, or **olive butt,** a hinge which in the bearing between the two leaves resembles a horizontally split olive.

o′ölite, or **oölitic limestone,** the granular variety of calcium carbonate, a building stone of fine texture, of which there are vast deposits in Lawrence, Monroe, and Owen Counties in Indiana.

o′pa (plural, **opæ**), in a Greek temple, the bed of a beam of floor or roof. 2. the space between the metopæ. 3. the space between joists.

opaion (o pi′yon), in ancient Greek and Roman work, an opening in the roof to allow smoke to escape. 2. a sort of lantern or clerestory.

Opalescent, a dark greenish gray gabbro "granite" with black and brown spottings, of coarse grain; quarried at Cold Spring, Minn.

o′pening, any aperture in a wall, usually door or window.

open space, in urban planning, that portion of a community site given over to roads, parks, and other land not containing the buildings.

open-string, descriptive of a stairway in which the ends of risers and treads are uncovered on the outside.

open valley, a roof valley where the shingles of the intersecting slopes leave open a space covered by metal flashing.

opepe (o pay′pee) (*Sarcocephalus diderrichii*), a wood from West Africa, with yellowish or pinkish sapwood and orange to golden yellow heartwood, darkening slightly upon exposure; texture coarse, grain frequently interlocked, hard, moderately heavy; used for flooring, furniture, panels, and veneer.

opera del duomo [It.], the workshop or museum of an Italian cathedral.

op′era house, a theater designed particularly for musical productions.

opisthodomus (o pis tho′do mus), the enclosed space in

the rear of the cella of a temple; the Roman posticum.

optostro'tum, Greek term for brick paving.

o'pus, work, in the sense of labor or its results.

orangery (ohr'anjerie), originally, a greenhouse for orange growing as part of a mansion; more commonly, a conservatory.

oratory (aw'ra toree), a small or private chapel.

orb, a boss at the intersection of vaulting ribs, perhaps originally to conceal the miters (8*c*). 2. a blank window or panel.

orchestra (ore'kestreh), in a modern theater, that sunken area directly in front of the stage in which the orchestra is seated. 2. the seating space on the main lower level of a theater.

or'der, in classical architecture, the column and its entablature (as in the Doric order, the Corinthian order), each giving its character to the whole building (11, 12, 13, 14).

ordinary (ord'nary), English and early American term for inn.

ordonnance (or'duh nuns), French term for the proper arrangement and composition of any architectural work leaning upon traditional law.

or'gan, originally, almost every kind of musical instrument used in churches, but for long confined to a valved wind instrument with a collection of pipes, played from a keyboard.

oriel (or'e el), a projecting window with its walls corbeled or supported by brackets.

oriele (ory el'), in medieval England, a small room at the end of the great hall in a manor house, perhaps formerly an oratory.

orient (or'e ent), to locate a building by points of the compass. 2. to locate a church so that the altar end is toward the east. In whatever direction the altar of a church is located by local considerations, the altar end is traditionally called the east end.

Oriental, a medium-grain pink granite with black and gray wavings; quarried at Morton, Minn.

oriental wood (*Endiandra palmerstoni*), also called Queensland walnut; an Australian wood varying in color from brown to gray or black, with pink streaks and a pinkish cast; used for veneer.

or'lo, or **or'le,** a fillet at the top or bottom of the shaft of a column. 2. the plane surface between adjacent flutes of a column or between channels of a triglyph; also called shank, femor, regela, and meros (12).

or'molu, goldleaf-coated bronze.

or'nament, detail that is incised, molded, painted, or otherwise added to a building, usually against a foil of plain surface, with the purpose of embellishment.

Ornamented English, that phase of Medieval architecture in England generally called the Decorated period; it occurred chiefly in the reigns of the three first Edwards.

ornate', ornamented to the verge of being overdone.

o′ro (*Pahudia rhomboidea*), also called tindalo; a wood from the Philippines, hard, heavy, and strong with pale orange heartwood turning to a deep wine-red color with age; used for interior finish, floors, doors, and veneer.

orphanage (or′fan idge), a building for the care and instruction of orphans.

orthog′onal perspective, a special type of orthogonal projection in which the rays are assumed to be not only parallel to each other but also perpendicular to the plane of projection. *See also* linear perspective.

orthog′onal projection, the graphic representation of a body upon a plane surface by drawing parallel lines to the surface from points on the body. *See also* orthogonal perspective.

orthograph′ic projection, a term loosely employed by American and English authorities to denote orthogonal projection.

orthostates (ortho sta′tees), in a Greek temple, the lower deep course in the naos walls.

or′thostyle, having columns in a straight line.

ossa′rium, or **os′suary,** a receptacle for the bones of the dead.

osten′sory, or **ostenso′rium,** a monstrance.

Ost′wald system, a widely used system for the designation and nomenclature of surface colors, developed by Wilhelm Ostwald of Germany and published in the Jacobson *Color Harmony Manual* obtainable from the Container Corporation of America, Chicago, Ill.

oubliette (oo blee et′), a dungeon in a stronghold, usually with a pit in which the victim really becomes "forgotten."

out′building, a minor structure separated from a building of which the former is a dependency.

out′house, a detached privy.

out′let, a distribution source of electrical current, such as for a lighting fixture, or a socket into which can be plugged the wiring for portable lamps and the like. 2. a discharge point in piping.

out′post inn, sometimes a synonym for motel, but more specifically designating what may be a branch establishment of a city hotel or an independent project, located well beyond the busy streets and affording the ample parking, ground-floor dining, and convention-assembly space that is lacking inside most cities.

o′verdoor, architecturally treated space over a doorway.

o′verhang, the projection of a member beyond the face below it; an upper story projecting beyond its supporting wall.

o′verhead door, a counterbalanced door that opens by following side tracks to a horizontal position above and behind the opening; used in garages, warehouses, etc.

o′vermantel, architecturally treated space above a fireplace mantel.

o′vershoot, the wide overhang of roof above first-story windows, as in the Dutch Colonial style. 2. the overhang of second story on the south side of a Pennsylvania barn.

o′verstory, *see* clerestory (7*g*).

o′verthrow, ornamental ironwork spanning a pair of gateposts.

o′volo, a profile or molding of convex section, its lower extremity receding from a vertical plane through the upper extremity (11*g*).

o′vum [Lat.], the egg, as in egg-and-dart molding (10*e*).

ovum mundi, *see* Great Monad (5*aa*).

ox′eye, a round or oval window, frequently in a dormer; an œil-de-bœuf.

P

pace, a dais. 2. a staircase landing. *See also* half-pace, quarter-pace, and footpace.

pack′ing, stuffing of oakum or the like to prevent leaking at a valve stem.

padauk, African (pah dowk′) (*Pterocarpus soyauxii*), a close-textured wood from the west coast of Africa; the heartwood is red to dark brown with red streaks and is used quarter-sliced for veneer; it is also used for carving.

Andaman padauk (*Pterocarpus dalbergioides*), a wood from the Andaman Islands, heartwood varying in color from yellowish pink to purplish red, darkening on exposure; strong, takes a smooth finish for cabinetwork, flooring, furniture, and veneer.

Burma padauk (*Pterocarpus macrocarpus*), a wood from Burma, close-textured with interlocked grain, yellow or golden reddish to dark, dull red with darker brown cross-bands; usually quarter-sliced for veneer.

pad′dock, a fenced enclosure adjoining, or near, a stable.

pad′lock, a self-contained lock having a pivoted bow or ring which is closed to lock.

pagoda (pa go′dah), in Far Eastern architecture, a tower-like or pyramidal structure, usually part of a temple (16*e*).

paillon (pay e′yon), the reflecting metal base for transparent lacquer, or gilded base for translucent coloring.

pai-loo (pay loo′), in China, a decorated gateway.

paint, a mixture of pigment in a liquid vehicle which, spread thinly on a surface, dries to form an opaque solid film.

paint′er, one who combines a knowledge of colors with their application for decorative and protective purposes. 2. an artist whose portrayal of objects or views is in color.

palace (pal′uss), a residence for royalty; by extension, a residence of especial magnificence.

palæstra (pal ess′trah), that part of the ancient Greek gymnasium given over to wrestling and the like.

pal′afitte, French and Swiss term for a lake dwelling.

palatial (pah lay′shal), palace-like, grand, of large size, and with elaborate amenities.

palatium (pah lay′shum), official palace of the Roman emperors.

palazzo [It.] (pah lot′so), a palace or a large residence.

paldao′ (*Dracontomelum dao*), a wood from the Philippines, Indo-China, and the West Indian Archipelago, possessing a great variety of grain and figure and a wide range of color, from grayish to greenish yellow with irregular, concentric, dark brown bands; used for veneer.

pal′ette, a board on which an artist spreads his colors. 2. the available color range for a project.

pal′ing, or **pale,** one of the upright members of a picket fence, fastened to top and bottom rails between posts.

palisade′, a fence of poles driven into the ground.

Palladian (pah lay′dee un), in the manner of Andrea Palladio, an Italian architect of 1518–1580; more specifically, the use of an arched opening closely flanked by square-head openings of smaller size and with the same base or sill.

Palladian motive, a generic term for the form characterized by a round-arched opening flanked by narrower, square-top openings beyond slender mullions.

palm (pahm), an ancient Hebrew and Chaldean unit of linear measure; 4 digits = 1 palm; 3 palms = 1 span; 2 spans = 1 cubit (1′–9.888″).

palm′ate, having lobes or leaves in fan shape, as the Greek anthemion (11*i*, 16*d*).

Palmer granite, a pinkish biotite granite of medium texture, from Maine.

palmette (pal met′), the conventionalized palm-leaf ornament, widely used in classical architecture; the anthemion (11*i*, 16*d*).

palmwood, *see* tepesuchil.

palosa′pis (*Anisoptera thurifera*), a wood from the Philippines and British Malaya, pale yellow with a pinkish cast, used for inexpensive furniture, interior finish, and veneer.

pampre [Fr.] (pam pr), an ornament composed of vine leaves and bunches of grapes, with which the hollow circumvolutions of twisted columns are sometimes decorated.

panache (pah nahsh′), that portion of a groined vault between two ribs.

pan-and-roll roofing tile, a roofing tile in two shapes, one of flat, rectangular section, the other a half-round section, for covering the joints of the flat sections (6*d*).

pancarpi (pan car′pee), Greek term for garlands and festoons of fruit, flowers, and leaves; a swag (16*j*).

pane, a sheet of glass for a comparatively small opening in a window sash or door. The term is rarely applied to large sheets of plate glass, as in a display window. 2. in ancient times, a side or face of a building.

pan′el, a sheet of material held in a frame usually of greater thickness.

pan′ic bolt, a door latch operated from the inside by pressure against a horizontal bar running practically across the full width of the door.

panier, or **pannier** [Fr.] (pan yay), a corbel form breaking the angle between a pilaster and the beam it supports.

panop′ticon, a building planned on a radial scheme, so that a single attendant at the center can observe the converging corridors.

pantograph (pan′to graf), a drafting instrument for copying at a different scale.

pan′theon, generic term for a temple dedicated to all the gods.

pan′tile, a curved roofing tile, somewhat like a prone letter S (6*a*).

pan′try, a room, usually between kitchen and dining-room, for handling and storing tableware and dry provisions. From the French *pain* (bread).

paoh-tah, in China, a temple, especially the tower-like forms of the Buddhists, always of an uneven number of stories.

papak′hu, the holy of holies in an Assyrian or Babylonian temple.

papier-mâché (pap yay mash-ay′), a composition of paper pulp and glue size, easily molded before it hardens.

paradis′us, in Medieval architecture, the cloistered forecourt of a church or cathedral.

par′apet, a low, retaining wall at the edge of a roof, porch, or terrace.

parascenium (para see′neum), one of the wings flanking the stage of a Greek theater.

paras′tas, or **parasta′ta,** one of the projecting side walls of a Greek temple *in antis.* 2. according to Vitruvius, a square post behind a column of a basilica for supporting the floor of an upper portico.

par′close, a screen of wood or stone separating chapels, especially at the east end of the aisles, from the body of the church.

paret′ta, roughcast embellished with surface pebbles.

pargeting, or **parge work** (par′jet ing, parj), back plastering; hasty plastering of the back of a wall or the back of the face withe to fill chance voids.

Par′ian marble, white, granular, saccharoidal marble from the Island of Paros in the Ægean Sea, much used by the ancients for statuary as well as building.

par′ish house, a building in connection with a church, where activities not so closely identified with worship are held.

park′ing, ground space devoted to the temporary occupation of vehicles, usually close to a building. 2. ornamental landscaped areas.

par′lor, the most formal room in a dwelling, often used for the entertainment of guests. The word is less used since the more informal living-room has largely supplanted the parlor.

par′odos, a passage used by the chorus of an ancient Greek theater.

parquet (par kay), a widely varying division of the main seating floor in a theater.

parquetry (par′ket ree), mosaic in flooring of wood.

parrell′, a chimney breast.

parsonage (par′son ij), the dwelling of a clergyman, often owned by the church he serves.

parstu′ga, three-room dwelling of the Swedes, the long rectangular plan of which consisted of two stugas joined by a vestibule and a third chamber.

part, or **minute,** a subdivision of the classic module. *See* module.

parterre (par tare), a level and patterned garden. 2. in an American theater, sometimes the seating section under the main gallery.

parti [Fr.] (par tee), the general scheme of a design, particularly in plan.

part'ing bead, or **part'ing strip,** a vertical guide strip on a double-hung window frame, separating the sashes.

partition (par tish'un), a wall dividing interior space.

partition block, light-load-bearing hollow masonry unit, made as thin as 2″, usually scored for plastering both sides.

par'ty wall, a wall built on a dividing line between plots of different ownership.

par'vis, the entrance court of a church or palace.

paschal (pass'kal), an architecturally important candlestick in ecclesiastical work, to receive the large paschal candle.

pas-de-souris [Fr.] (pah duh soo ree), steps from the moat to an entrance into the castle or stronghold.

passage, or **passageway** (pass' ij), a corridor or other horizontal means of intercommunication between elements of an interior.

passerelle [Fr.] (pas serel), literally, a footbridge.

pass'key, *see* master key.

pasticcio [It.] (pahs tee'tcho), or **pastiehe,** a composition made up of fragmentary parts of other works.

pastiche, *see* pasticcio.

pastophoria (pass to for'ea), in Greek antiquity, apartments near the temple for housing the priests.

patand', in early English carpentry, a sill or bottom member of a frame.

patera (pah tare'ah), a circular, dishlike ornament in classical architecture. In medieval times it was applied to the square, floriated designs in great variety, frequently used to interrupt moldings (9*c*).

patina (pah teen'ah), the color and texture added to a surface by time and various allies.

patio (pah'tyo), an open court enclosed on three or four sides by elements of a building.

patron [Fr.] (pat ronh), teacher, master.

pave'ment, or **pav'ing,** durable floor, walk, or road surfacing.

pave'ment light, transparent or translucent element in paving to light a space beneath; vault light.

pav'er, an occasional term for quarry tile.

pavilion (pah vil'yun), originally a temporary or movable shelter, sometimes merely a tent; a small outbuilding. 2. a wing or section of an institutional building, such as a hospital. 3. a building for temporary use, as in an exposition.

pavonazzo (pavvo not'so), descriptive of brilliantly veined marbles.

peaked roof (peekt), a roof rising either to a point or a ridge.

pear, alligator, *see* avocado.

pearl molding, one simulating a string of beads (10*d*).

pearwood (pare'wood) (*Pyrus communis*), a native of Europe and Asia, long cultivated in the U.S.A., although most of the wood comes from France or Germany; almost flesh-colored with light and dark shadings; used chiefly for veneer.

peb′ble dash′ing, mortar or stucco with a surface of partly imbedded pebbles.

pecans′ (*Carya illinoënsis, C. aquatica, C. cordiformis*, and *C. myristicaeformis*), natives of the U.S.A. with heartwood reddish brown in color, with darker brown stripes, and sapwood varying from pale red to white; can be stained and finished to resemble walnut; used for interior finish, furniture, and veneer.

pecky cypress, *see* cypress.

ped′estal, a base for a column, or for a piece of sculpture or the like (12, 13).

ped′iment, the triangular face of a roof gable, especially in its classical form.

pediment arch, *see* miter arch (1*o*).

peke′a (*Caryŏcar* spp.), trees of tropical America, the yellowish or grayish wood of which is valued for timber.

pele, a small, fortified tower or keep of the Middle Ages, along the Scottish and English border.

pel′let molding, a flat band bearing a range of discs, found in Norman architecture (9*n*).

pelourinho, a decorative shaft or column set in a public square of a Portuguese city as a token of municipal rights.

pen′dant, or **pen′dent,** an ornamental member suspended from above.

pendant post, a member in medieval roof framing (7*h*).

penden′tive, a triangular segment of vaulting used to effect a transition at the angles from a square or polygon base to a dome above (7*b*).

penetrale (penna trah′lay), a holy of holies in a temple, generally containing an altar to Jupiter Hercæus.

penetra′lia, small chapels dedicated to the penates in the innermost part of Roman houses; depository of the family's valuables.

penitentiary (penit ten′sharee), a prison. 2. a small building in which the penitent of a monastic order confined himself. 3. that part of a church to which penitents were admitted during services.

Pennsylvania bluestone, also called Wyoming Valley stone, a fine-grain, compact, hard sandstone of gray-red, gray-green, or blue-gray; used for trim, paving, etc.

pen′tacle, pental′pha, or **pen′tagram,** a five-pointed star enclosing a pentagon, not infrequent in medieval tracery and decoration (5*y*).

pen′tastyle, in classical architecture, having five columns across the main façade.

Pentel′lic marble (*Marmor pentalicum, greco fino*), a white to grayish crystalline marble from Mount Pentelicus, between Athens and Marathon in Greece. It was used in the Parthenon.

pent′house, enclosed space above the level of a main flat roof, as the top of an elevator shaft or an above-roof apartment.

pent roof, a roof of a single sloping plane (6*j*).

pep′peridge, *see* gum, black.

pequia peroba (pee kwi′ah) (*Aspidosperma tomentosum*), a wood from Brazil that is frequently confused with peroba; strong, yellowish in color, used for general construction work, flooring, doors, and furniture.

per′close, an enclosing barrier, such as a railing, protecting an area or an object.

pergola (pur′go lah), an arbor or colonnade supporting open roof timbers, often vine-covered.

perib′olus, or **perib′olos,** the wall bounding an enclosure, or the enclosure itself, more particularly around a temple.

per′idrome, the space between the peristyle and the walls of a temple.

period′ical room, in libraries, clubs, and the like, a room in which may be found the current periodical publications.

perip′teral, having a row of columns around the cella of a temple.

per′isphere, a spherical form used in connection with the trylon at the New York World's Fair of 1939.

peristerium (pare eh ste′reum), or **locus columbæ,** the place above an altar where was hung the silver dove representing the Holy Ghost.

per′istyle, the outer colonnade surrounding a temple or other structure, or a court.

peristy′lith, a circular group of upright stones enclosing a burial mound.

peristyl′ium, in ancient Rome, a court with colonnade on three or four sides.

pero′ba, pequia, *see* pequia peroba.

rosa peroba (*Aspidosperma* spp.), woods from Brazil called by many confusing names; rose red to yellowish color with darker streaks, fading to brownish tones; used for flooring, fine furniture, interior finish, and veneer.

white peroba (*Paratecoma peroba*), also called peroba do campo; a wood from Brazil, of a pale, golden olive or brownish color, with medium texture; said to be stronger than teak; used for structural work, interior woodwork, and veneer.

perpen′der, or **per′pend stone,** a stone extending through the thickness of a wall and finished on both ends.

Perpendic′ular Gothic, an English development of Gothic architecture after 1350, characterized by emphasis of vertical lines.

perpeyn wall (pur′pane), a projecting pier, buttress, or pilaster, to sustain additional weight upon or against the wall.

per′ron, an arrangement of exterior entrance steps, usually impressively elaborated.

perspectif cavalière [Fr.] (per spek tif kavva lee air), a linear perspective in which the projection is not necessarily perpendicular to the picture plane, and is thus distorted.

perspec′tive, *see* linear perspective.

pet′cock, a small valve on a pipe line, boiler, radiator, or the like, for draining or testing.

petroglyphy (pet rog′leh fee), primitive stone carving.

pew (pyou), a benchlike seat for a church interior.

pew′ter, an alloy of four parts of tin and one of lead.

pharmacy (far′mus see), a building or room for the compounding and dispensing of drugs.

phon (fahn), unit of sound as received by the average human ear.

phosphor-bronze (foss′for), an alloy metal in which copper, tin, and very little phosphorus are fused; it can be extremely ductile, tough, or very hard.

photoelec′tric eye, or **photo-electric-cell-operated relay,** a device depending on the interruption of a fixed beam of light to act as a trigger to door-opening mechanism, counting machines, sorting machines, and many other such operations.

photomural (fo′to mew′rul), a mural in the form of an enlarged photograph or montage.

piano nobile [It.] (pee ah′no no′billay), the principal story of a house, usually one flight above the grade.

piazza (pee az′zah), in Italy (pee ot′sah), an open space or public square in a city. 2. a covered gallery or veranda.

pick′et, one of the upright wooden members supported by upper and lower rails between posts in a type of fence; a paling.

pic′ture mold, a molding at the upper part of a wall, or forming the lower edge of an interior cornice, rounded at its top to support picture hooks.

piedroit [Fr.] (pyay drwah), a pier or small pillar, partly hidden within a wall; it differs from a pilaster in having neither base nor cap.

piend (peend), an arris.

pier (peer), an upright structure of masonry to serve as a principal support, whether isolated or part of a wall.

pil′la, a masonry support for roof timbers that is superimposed on a column. 2. in Italy (pee lah), a free-standing holy-water font.

pilaster (pill ass′tur), an engaged pier of shallow depth; in classical architecture it follows the height and width of related columns, with similar base and cap.

pile, a columnar support that is driven into the ground as part of a foundation; its lower section is usually of wood, driven to refusal, this being capped with a concrete cylinder if greater length is required.

pil′lar, a columnar support but not a classical column.

pil′low, a supporting member of cushion shape, usually at the top of a column.

piloti (pill ot′ee), a heavy column, usually of reinforced concrete, supporting a structure above an open ground-level space.

pinacotheca (pinna ko the′ka), Greek term for a picture gallery.

pine, eastern white (*Pinus strobus*), the first lumber used by the early settlers in America; soft, fine-textured, easily worked; heartwood endures under exposure; now largely knotty second growth and replaced by western white pine (*Pinus monticola*) under the names of California and Idaho pine.

Norway pine, *see* red pine.

Parana pine (*Araucaria angustifolia*), a wood—not a true pine—plentifully exported from Brazil; warm, yellowish brown in color, with a closer and finer grain than the better-known pine; used for many purposes.

ponderosa pine (*Pinus ponderosa*), a tree of the Rocky Mountain and Pacific Coast regions, with wood moderately light, rather uniform in texture, easy to work; used widely for millwork of doors, frames, and sash.

red pine (*Pinus resinosa*), a member of the yellow-pine group, growing in Canada and the Lake states; more contrast in texture, heavier, stronger, and somewhat more resinous than the eastern white pine with which it is sold in the lower grades.

southern yellow pine, woods of the southeastern states, consisting chiefly of loblolly (*P. taeda*), slash (*P. caribaca*), longleaf (*P. palustris*), and shortleaf (*P. echinata*); the lumber is relatively strong and dense. The wood characteristics of the species overlap according to age and growth conditions. They are well fitted for heavy and light framing and for boarding. Southern yellow pine is one of the two most extensively cut woods in the U.S.

sugar pine (*Pinus lambertiana*), grown in California, southern Oregon, and Mexico. Large trees yield wide and thick sizes of lumber for millwork.

pinnacle (pin′eh kl), a terminal ornament or protecting cap, usually tapered upward to a point or knob and used as a high point of a roof, a buttress, or the like (7*a*).

pintle (pin′tl), a pin completing the junction of two members and leaving one or both free to pivot upon it.

pipe, a tubular conduit for liquid or gas.

piscina (pih see′nah), in ecclesiastical architecture, a basin of stone or marble in which the chalice is washed after the rite of the Eucharist.

pisé (pee zay′), or **pisé de terre,** rammed-earth wall building.

pit, of a theater, formerly the part on the ground floor between the lower range of boxes and the stage; more recently, a much-reduced area for the stalls and reserved pit seats of the English theater.

pitch, the degree of inclination, as of a roof plane or a flight of stairs. 2. a coal-tar product used for flat-roof covering and paving, fluid when hot.

placage (plak′ij), a thin application of material and architectural detail to an otherwise bare wall.

plafond [Fr.] (plah fonh), a ceiling treatment upon the underside of a floor. 2. a ceiling of a room, flat or vaulted. 3. any soffit.

plan, a graphic representation of a building as cut by an arbitrary, horizontal plane, although it may include surrounding objects (paths, steps, planting) as seen from above (16*l*).

plan′cer, or **planceer′,** the soffit of a cornice. The French term is *plancher*.

plane, American, *see* sycamore, American.

oriental plane (*Platanus orientalis*), a tree that grows in southeastern Europe and adjacent Asia, producing a wood that is pale yellow to light red; used for cabinetwork, furniture, and flooring.

plan′etar′ium, a room or building with a domed ceiling on which are projected representations of the planetary system in various phases.

planim′eter, an instrument to measure an area by tracing its perimeter.

plan′ish, to make smooth with a plane, or by light hammering. 2. to polish.

plank, a length of wood having rectangular section not under 1½″ nor over 3½″ in thickness and not under 6″ wide.

plant′ed, fastened on or tongued in, as a molding separately wrought and then applied.

plaque (plak), an applied or inset decoration, usually of round or oval shape.

plas′ter, a mixture of lime, sand, water, and gypsum, applied as a thick paste upon a firm base of masonry or lathing to form, when hard, a smooth and nearly impervious surface for wall or ceiling.

plas′ter bead, a built-in edging, usually of metal, to strengthen a plaster angle.

plas′terboard, a composition sheet in various thicknesses used as a base for a thin finish coat of plaster.

plas′ter of Paris, calcined and finely ground gypsum.

plas′tic, a generic term for materials that may be molded, including those formed by extruding.

plas′ticine (plas′teh seen), a modeling clay that retains its plasticity without the addition of moisture.

plat, to make a plan of land divisions, streets, etc.

plat band, a flat band or string course with a projection less than its breadth.

plate, in wood-frame construction, the horizontal member capping the range of exterior wall studs and supporting the rafters.

plate glass, glass cast in sheets and polished.

plateresque′, designating Spanish work that reflects an effort to build in the Italian style; it originated in the sixteenth century and implied a fancied resemblance to work of the silversmith (Sp. *platero*).

plate tracery, tracery formed by piercing a single large stone.

plat′form, a raised section of flooring, as a dais or simple stage.

play, clearance for movable parts—sash, drawers, or the like.

play'house, a theater. 2. a small house for children's play.

ple'num, or **plenum chamber,** a container into which air is forced for slower distribution through ducts.

ple'num system, provision for ventilation of an interior in which fresh or conditioned air is forced into a plenum chamber, from which it finds its way through ducts to the various rooms.

plex'iform, resembling weaving or plaiting, as in certain Romanesque and Celtic ornamentation.

Plex'iglas, trade name for a group of plastic products, among which the transparent sheet form is most common.

plinth, the base block of a column, pedestal, or other isolated object (12). 2. the base block at the juncture of baseboard and trim around an opening.

plot, a definitely limited piece of land, as a building plot, that is, the piece of land on which a building stands or is to be built.

plotting, the laying out, in drawing, of a group plan or the governing points of a curve or graph.

plow, to cut a groove, as in tongue-and-groove boards (4*n*).

plug, a stopper for a plumbing-fixture drain opening. 2. a male-threaded casting for closing the end of a pipe line. 3. a terminating fixture for the wires of portable electric lamps or the like by which connection is made with an outlet socket.

plumb (plum), accurately upright.

plumb bob, a weight, usually pointed, suspended at the lower end of a cord, with which to test verticality.

plumber (plum'er), a workman skilled in plumbing.

plumbing (plum'ing), the craft of installing pipe lines, valves, fixtures, etc., for water, sewage, and gas.

plunge (plunj), a small swimming pool.

plu'teus, in Roman architecture, a dwarf wall or parapet, as between columns.

ply, lamination, twist, fold, as three-ply.

ply'wood, laminated wood in sheet form, alternate laminations changing direction of grain.

poché [Fr.] (po shay), in a plan, the blacking of areas that represent wall sections. The verb is *pocher*, having the same pronunciation.

podium (po'de um), the mass of masonry on the flat top of which a classical temple was built. 2. an elevated station point for the conductor of an orchestra.

Point'ed architecture, an occasional term for Gothic.

point'ing, the final filling and finishing of mortar joints that have been left raw or raked out.

polychromy (pol'ee kromee), decoration in colors.

polystyle (pol′ee stile), in classical architecture, many-columned.

pom′mel, or **pomel,** a knob terminating a conical or domical roof.

pool, a swimming pool; a garden pool.

pop′ie, pop′py, or **poppyhead,** the ornamental terminal of a pew end (8*e*).

pop′lar, yellow (*Liriodendron tulipifera*), or **tulip poplar;** a wood found southeast of the Mississippi River, soft, fine-textured, light; often called whitewood; used for doors, sash, general interior woodwork, and veneer.

porch (portch), a roofed space outside the main walls of a building and at an entrance.

porphyry (pore′firee), a fine-textured and hard stone, mostly in crimsons and greens, taking a high polish.

por′tal, a principal entrance.

portcul′lis, a lifting gate with sharp spikes at the bottom, used at the entrance to a stronghold.

porte-cochère (port ko share′), a shelter for vehicles outside an entrance doorway.

por′tico, an entrance porch.

Port′land cement, the widely used hydraulic cement, so called because of a fancied resemblance to England's Portland stone.

Port′land stone, a limestone found in the Isle of Portland, England.

posada (po sah′deh), in countries of Spanish influence, an inn.

post, an upright supporting member.

post-and-lin′tel, description of trabeated construction; that is, upright supports bearing beams.

pos′tern, a door of secondary importance, often beside a large gate.

post′flare, the straight or curved enlargement of a post towards its top to serve as a capital or bracket for the better support of the weight above.

postiche (poss teesh′), applied inappropriate ornament.

posticum (poss′teh kum), the space in a temple in the rear of the cella; opisthodomus.

post office, a building or office for the mail service.

postscenium (post see′neum), in ancient theaters, the back of the stage where the machinery was kept and where the actors dressed.

Potsdam sandstone, *see* Malone sandstone.

pounce, to transfer the elements of a drawing by rubbing powder through holes pricked through the lines of a paper pattern.

pow′der room, originally an anteroom in which to powder wigs; later, a retiring-room for ladies.

poyntell′, a pavement of small lozenge-shaped tiles, or square tiles laid diagonally.

pozzuolana (pot soo o lah′nah), an Italian volcanic sand which, when pulverized and mixed with slaked lime, forms a hydraulic cement.

præcinctio (pre sink′teo), a balteus (13).

prætorium (pre to'reum), the official residence of a governor (prætor) of a Roman province.

pre'cast, having received its final form before introduction into a structure, as precast concrete slabs, precast reinforced lintels, and the like.

precedent (press'uhdent), usage in a previous period.

predel'la, the broad step at the base of an altar. 2. a gradin.

prefab'ricated, descriptive of units that have been manufactured before arrival at the building site.

prefecture (pre'fek choor), a building housing the offices of a governor or administrative official.

pre'miated, distinguished by an award of merit in competition.

prem'ises, a building and its grounds.

presbyterium, or **presbytery** (pres bit ee'reum, pres'bitree), in a church, the space in the chancel set aside for the clergy.

presid'io, an outpost or fort of Spanish America.

pressed brick, brick molded to a compact smooth face by mechanical pressure, as differentiated from brick made by the lighter pressure of filling a mold with the clay.

prie-dieu (pree deu), a kneeling desk for prayer.

pri'maver'a (*Cybistax donnell-smithii*), a wood widely dispersed in tropical America, yellowish white to light yellowish brown in color; when quarter-sliced, it produces a straight-striped or highly figured veneer.

priming (pri'ming), a ground coat in painting.

pri'ory, a monastery headed by a prior or prioress.

prism glass, glass designed to change the direction of light rays by refraction.

prison (priz'un), a building in which lawbreakers may be confined.

priv'y, a small building to shelter the primitive and unsanitary prototype of the water closet.

prix [Fr.] (pree), prize, as Grand Prix de Rome.

procathe'dral, a church used temporarily as the cathedral of a diocese while the cathedral remains unfinished or is under repair.

prodo'mus, in ancient architecture, the portico before the entrance to the cella of a temple.

pro'file, the outline of the exposed face of a cross section, as of a molding (11*b*–*g*).

pro'gram, a list of requirements, conditions, and other governing data in an architectural competition or architectural problem. 2. a plan of operation with time and financing elements, division of responsibilities, and the like, for a building project.

projection (pro jek'shun), the representation of a body on a plane. 2. the extension of a member beyond another.

projet [Fr.] (pro zhay), an architectural problem. 2. the main elements of an architectural scheme, more or less roughly sketched in advance. *See also* parti.

pronaos (pro na′us), the portico of a temple in classical architecture, or the space in front of the cella.

propor′tional divi′ders, an instrument consisting of two double-pointed bars joined by a movable pivot, enabling lengths picked up by the points of one end to be enlarged or reduced by the opposite pair of points in a proportion established by the movable pivot.

propylæum (pro pil lee′um), an imposing gateway in front of and separate from a temple. Propylæa (plural), the entrance to the Acropolis at Athens.

propylon (plural, **propyla**) (prope′elone, prope′elah), in ancient Egyptian architecture, a gateway before a temple.

proscenium (pro see′neum), the wall and its arched or rectangular opening between stage and orchestra in a theater.

pro′stas, an antechamber or a vestibule. 2. the portion of a temple included between the antæ of a portico *in antis*.

pro′style, in classical architecture, having columns only across the front of a temple.

protectory (pro tek′toree), a building for the care and education of wayward or destitute children.

prothe′sis, a chapel as part of a building of the Greek Church.

prothyride, *see* ancon (2*i*).

prothy′rum, or **prothy′ron,** a porch at the outer door of a house. 2. a portal.

protrac′tor, a drafting instrument for laying out angles.

prytaneum (prit anee′um), in ancient Greece, a sort of town hall. 2. a state dining-room. 3. a guest house.

pseudo-dipteral (syoo do dip′teral), descriptive of classical dipteral temples in which the inner line of columns is omitted but where the space they would have occupied is retained.

pseudo-perip′teral, descriptive of classical temples having columns across the front and on the sides to the depth of the portico, the sides and rear of the cella having columns engaged upon their walls.

pseudo-pro′style, descriptive of classical temples in which the front portico columns are located closer to the cella than the space of the regular intercolumniation.

pteroma (ter o′mah), the space between cella walls and peristyle of a temple; also called ambulatio.

pteron (ter′on), in classical architecture, that which forms a side or flank.

pub′lic build′ing, any building which the public has the right to enter.

pub′lic hous′ing, dwelling units provided by a municipality, upon a specified basis of tenant selection, with or without subsidy.

pueblo (pweb′lo), a communal dwelling of the Indians of the southwest U.S.A., entered from the top by ladders.

Pueblo sandstone, a fine-grain, soft gray, white- and gray-veined stone quarried along Turkey Creek, Colo.

pug′ging, a filling between floor joists or studding, of rough plastic material.

pulpit (pull′pit), an elevated reading desk for a preacher.

pulvi′nar (plural, **pulvinar′ia**), originally, the cushions on which statues of the gods were set in the temples. 2. the side bolster form of an Ionic capital, terminated by the volutes (13).

pul′vinated, convex in face, as a molding or certain types of frieze (10*h*).

pump room, a dispensing-room in a spa; a kursaal.

puncheon (pun′chun), a short upright member in framing; a stud. 2. a log adzed to show one plane surface.

punk′ah, a ceiling fan common in India and other warm climates.

Pur′beck marble, a dark blue-green stone marked by gray fossils.

Pur′beck stone, a buff limestone bearing many fossils, from the Isle of Purbeck, England.

purfled (pur′fld), ornament representing embroidery, drapery, or lacework.

pur′lin, a horizontal member resting usually on trusses and supporting the roof rafters.

purpleheart, *see* amaranth.

push, a small knob or button, such as a bell push, an electric pushbutton.

push′button, a button-operated electric switch, the pushing of the button against its spring momentarily closing the circuit.

put′log, a horizontal support for the planking of a scaffold; a ledger.

put′log hole, a small recess in masonry for the support of scaffolding; a columbarium.

put′ty, a stiff, doughlike material consisting of pigment and vehicle, used for setting window panes and filling imperfections in wood or metal surfaces.

pycnostyle (pik′no stile), having intercolumniation of 1½ diameters.

py′lon, a truncated pyramidal form characteristic of Egyptian monumental architecture, where it was used largely in gateways (16*n*).

pyramid (peer′amid), a huge masonry form, originally marking the grave of an Egyptian pharaoh; square in base with triangular sides meeting at a point.

pyramidon (peer am′idon), the small flat pyramid terminating the top of an obelisk.

Pyrenesse Black-and-White, a dark brownish black marble from France, with thin and broad golden veins in haphazard pattern. The veins are glasslike, and the entire mass is crazed with very fine cobweb-like veins. A marble of wide variation but consistent in color value.

pyx (pix), a receptacle for the Host, in the celebration of the Eucharist.

Q

quad, en enclosed court, or quadrangle.

quad′ra, a square architectural frame, as for a bas-relief sculpture. 2. a fillet above and below the scotia in the base of an Ionic column (13). 3. the plinth block of a podium.

quad′rangle, a rectangular court bordered by a building or buildings.

quad′rel, a square tile or similar unit.

quadrifores (kwad re for′ays), in ancient architecture, folding doors, their height divided in two parts.

quadriga (kwad ree′gah), a four-horse chariot, used as a triumphal motif in sculpture.

quadripartite (kwad re par′ tite), having four divisions, usually describing groined vaulting.

quadriporticus (kwad re por′ tekus), in ancient Roman houses, an atrium or court enclosed by a portico.

quan′at, or **ghan′at,** the ancient Persian system of distributing water underground by gravity.

quan′tity surveyor, in England and certain of her colonies, one who draws up lists of quantities—labor and materials—upon which contractors' tenders are based.

quar′rel, a diamond-shaped pane of glass. 2. a minor piercing in tracery. 3. a small square or diamond-shaped paving unit. *See also* quadrel.

quarry (kwar′ree), a natural deposit of stone. 2. a square paving tile. *See also* quadrel. 3. a small diamond-shaped or square sheet of glass for leaded work.

quar′ter, medieval term for a stud.

quar′tered, or **quar′ter-sawn,** descriptive of lumber that is sawn from the log approximately radially.

quar′terfoil, *see* quatrefoil (9*e*).

quar′ter-pace, a landing interrupting a stair where a turn of 90° is made.

quar′ter-round′, a molding having a profile of a quadrant of a circle; an ovolo or echinus (11*g*, 12).

quatrefoil (kat′r foil), a four-lobed figure in variations (9*e*).

quattrocento (kat′ro chen′to), the fifteenth century or early Renaissance in Italy.

Queen Anne, designating a style developed in England in the early eighteenth century.

queen bolt, an iron rod substituting for a queen post.

queen closer, a portion of a brick smaller than a half length, to complete a dimensioned course.

queen post, one of two vertical members flanking the king post of a truss; if more than one such is used between the center and the end, the queen post may itself be flanked by secondary queen posts.

quick′lime, calcium oxide; freshly burned lime ready to be slaked; it combines with water to form slaked lime or lime putty.

quick′sand, an unstable volume of sand and water, usually in or near the sea, a lake, or a river.

quilt′ing, insulation material between two sheets of paper.

quin′cunx, an arrangement grouping of five objects so that one is at each corner of a square and one in the center.

Quincy granite, a hornblende pyroxene granite of Quincy, Mass.; from medium gray or bluish gray to a very dark bluish gray, all with blue or blue-black spots; its texture is from medium to coarse with even grain, taking a high polish because of the absence of mica.

quinquefoil (kanh′keh foil), a five-lobed figure in variations typified by the trefoil and quatrefoil; cinquefoil (9*h*).

quinta (kin′tah), a country estate (Portugal, Madeira, and Spain).

quirk (kwirk), in moldings, a small channel such as is commonly used to end a series of moldings against a plane, or flanking a bead.

quoin (koin), one of the corner stones of a wall when these are emphasized by size, by more formal cutting, by more conspicuous jointing, or by difference in texture (16*m*, *p*).

Quonset hut (kwahn′set), a semicylindrical shelter of corrugated steel, insulated; designed chiefly for military use; takes its name from the place of manufacture in Rhode Island.

R

R.A., abbreviation for registered architect.

rab′bet, *see* rebate (4*h*).

race′way, a channel for electric wire, cable, or bus-bar. Broadly speaking, this includes rigid or flexible metal conduit, but in common parlance a raceway is generally understood to be a rectangular duct, as differentiated from the tubular conduit.

rack′ing, preparing a masonry wall for later extension which will be added without breaks in the coursing.

ra′diant heating, a system in which floors or walls, or both, are heated, thus warming the persons within the room.

radia′tion, direct, a system of heating which supplies heat directly from radiators in the room itself.

indirect radiation, a system which heats by a supply of air which has been heated by radiators outside the room.

radiator (ray′de atur), a hollow vessel of material that is a good conductor of heat; connected with a pipe-line supply of steam or hot water, it serves to heat the air that impinges on its outer surface.

raft′er, a supporting member immediately beneath the roofing material or the roof boarding.

hip rafter, one at the junction of a hip-roof slope and the main roof.

jack rafter, one of the short rafters in the angle of a hip roof.

valley rafter, one in the trough of two roof surfaces.

rag′lin, the raked joint in masonry to receive flashing.

ragwork, masonry of undressed flagstone or other flat pieces.

rail (rale), a horizontal member in a panel frame, as in a paneled door between the stiles. 2. the top member connecting the posts of a fence or a row of balusters. 3. handrail, a rail supported on short brackets along the wall of a stairway, to be grasped by the hand.

rail′ing, a guard rail, or series of them, on posts or balusters.

rain leader, or **rain conductor,** a pipe, usually of metal, of round or rectangular section, to lead rain water from an eaves gutter to a drain below; a downspout.

rain-water head, the top of a leader, usually enlarged, where it receives water from the eaves gutter.

rake, a slope or inclination, as of a roof, gable, or stair string. *See also* pitch.

rak′ed joint, a joint in masonry which has been cleaned of mortar for a short distance back of the face to permit of further joint treatment or to form a key for plastering.

rake mold, the molding just under the sloping edge of a roof.

ram′bler, a popular name in some localities for a dwelling of one story and rambling plan.

ram′med earth, a system of wall building with earth tamped into forms, practised in southwest and south central U.S.A., and also in the south of France where it is called *pisé*.

ramp, an inclined walk or driveway. 2. the concave bend of a handrail where a sharp change in level is required, as at the post of a stair landing.

ram′pant arch, *see* arch (2*e*).

ranch house, originally the main dwelling on a stock farm; designating a style of West Coast dwelling of which the above was the prototype.

ran′dom ashlar, masonry of square- or rectangular-face stones, with neither vertical nor horizontal joints continuous.

ran′dom masonry, that in which the course heights vary in size.

ran′dom widths, the term used in describing flooring boards or shingles supplied in varying widths.

range, the cooking apparatus for the kitchen. 2. a line of buildings having one ownership, purpose, or control.

rath, a Dravidian rock-cut temple of India.

rathaus [Ger.] (raht′howce), the building housing the administrative offices of a municipality.

rathskeller [Ger.] (rahts′keller), a room, originally a cellar, in which beer and other refreshments are served.

Raymond granite, a biotite-muscovite, light gray, with biotite mica in excess of the muscovite, and an occasional crystal of black hornblende; this is a medium-fine-grain granite of California.

rayonnant [Fr.], descriptive of a type of French Gothic tracery which emphasized radial lines.

read′ing-room, that part of library, club, or other institution in which a prospective reader will find suitable quiet, seating, lighting, and perhaps delivery service of books.

re′al estate, land and what is built upon it.

re′bate, or **rabbet,** a sinkage cut in one wood member to receive the edge of another (4*h*).

receptacle (re sep′takl), a fixture interrupting an electrical supply circuit, into which a plug connection may be made for an extension or branch circuit.

recess (re sess′), a sinkage in a wall plane, usually right-angled as differentiated from a niche.

Rectilinear (rek ti lin′e ar), a synonym for the Perpendicular period in English Medieval architecture.

rectory (rek′toree), residence of a rector, the clergyman in charge of a parish, or the head of certain educational institutions.

redan [Fr.] (ray danh), a buttress of V-shape projecting from the lower side of a wall crossing a slope.

red lead, tetroxide of lead, widely used as a pigment in linseed oil for painting metal as protection against rust.

red′wood (*Sequoia sempervirens*), a tree of California, the lightweight, reddish wood of which is quite decay resistant and is used in building for both exterior and interior work, and for structural timber.

reed′ing, a molding, or a surface, made up of closely spaced parallel, half-round, convex profiles.

reel-and-bead, *see* bead-and-reel (10*c*).

refectory (re fek′toree), a dining-room in the house of a religious order.

reflected plan, a graphic horizontal section, shown looking up instead of down, as in the normal plan (14*e*).

reflector (re flek′tor), a polished surface to reflect light in a desired direction. 2. a baffle to reflect heated air.

reform′atory, a prison school for juvenile offenders.

refrac′tory, a heat-resisting unit for furnace lining and the like.

refrigerator (re frij′erator), a compartment for keeping food, and the like, at low temperatures.

Regency (ree′jen see), a period of French architectural style roughly corresponding to the term of 1715–1723, when Philip of Orleans was regent; a period of transition from the style of Louis XIV to that of Louis XV. In England the term covers the architecture of more than their Regency (1811–1820); it extended from 1800 to the early years of Victoria's reign.

register (rej′ister), the valved end of a duct for incoming or escaping air.

registra′tion, the process of determining and certifying an architect's competency to practise under state laws.

reg′let, a molding of rectangular profile such as traces the pattern of a raised fret (11*a*).

regula (reg′yoo lah), the fillet in a Doric entablature that bears on its underside the guttæ (12).

Reignier work, ornamental wood inlay in colors, in the manner of buhl work.

reinforced concrete (re in forst′), concrete in which have been embedded, preliminary to the pouring, steel bars or mesh to give tensional strength.

reinforcement (ree in force′ ment), specifically, the strengthening of concrete by inserting steel bars or wire mesh in the forms before pouring. 2. added strengthening.

reinforc′ing rod, soft-steel rod, usually with slight surface projections, to lend tensional strength when properly embedded in concrete. The surface corrugations give the name "deformed" to such rods.

Reisner work (rise′ner), surfacing of inlaid colored woods, a seventeenth-century German practice.

relevé [Fr.] (relleh vay), a measured drawing of old work. 2. a restoration.

relief′, *see* rilievo.

reliev′ing arch, *see* arch (1*c*).

relievo, *see* rilievo.

Renaissance architecture, an architecture resulting from a rebirth of interest in, and knowledge of, earlier classic forms and from a revolt against medieval forms and habits. Starting in Italy in the fifteenth century, it spread throughout Europe, strongly affected by regional influences. Characterized by the re-use of the classic orders and emphasis on pictorial impact, Renaissance architecture is a generic term for widely differing design in Italy, England, France, Spain, Germany, the Netherlands, and the Americas, up to the end of the nineteenth century.

ren′der, to add the finishing stage of a drawing, usually in washes. 2. to make a presentation drawing.

rendu [Fr.] (rahn deu), the coloring of a drawing. 2. the finished projet. 3. the delivery of a projet.

Renfrew, a British fossiliferous marble, dark gray verging on black, with bright red and white veins.

replum [Lat.] (rape′lum), the panel of a framed door.

repoussé (reh poo say′), with pattern or design in relief, as in embossed metalwork.

reredos (rare′eh doss), a screen forming a background for an altar. If not a screen but a treatment of the east wall, as is usually found in Spanish ecclesiastical architecture, it is called a retable.

reservoir (rez′er vwar), an artificial pond, lake, basin, or cistern for the collection and storage of water.

res′idence, a dwelling of the more imposing type and size.

resin (rez′in), a solid or semisolid, water-insoluble, organic substance with little or no tendency to crystallize. An alkyd resin is one made from polyhydric alcohols and polybasic acids. A phenolic resin is a synthetic resin made from phenols and aldehydes.

respond′, in Medieval architecture, a half pillar or pier attached to a wall to support an arch.

ressaunt (res sawnt), early English term for an ogee molding (12).

ressaunt lorymer, *see* roll molding.

ressaut [Fr.] (resso), the projection or recession of one member as compared with an adjoining one.

restaurant (res′taw rahnt), a place where prepared food is sold and served.

rest′ house, an inn for travelers in India.

restora′tion, rebuilding to approach as nearly as possible the original form.

reta′ble, the background of an altar when the altar stands against it; usually with shelves for candles, niches, and symbolic ornament.

retain′ing wall, a wall built to retain a bank of earth, as at a change in grade levels.

reticulation (re tik yoo la′ shun), irregular network pattern, particularly in elaborate masonry or quoins.

retrochoir (reh′tro quire′), the chapels and other parts behind and about the high altar.

return′, the right-angled change of direction of a molding or group of moldings, terminating the run. 2. a corresponding termination of a projecting member of any kind, including a wall.

reveal, or **revel** (re veel′), the depth of wall thickness between its outer face and a window or door set in an opening.

revet′, to face with masonry, as an embankment.

revolving door, a widely used type for entrances to public and commercial buildings, having four leaves pivoted at their inside stiles and enclosed in a circular vestibule (16*a*).

rez-de-chausée [Fr.] (ray deh sho sa), ground floor.

rhe′ostat, an apparatus for regulating the flow of electric current.

rib, a transverse or diagonal structural member of arched vaulting, usually emphasized; between the ribs the vaulted ceiling is sprung (8*a*, *h*).

R.I.B.A., Royal Institute of British Architects.

rib′bon, a horizontal board let into the face of studding, to support on its upper edge the floor joists, in balloon-frame construction; also called a ledger board.

rib′bon development, extension of urban growth along radial highways.

ridge, or **ridgepole,** the top horizontal member of a sloping roof, against which the upper ends of the rafters are fixed (7*f*).

ridge roll, the half-cylindrical surface, usually of metal, for finishing a roof ridge.

rift, or **riven,** said of wood split or sawn with the grain.

rilievo [It.] (rilly a′vo), ornament in relief. There are three degrees: alto-rilievo, mezzo-rilievo, and basso-rilievo, representing great projection, about half projection of a figure, and slight projection.

rim lock, a lock designed to be affixed to the surface of the door, as differentiated from the mortise lock, which is let into the edge of the door.

rinascimen′to [It.], renaissance.

rinceau (rin so′), a strip pattern of ornament, usually in low relief, conventionalizing an undulating vine bearing leaves and fruits or flowers (15*b*).

ring road, concentric rings, circumferential street, or **circular highway,** in urban planning, units of a plan that complement radial thoroughfares and incidental gridirons.

rink, an enclosed space with a floor adapted to ice skating or roller skating.

rip, in sawing lumber, to saw with the grain.

rip′rap, broken stone for foundation filling or for laying up a retaining wall without mortar, or for breakwater or mole construction.

rise, the vertical measurement between two successive treads in a stair. 2. the height of an arch from springing to crown (1*b*).

ris′er, the vertical member between treads of a stair. 2. a vertical pipe main.

rive, to split with the grain, as rived or riven cypress shingles.

riv′eting, fastening metal together by the insertion through a drilled hole of a short soft-metal pin with a head on one end, the other end being cramped while hot into a similar head.

rocaille (ro ki), rococo.

rock-faced, descriptive of stone laid up as masonry with faces as received from the quarry.

Rocklin granite, a light-colored granite of California, somewhat similar to Raymond granite.

rock temple, a temple formed by hewing out the space in a practically vertical rock cliff, as at Abu-Simbel, Egypt; Ellora, India; and Petra, northern Arabia.

rock tomb (toom), a tomb excavated from the solid rock, as found in Egypt and elsewhere.

Rockville, a coarse-grained granite with feldspars ½″ to ¾″ across; color is pinkish gray, and it consists of pale pink feldspar, quartz, and black mica; quarried at St. Cloud, Minn.

Rockwood oölitic limestone, a light gray or buff even-textured variety quarried near Rockwood, Franklin County, Ala.

rock wool, or **mineral wool,** a loose fibrous material, made from certain kinds of rock and molten slag, used for insulating purposes in walls, roofs, floors, etc.

roco′co, a type of Renaissance ornament combining in profusion rocklike forms, scrolls, and crimped shells, often without organic coherence but presenting a lavish display of decoration. 2. excess in decoration.

rod′ding, the act of compacting freshly poured concrete in its form by freeing the mass of air pockets with repeated stabs of a rod; such compacting is now more efficiently done with a vibrator.

Rojo Alicante, a Spanish marble of considerable variation in ground color—light to dark red—and with irregular splotches of red-buff and red rather evenly distributed, with white lightning-like veining.

roll-and-fillet molding, a molding of convex face with a square fillet projecting from the middle of the profile, found in Medieval architecture.

roll molding, a cylindrical form occurring chiefly in Early English and Decorated periods of Gothic. With a slight edge at one part, it is called a scroll or edge molding, or a ressaunt lorymer (8*f*).

roll roofing, composition sheet roofing which is laid and overlapped from a roll of the material.

Roman arch, the round arch (1*b*).

Roman architecture, an architecture largely of pozzuolana concrete, faced with brick, stone, and marbles, carried on under the Roman Empire, not only in Italy but elsewhere in Europe and in North Africa and western Asia. It may be considered as dating from 146 B.C. until 365 A.D. In Roman architecture is seen the combination of the trabeated Greek style with the arcuated forms of the earlier Etruscans, in meeting the greater engineering needs of a more complex civilization—aqueducts, public baths, city walls, bridges, forums, basilicas, and the like.

Roman Breche, an Italian brecciated marble containing large and small fragments of grayish blue and white, more or less outlined with golden red veins. It more nearly approaches a blue aspect than does any other marble.

Romanesque architecture, various phases of European architecture that were based on Roman forms, usually more specifically labeled as Italian Romanesque, French Romanesque, and German Romanesque. The growing use of the pointed arch and the Gothic conception of balanced thrusts, in the twelfth century, marked the end of what was not one style but rather a group of transitional local styles.

rondelle (rahn del′), a small disc of glass as used in leaded windows.

rood, a crucifix as used in the chancel of a Christian church.

rood beam, a beam or bottom chord of a truss near the front of a chancel, on which the rood is borne.

rood loft, a gallery over the rood screen.

rood screen, a screen in the chancel, supporting the rood.

rood spire, a spire built over the intersection of nave and transepts.

roof, the weatherproof top shell of a building.

roof guard (gard), a device to check snow from sliding off a pitched roof.

roof′tree, the ridge of a roof; by extension, the dwelling.

roof truss, any type of truss used for roof support.

room, an enclosed space inside a building, usually given a specific name, as dining-room, bedroom, etc.

rope molding, a molding simulating the twisted strands of cordage.

rosace, rose, or **rosette,** an ornamental centerpiece in a ceiling.

rosamay (*Dysoxylum fraseranum*), known also as Australian rosewood and rose mahogany; a wood from Australia suggesting mahogany, with its fine texture; is easily worked and with some fragrance; used for fine cabinetwork.

rose, a guard plate or escutcheon between a doorknob and the door, with perforation for the shank.

Ro′sendale cement, a light hydraulic cement first made about 1837 in Rosendale, Ulster County, N. Y.

rosette′, a conventionalized circular floral motif, usually sculptural.

rose window, a circular window, particularly in church architecture, the tracery of which loosely suggests a rose; if the radial lines are strongly emphasized it is sometimes called a wheel window or catherine wheel.

rose′wood, African, *see* bubinga.

Australian rosewood, *see* rosamay.

Brazilian rosewood (*Dalbergia nigra*), a hard, close-textured wood, of dark purple or red to tawny shades; highly prized for cabinetwork and useful as veneer.

East Indian rosewood (*Dalbergia latifolia*), a wood varying widely in color, from dark purple and almost black through many shades of red into yellow; used for furniture and veneer.

Rosso Antico, an Italian marble, deep red with white and black markings. 2. a felsitic-base eruptive rock used by the ancient Egyptians for statues.

ros′trum (plural, **rostra**), a raised dais or pulpit for the use of a public speaker.

rotun′da, or **roton′do** [It.], a space circular in plan and covered by a dome.

Rouge Jascolin, an Italian marble having bold swirling masses of mixed red, cream, and rose.

roughcast (ruff′kast), coarsely textured exterior plaster or stucco. *See also* pebble dashing.

rough flooring, the underflooring of rough lumber, usually square-edged, upon which a finish floor is laid.

rough hardware, a term including bolts, nails, spikes, and the like, as distinguished from the finish hardware.

rough′ing-in′, the installation of a plumbing system, exclusive of its fixtures.

round, or **in the round,** sculpture in full three-dimensional form, as opposed to sculpture in relief.

round arch, an arch of semicircular form, also called Roman arch (1*b*).

roun′del, a small circular window or panel; an œil-de-bœuf. 2. a bead molding. 3. a semicircular bastion.

round′house, a shelter for locomotives, centering upon a turntable.

row house (ro′howce), a house of a row, joined to its neighbors by party walls and covered by the same roof.

rowlock arch, an arch of brick, used chiefly as a relieving arch (1*c*) and formed of concentric courses of headers.

rowlock cavity wall, cavity wall of brick in which all brick in both withes are laid on edge (3*j*, *k*).

rubbed brick, brick selected for color and rubbed to a smooth surface on one or two vertical faces, as for window and door jambs and heads; gauged brick.

rub′ble, broken, untrimmed stone used in masonry. Random rubble is masonry laid with no course lines, as the stone comes.

ruden′ture, similar to cable but frequently used on a shaft without the flutings.

ruderation (roo der a′shun), a method of laying pavements of small stones, mentioned by Vitruvius.

Rum′ford fireplace, a form invented by Count Rumford to throw more heat into the room and less up the chimney.

run, of stairs or rafters, the distance between the end supports.

rus′tic woodwork, structure, wall panels, or screens made of unpeeled logs and saplings.

rustica′tion, or **rustic work,** masonry in which the principal face of each stone is rough, reticulated, or vermiculated, with a margin tooled smooth along rectangular edges; or the principal face may be smooth and surrounded by a bevel margin returning to the plane of the wall (16*p*).

rust joint, in piping, a tight connection effected by induced rusting of the pipe ends; iron filings and sal ammoniac are used.

S

sabi′no (*Magnolia splendens*), endemic to Puerto Rico with a hard, fine-grained wood, brown in color; very scarce.

sacellum (sah sel′um), a minor shrine of ancient Rome. 2. an enclosed roofless space.

sacrarium (sah kra′reum), in ancient Rome, a shrine in a private house. 2. the sanctuary of a church. 3. a piscina.

sacristy (sak′ristee), a room where church vestments and sacred vessels are kept, and where the clergy robe.

sad′dle, a flat strip of wood or metal projecting above the floor between the jambs of a door; a threshold.

sad′dle bar, an iron bar to which the cames of leaded glass are fastened for reinforcement.

safe, a strongbox. 2. a shallow pan with waste pipe, to gather and lead away an overflow.

safe-deposit box, a small receptacle, usually in a tier in the strong room of a bank, which one may rent for the safekeeping of documents and the like.

safe-deposit vault, a strong room, usually in a basement, to provide secure storage.

safe′ty valve, a valve for a steam boiler, set to open automatically at a given pressure.

sagitta (sah jeet′ah), rare term for the keystone of an arch.

sal′amander, a portable box stove for use as an aid in drying plastered walls.

sa′lient, a projecting mass.

salmon brick (sah′mun), one of the more lightly burned upper bricks of a kiln.

salon (sah lonh), a reception room. 2. an exhibition room. 3. a gathering in either of the foregoing.

saloon′, the public room of a passenger vessel. 2. a place for the sale and consumption of liquors.

salutatorium (sah loo tah to′reum), in medieval building, a porch or a portion of a sacristy where clergy and people could confer.

sam′ple room, a room, usually in a hotel, for the display of merchandise by a traveling salesman.

sanatorium (sanna to′reum), a building for convalescent invalids.

sancta bell (sank′tah), in a church, the bell announcing the beginning of the Sanctus or the approaching elevation of the Host.

sanctuary (sank′chew airy), that part of a church where the principal altar is situated.

sandarac (san′darak) (*Tetraclinis articulata*), a tree of North Africa, the wood of which is dark and hard; also called Algerian thuja; *see* thuja burl.

sand′blasting, a process of cleaning, or engraving through a frisket, employed on masonry faces, glass, or other hard surfaces, using sand propelled by compressed air.

sand finish, a final coat of plastering, usually of lime and sand, floated smooth.

sand′ing, sandpapering wood to a smooth surface.

sand′stone, sedimentary rock of non-crystalline formation, resembling cemented sand.

sand′wich, or **structural sandwich,** a strongly bonded union of two thin, strong, hard outer skins with a core of relatively light-weight material possessing insulating properties; the sheet used in walls, partitions, and roofs.

sanguine (sang geen′), a blood-red iron oxide crayon.

sanitarium, *see* sanatorium.

san′itary engineering, the science of guarding health through proper water supply, sewerage, and the like in the individual building and in a far broader field in public utilities and municipal, county, and state works.

sapele (*Entandrophragma cylindricum*), or **aboudikro,** a wood from West Africa having sapwood of a yellowish tint and heartwood light red, darkening on exposure to reddish brown with pronounced dark, straight stripes; used for veneer.

sap′wood, that portion of a tree just beneath the bark, consisting of the young growth.

Saracen′ic, or **Moham′medan architecture,** a term designating the architecture of a religion rather than of a country or a people; an architectural flavor imparted by the Mohammedan religion to building in Arabia, Persia, Mesopotamia, Syria, Palestine, Egypt, North Africa, and Spain, inevitably showing wide geographical differences. Largely of mosques and tombs, the work is characterized by geometrical decorations on the wall surfaces, by bulbous domes, by minarets, and by pointed, multi-foil, and horseshoe arches.

sarcophagus (sahr koff′eh guss), a stone tomb of coffin size or larger.

Sarrancolin, a breccia marble quarried near Sarrancolin in the French Pyrenees. The colors are widely variable, with gray, yellow, and red predominating.

sash, a frame for glass to close a window opening or as part of greenhouse construction.

sash balance, a counterpoised weight, or a spring with equivalent pull, to balance a sash of a double-hung window.

sash bar, a muntin.

sash cord, a small rope attaching one side of a window sash to its counterweight.

sash weight, a counterweight for a window sash.

Sassanian architecture (sass sa′nean), a period in Persian architecture about the fifth and sixth centuries A.D.

sat′ellite, in urban planning, an outlying community unit of secondary importance, dependent upon the larger city.

satinee (sah teen'ee) (*Brosimum paraense*), a wood from South America, of a rich red, medium texture, not difficult to work; it takes a good polish and is used for veneer.

satinwood, Brazilian (*Euxylophora paraensis*), a wood from Brazil, frequently substituted for the satinwood from Ceylon or San Domingo; bright golden yellow in color; hard; texture medium, uniform; used for veneer.

Ceylon satinwood (*Chloroxylon swietenia*), an East Indian tree valued for use in fine cabinetwork and veneer; pale golden color with lighter ripple.

West Indian satinwood (*Zanthoxylum flavum*), or **aceitillo,** a bright golden wood from the West Indies used for veneer.

saturation, the percentage of hue in a color. Quality factors in color are hue, saturation and brightness.

saw-tooth roof, a roof form sometimes employed for industrial plants, having a succession of monitors in sawtooth shape, providing natural light from one direction.

scab'ble, to rough-dress stone to an approximately plane face.

scabellum (skah bel'um), a moderately tall pedestal for statuary.

scaf'fold, a temporary structure for the support of plank footing and platforms as aids to workmen in carrying up a wall.

scagliola (skah lee o'lah), simulation of colored marbles in plaster; first used soon after 1600.

scale (skayl), a measuring strip as an aid in proportional drafting. 2. in architecture, harmonious relationship of parts to one another and to the human figure.

scal'ing, the ascertaining of dimensions from a proportional drawing by comparison with a scale.

scallage, or **scal'lenge** (skayl' ij, skal'lenj), a local English term for lychgate.

scalpturatum opus [Lat.] (skalp tyoor ah'tum o'puss), a use of inlaid colored marble, first introduced into Italy between 147 and 103 B.C.

scamilli impares [Lat.] (skah meel'ee im pa'rees), the slight bowing upward of apparently horizontal lines, as in the Parthenon.

scamil'lus, in ancient Roman architecture, a block of stone supporting the pedestal of a statue or the plinth of a column. 2. in Greek architecture, a surplus bevel of stone adjoining a sharp edge, to prevent chipping when the block was being set.

scandula (plural, **scan du'læ**) (skan dyoo'lah, -li), a wooden shingle as used on the early buildings of Rome.

scantling (skant'ling), a minor timber, not over 4″ square in section.

scape, or **scapus** (skape, skape' us), Greek term for the shaft of a column. 2. apophyge (12)

scarf (skarf), or **scarf joint,** a lapped joint for timber, in variations.

scena (see′nah), a wing of an ancient theater, containing performers' robing-rooms.

scheme (skeem), the chief elements of a composition and their interrelationship; usually the preliminary stage of a design; a parti.

scheme arch, or **skene arch,** a segmental arch (1*d*).

schist (shist), roughly, a rock or building stone that splits.

schloss [Ger.], the castle of a feudal lord.

school (skool), or **schoolhouse,** a building in which students of the elementary grades receive instruction.

school′room, a room where students gather for general assembly purposes.

scissors truss (siz′zers), a form of truss which serves without a bottom horizontal chord (4*m*).

sconce (skonce), a side-wall bracket fixture for holding one or more candles.

sconcheon (skon′shun), that portion of the side of an aperture extending from the back of the reveal to the inner face of the wall.

score, to scarify a surface to make a better bond for the plaster or cement which is to follow.

Scotch bond, in brickwork, same as English garden wall bond (3*f*).

scotia (sko′shah), a concave molding with a profile not unlike a section of a parabola (11*c*).

scratch coat, the first rough coat of plaster, scored before completely set, to give better adhesion of the coat to follow.

screed, a guide strip to establish the proper thickness of plaster or concrete over a surface.

screen, a thin partition, often with openwork. 2. insect screen; wire-mesh protection for door and window openings.

screw stair, a spiral staircase about a slender pole.

scribe, to cut the edge of one member in an irregular line so as to fit snugly against another, as around moldings or against masonry.

scriptorium (skrip to′reum), a writing-room, usually of a monastery.

scroll (skrole), a volute. 2. a band, usually in relief, to contain an inscription. 3. a band of flowing ornament.

scroll′work, openwork cut with a jigsaw.

scul′lery, English term for a sort of kitchen pantry where pots and pans are cleaned and stored.

sculp′tor, an artist who works in three-dimensional forms, either by cutting from the solid or by building up with modeling clay or the like.

sculpture (skulp′choor), the work of a sculptor.

scutcheon (skutch′un), an escutcheon. 2. an old name for angles of buildings or parts thereof when these were greater than a right angle.

scuttle (skut′l), a hatchway, usually in a roof, with removable cover.

seal (seel), to apply an inner wall surface, as of plaster or matched boarding. 2. the water head in a plumbing trap.

seam (seem), a sheet-metal joint.

seasoned (see′zund), applied to wood or timber, dried (not necessarily by kiln) and hardened by aging after being cut.

seat (seet), a place upon which to sit, usually built in. 2. a residence, as a country seat.

seat′ing, or **seating capacity,** a measure of size for a church, an auditorium, a theater, or the like.

se′cret dove′tailing, a dovetail joint on a miter where the wood on the exposed face is undisturbed (4*b*).

se′cret nail′ing, of flooring or matched sheathing, where the nails are driven through the tongue but not the face; blind nailing.

sectilia (sek til′yah), paving of hexagonal units.

section (sek′shun), a drawing representing the elevation of an imaginary plane cutting through a building or other object. Sections in architectural parlance are usually vertical planes; horizontal plane sections are plans (7*g*, 16*l*).

sec′troid, the warped surface between groins in vaulting.

sedile (plural, **sedilia**) (seh di′lee, seh dil′yah), a formal seat for the clergy, usually built along the chancel wall of a church.

segmen′tal arch, *see* arch (1*d*).

seicento (say chen′to), the seventeenth century in Italian art.

seigniory (seen′yurry), the residence of a lord in southern Europe.

se′kos, in ancient Greece, a sanctuary; sometimes the whole naos of a temple.

semi-arch (sem′e artch), half an arch, as in an abutment or a flying buttress (7*g*).

semidetach′ed, descriptive of a pair of houses with a party wall between.

semidome (sem′e dome), a half-dome, as one over a semicircular niche or apse.

sem′inary, a school of special purpose, as for theology.

se′na, *see* narra.

septic tank, a tank in which occurs the disintegration of organic matter in sewage by bacterial action.

sepulcher (sep′ul ker), a tomb of masonry or one cut out of the rock.

seraglio (ser ah′leo), residence of a sultan.

seraya (ser i′ah) (*Shorea* spp.), also called meranti, a wood from the Malay Peninsula, Borneo, and Singapore, frequently marketed as Philippine mahogany; heartwood pink to purple-brown.

serpentine (sur′pen teen), curving alternately to right and left. 2. a building stone, hydrous magnesium silicate, generally dull green in color and often mottled; the presence of iron may lend red or brown. In its fibrous form it resembles asbestos. In polished slab form it is used as one would use marble.

serrurerie (serroo ra ree), French term for wrought-metal work.

service stair, a secondary stairway for service.

set, the hardening of plaster or cement after its plastic state.

set′back, the recession of an upper part of a façade, due to smaller area of upper floors; the setback is usually an answer to certain zoning restrictions.

set′tlement, the failure of the soil to hold a structure's foundations where first located, or uneven failure in compression by members in the structure itself.

sev′ery, a bay of a vault.

sewage (soo′idj), waste matter mainly in liquid form carried from places of habitation by the drainage lines of a plumbing system.

sewage disposal, the use of subsoil bacterial action, filtering, and the like to purify the water of sewage.

sewer (soo′er), a conduit for sewage and storm water.

sewerage (soo′er idj), provision for a sewer system.

sexpar′tite, descriptive of the six-part groined vault.

sgraffia′to, *see* sgraffito.

sgraffito (zgraf fee′to), or **graffito,** plaster surfaces made decorative by scoring a pattern upon them while soft, sometimes revealing an undercoat of different color.

shack, a rudely constructed shelter of small size.

shade, a fabric screen to obstruct the light passing through a window, usually hung from a spring-actuated roller.

shad′ow, indication on a drawing, sunlight intercepted; the conventionalized sun location is assumed at an angle of 45° above the horizon and 45° in left front of the plane of the picture (16*o*).

shaft, that portion of a classical column between base and capital (15*g*). 2. a chimney stack. 3. an elevator well.

shake, a split in timber. 2. a hand-split shingle widely used in the Pacific Coast states of the U.S.A.

shale, a clayey rock, easily broken and tending to lamination parallel with the bed.

shank, the plain space between channels of a triglyph. Vitruvius gave it the name of femor (12).

shan′ty, a shack, a rude wooden shelter. 2. the office of a contractor on a construction job.

shear (sheer), the strain upon, or the failure of, a structural member at a point where the lines of force and resistance are perpendicular to the member.

sheathe (sheethe), to apply a covering of boards or other surfacing to the inside or outside of a structural frame.

sheath′ing paper, tough, water-resistant paper applied over studding or over sheathing, to be itself covered by shingles, siding, or other outside facing.

shed, a lightly built subordinate shelter, usually one story high, not always fully enclosed, and sometimes a lean-to.

shed roof, a roof having only one sloping plane (6*j*).

sheet, a thin piece of material, as glass, veneer, or rolled metal.

sheet′ing, or **sheet piling,** a line of planks, often tongued and grooved on the sides, driven endwise into the ground to protect subgrade operations.

shelf, a ledge or setback. 2. a horizontal board or slab of other material to serve as a resting place for small objects, as a bookshelf, a mantelshelf, a linen shelf.

shellac (shel ak′), a type of varnish consisting of lac carried in alcohol as a solvent.

shel′ter, generic term for buildings serving as habitations for humans.

shelv′ing, shelves. 2. material prepared for the building of shelves.

sher′ardizing, a process that coats the surface of iron or steel with a condensation of volatile zinc dust, for protection against corrosion. Named for the inventor, Sherard Cowper-Coles.

shim, to increase the height of a support by inserting a thin wedge-shaped or flat piece of hard material between the support and what rests upon it.

shingle (shing′l), a wedge-shaped piece of wood as used in overlapping courses to cover a roof or an outside wall surface; the name is also given to similar units made of other materials.

shingle tile, a flat ½″ clay tile, usually 12″ to 15″ by 7″, used chiefly for roofing and laid like shingles.

ship′lap, a beveled or rebated jointing of two boards to form a weather-resisting outside wall surface (4*o*).

shod′dy work, careless, unworkmanlike results.

shoe (shoo), a scantling laid upon a floor to form a base member for partition studding.

shop, a building or lesser space for a retail sales business. 2. a space set aside for making repairs or small manufacturing.

shop drawing, working drawing by a manufacturer to indicate how he would carry out some detail of the architect's drawings and specifications.

shop′ping center, that portion of a city, town, or neighborhood in which are grouped retail stores.

shor′ing, temporary buttress-like supports to prevent collapse of a building under alteration or of a structure adjoining a new operation.

short circuit, or **short,** a connection, by reason of low resistance or accident, by which a designed electrical circuit is nullified.

shot-sawn, descriptive of a finish given building stone by using chilled-steel shot in the sawing process. Also called chat-sawn.

show′er, or **shower bath,** the floor receptacle and plumbing providing means of bathing by overhead spray.

show′room, a room for the display of merchandise.

shrine, a building, or a particular place in one, that is held sacred.

shrink'age, contraction of a material through cooling or drying.

shut'ter, an extra closure for a window or door, usually of wood, paneled, and one of a pair hinged at the outside jambs.

shut'tering, closures for shop windows and similar large areas, of metal or wood. 2. English term for form in which concrete is to be poured.

side light, a source of artificial illumination located on an interior wall or partition. 2. one of a pair of narrow windows flanking a door.

side'walk, paving for pedestrians, flanking a street.

siding (si'ding), exterior wall covering of horizontal boards nailed to a wood frame.

siedlung [Ger.] (plural, **siedlungen**) (zeed'loong), integrated housing as a community unit.

sik'ra, or **sikhara,** a tower form or spire of northern India.

silica gel, a substance used in dehumidifying because of its ready absorption of moisture, and the readiness with which it gives up this moisture when heated.

sill, the horizontal member immediately supported by a foundation wall or piers, and which in turn bears the upright members of a frame. 2. a horizontal closure at the bottom of a door frame.

sillcock, or **hosecock,** a faucet or hose connection, usually on the exterior of a building about sill height.

si'lo, a tower-like building to hold cut fodder or ensilage until ripened for cattle food.

sima (see'mah), the rain gutter of a classical building.

sink, a washbasin for kitchen, pantry, or janitor's closet, provided with plumbing.

sink'age, a recess or set-back panel of slight depth, usually occurring in wall, ceiling, or floor.

siparium (see pa'reum), ancient Roman screen used as a theater drop-curtain.

siphon trap, *see* S-trap.

S-iron, the visible exterior end of a tie rod used to hold masonry walls together or to secure interior framing to a masonry wall; the end is often like a letter S.

sissoo' (*Dalbergia sissoo*), a hardwood from India in a warm brown with golden or deeper brown streaks, used for veneer.

site, a specific plot of ground, as where a building is located or is to be erected.

sit'ting-room, an informal room in a dwelling, where family and friends gather.

sitz bath, a bathing bowl, common in Europe, wherein one may bathe the midsection of the body.

size, measurement in extent. 2. a liquid coating composition, usually transparent, for sealing a porous surface preparatory to application of finishing coats.

skel'eton construction, that in which a steel frame carries all the weight, in contrast to the earlier bearing walls of masonry; the term might rationally be applied also to construction having a frame of reinforced concrete.

sketch, a hastily made drawing. 2. a preliminary presentation drawing in the field of design —plan, elevation, or perspective.

skew (skyoo), a bevel-faced member, particularly a stone at the eaves end of a gable.

skew′back, the beveled support at either end of a segmental arch.

skim coat, the final thin coat of plastering.

skintled brickwork (skin′tulled), a method (a short-lived fancy) for laying up brick with extreme irregularity of the front face.

skirtboard, or **skirt′ing,** a baseboard or finishing board at junction of interior wall and floor.

skylight (ski′lite), a glazed opening facing upward.

sky′scraper, a very tall building, usually of skeleton construction.

slab, the outside lengthwise cut of a log. 2. a thick plate of material, as a slab of stone, concrete, or glass.

slake, as applied to lime, to add water, starting a chemical action resulting in lime putty.

slat, a thin strip, usually of wood, as used in a louver or blind.

slate, thinly laminated rock as split for roofing, paving, and the like.

sleep′er, a timber laid on the ground or in concrete flush with the surface, on which to nail flooring.

slide, a flat board, usually beneath the counter shelf of a dresser, desk, bookcase, or the like, that may be partly withdrawn to serve as a support. 2. a sliding closure for an opening, as between kitchen or pantry and dining-room.

slide rule, an instrument for making certain calculations or computations logarithmically.

slim′line lamp, instant-start, single-pin, hot-cathode fluorescent lamp.

slip sill, a stone sill for window or door which does not project into the wall beyond the jambs.

slop sink, a low, deep sink for service or janitor use.

slum, a section of a city or town in which many of the habitations have deteriorated to such an extent that they menace the health and security of the whole community.

slump, or **slump test,** a routine test to determine the consistency of freshly mixed concrete.

slype, a passageway, such as from transept to chapter house or from cloister to deanery.

smoke test, a test to determine the tightness of a piping system, by filling it with smoke and tracing the odor.

snack′et, provincial English term for a casement hasp.

snake′wood (*Piratinera guianensis* and other species), also called letterwood, a wood from northern South America to southern Mexico, reddish brown streaked with black lines, very hard and heavy; used for veneer and inlay.

snibill (sny bill), a true hinge, having a pintle. *See also* hinge loop.

snow guard, a device, usually in the form of projecting wires or the like, on the roof slope, to prevent or at least hinder snow slides.

soap, a half-brick-shaped unit of brick or tile cut longitudinally.

socle (so′kl), a foundation block, higher than a plinth, for sculpture and the like; sometimes carried along or around a building as a continuous socle.

so′dium-va′por lamp, a light source used chiefly in street lighting, utilizing electric discharge in this vapor; the yellow color of the light approaches the point of maximum luminosity in the spectrum.

sof′fit, the finished underside of a lintel, arch, or other spanning member, usually overhead.

soft′wood, lumber of the coniferous trees as distinguished from the hardwoods.

soil pipe, or **soil stack,** the drainage main, chiefly vertical, into which branch lines drain plumbing fixtures.

so′lar heat, heat trapped from the sun's rays.

solarium (plural, **solaria**) (so la′reum, so la′re ah), a room the walls and sometimes roof of which are glazed to admit an abundance of sunlight.

soldering (sod′er ing), making tight a junction of metallic sheets, piping, and the like by the application of a molten alloy of lead and tin.

sol′dier course, usually descriptive of brick standing on their ends with edge to the front.

sole, or **shoe** (shoo), a scantling laid upon a floor to serve as a base for partition studding.

so′lenoid valve, a valve opened by electromagnetic action and closed by gravity.

Sol′omon's seal, or **magen-Dawid** (David's shield), a symbol of Judaism, two intertwined equilateral triangles (5*z*).

Somes Sound granite, a biotite granite of Maine; coarse, inclined to medium grain in a light grayish buff.

som′mer, *see* summer beam.

soor′kee, in India, a mortar of lime, pulverized brick, and water.

sotto portico [It.], a covered public way beneath the overhanging upper story and behind the columns of a façade.

sound′ing board, a reflector made of resonant material, set above and behind a pulpit, bandstand, or the like.

soundproofing, insulation in the form of sound-deadening material in walls, ceilings, or floors.

sow′del, *see* saddle bar.

spack′ling, or **sparkling,** a putty-like material for the filling of cracks and holes in plaster, sometimes in wood, to prepare the smooth surface for further finishing.

spall, to split off from the surface, as stone that is bearing undue pressure near its face or is acted upon by weathering.

span, the distance between the supports of a beam, arch, or the like.

span′drel, the surface at the side of a half-arch between a vertical line at the bottom of the archivolt and a horizontal line through its top (1*b*). 2. in skeleton-frame buildings, the panel of wall between adjacent structural columns and between windowsill and the window head next below it.

span′drel beam, a beam designed to support the window or windows and wall of a story height between neighboring upright columns.

Spanish architecture, comprising chiefly the adaptation and development of Renaissance architecture originating in Italy.

Spanish roofing tile, a rounded-top, interlocking side-joint tile about 9″ x 13″ (6*h*).

spar, old term for a timber.

spark′ling, *see* spackling.

spar′ver, a canopy frame over a dais or bed.

specification (spess ifi ka′shun), a description, for contract purposes, of the materials and workmanship required in a structure, as also shown by the related working drawings.

specus (spee′kus), the water channel of an aqueduct.

spel′ter, zinc in ingot form.

spe′os, in ancient Egypt, a rock temple.

spere, the screen set across the lower end of the hall in domestic buildings of the Middle Ages.

speroni (sper o′nee), wall buttresses; anterides.

sphæristerium (sfee riss tee′reum), in ancient classical architecture, a ball court, usually part of a public bath or gymnasium.

sphinx (sfinx), a fabulous creature, common in Egyptian sculpture. The androsphinx represented the body of a lion with the head of a man; the criosphinx, the body of a lion and the head of a ram; the hieracosphinx, the body of a lion and the head of a hawk.

Great Sphinx, an Egyptian monument near the Pyramids of Gizeh, partly natural rock and part masonry, with a shrine, built against the breast and between the forepaws, of an image of Harmachis, the Egyptians' god of the morning.

spier, a fixed screen functioning as a partition.

spig′ot, a plug for a cask; by extension, a faucet.

spike, a heavy type of nail, of use in fastening large timbers.

spile, the term used in some localities to designate a pile, a columnar support driven into the ground.

spina (spee′nah), the podium wall bisecting the classical hippodrome.

spin′dle, a small axle, as the spindle of a vane or the spindle on which doorknobs are fixed. 2. a short turned part, as that on a baluster.

spira (spee′rah), a group of moldings on the base of a column or pilaster.

spi′ral staircase, a flight of stairs winding around a central vertical support or open space.

spire, a tall tower roof, tapering upward to a point. 2. in ancient architecture, the base of a column; sometimes the astragal or torus.

splay, a beveled or slanted surface, as the splay of a window embrasure.

splice, a joint formed by overlapping and binding together two members.

spline, a flexible strip with provision for holding it in desired curves, used as a drafting aid. 2. a thin strip forming a key between two boards or planks and locking their edges together; usually the spline is of rectangular section, but sometimes of X-section (4*i*).

split system, in heating, an installation utilizing two simple systems, such as radiators and also indirect warm air.

spoil, unwanted material removed from an excavation.

spring, of an arch, the initial rise from the impost (1*b*).

spring′er, the masonry unit lying first above the impost of an arch. 2. a rib of a groined vault.

springhouse, a small house built to enclose a spring and used for storing dairy products and other foods in lieu of refrigerating equipment.

sprin′kler, or **sprinkler system,** a water valve opened by the melting of a fusible link, used in series as an automatic aid in quenching interior fires.

spruce, an important wood with a number of species, including eastern spruce (*Picea rubens*, *P. mariana*, and *P. glauca*), Engelmann spruce (*P. engelmanni*), and Sitka spruce (*P. sitchensis*), of which the Sitka is in wide use; a strong, light, shock-resisting wood used for interior and exterior finish, siding, and general construction.

European spruce (*Picea excelsa*), a wood imported from the Baltic as white fir, white deal, or Norway spruce, and also from Canada, where it is called yellow spruce; a white, straight-grained, even-textured, tough, light wood used for interior construction.

sprue (sproo), a projecting inlet in a mold through which metal is poured for a casting, the resulting surplus projecting metal being removed later.

spunware, circular forms of thin metal produced by spinning.

square, a plane figure having four equal sides and four interior right angles. 2. an area of flooring, roofing, or the like, 10′ square. 3. an open or parked rectangular space in a community. 4. an instrument, sometimes combined with measure, for determining right-angledness. 5. adjective, descriptive of lines or planes at right angles to each other.

squinch, an arch or corbeling at the upper interior corners of a square tower, for the support of a superstructure of octagonal or circular form (7*c*).

squint, an oblique opening in the interior wall of a medieval church to afford a view of the high altar for persons in the transepts or aisles; a hagioscope.

sta'ble, a structure, or part of one, for the sheltering of horses or cows, etc. 2. (adjective) set firmly in place.

stack, a vertical range of bookshelves. 2. a chimney, particularly a large or tall one. 3. a vertical range of piping with branches, for heating or plumbing.

stad'huis, in the Netherlands, a town house or a city hall.

stadium (plural, **stadia**) (sta'deum, sta'de ah), a circular, oval, or round-ended sports amphitheater.

staff, a short-lived exterior wall covering resembling stucco, used chiefly for exposition buildings and the like.

staff bead, an angle bead, a vertical member protecting or decorating the salient angle of a wall, particularly when it engages plaster, stucco, or staff. 2. the outside molding member of an exterior architrave, fitting snugly against the adjoining wall.

stage, a platform raised above the floor level at the front of a theater, lecture hall, classroom, or the like.

staging (stayj'ing), temporary platform working space in and about a building under construction or repair. 2. scaffolding.

stag'ger, to arrange in parallel rows but with objects in one row opposite spaces in the next.

stain (stane), color in a dissolving vehicle, which, when spread on an absorptive surface, penetrates and gives its color to the wood or other material.

stain'ed glass, glass given desired color in its "pot-metal" state. 2. such glass disposed in decorative or pictorial compositions with the use of lead cames, metal frames, and stiffeners.

stain'less steel, an alloy of steel that is resistant to rust and corrosion.

stair, a step, alone or in a series, facilitating walking from one level to another.

stair'case, a series of steps or flight of stairs, possibly with landings, and with handrail, newels, etc.

stair'way, a flight of stairs not necessarily cased in or enclosed.

stake out, to mark, with stakes driven into the ground, the location of a proposed structure.

stall (stawl), an individual compartment, three sides closed and sometimes a gate or door on the fourth, for horse or cow in a stable. 2. a theater seat with arms. 3. a seat for the clergy in the chancel of a cathedral or church.

stam'ba, an isolated pillar serving as a memorial.

stanchion (stan'chun), a vertical post, two of which are used to confine a cow in a stable, flanking the animal's head. 2. an upright bar between mullions of a window.

standing waste, a vertical, overflow pipe inserted in the customary bottom outlet of a bowl or tank.

stand'pipe, a cylindrical reservoir, usually of metal.

stan'za [It.], a room.

sta′ple, a double-pointed U-shaped piece of metal.
star molding, a common molding in Norman architecture.
stasid′ion, a stall in a Greek church.
state house, a capitol of a state in the U.S.A.
state′room, a sleeping compartment on a ship or train.
Sta′tion of the Cross, one of fourteen shrines in a church, marking successive scenes in the Passion of Christ.
station-point perspective, or **centrolinear projection,** a form of linear perspective in which the point of sight is assumed to be fixed and the line of sight is perpendicular to the plane of projection.
stat′uary, statues collectively.
stat′ue, a sculpture of a human or animal figure.
statuette′, a statue of less than half life size.
stat′umen, a lime-and-sand mortar used in ancient Rome in paving.
stay, a prop.
steam fitter (steem), a workman skilled in piping for steam or hot-water heating.
steam pipe, a pipe for carrying steam.
ste′atite, soapstone in slab form, as for hearths, fireplace facings, laundry tubs, and the like.
steel, an alloy of iron that is of chief interest to the architect in the following varieties:

chromium steel, an alloy of steel possessing extreme hardness; it can be machined when annealed; used chiefly for bearing plates.

hard, or **high-carbon steel,** containing over 0.5% carbon, used for springs, tools, and the like.

manganese steel, an alloy of steel that, in the form of castings, has great resistance to abrasion; it cannot be machined.

medium, or **medium-carbon steel,** containing from 0.25% to 0.50% carbon, used for rolled structural forms, reinforcing bars, and the like.

nickel steel, an alloy of steel possessing greater strength than carbon steels; it is rolled in the standard sections.

soft, mild, or **low-carbon steel,** containing up to 0.25% carbon, of great ductility, as in its use for drawn wire.

steel-frame, describing a building in which the support is achieved by a closely knit structure of steel.
steel′worker, a workman skilled in structural steel or reinforcing for concrete.
steen′ing, brickwork without mortar, as in a leaching cesspool.
stee′ple, a tower and spire, usually on a church.
stele (stee′lee, or stay′lee), an upright slab of stone bearing an inscription and sometimes bas-relief sculpture.
step, one unit—tread and riser—alone or in series in a flight of stairs.
step bracket, a bracket form, carved or sawn, for ornamenting the end of a step in an open-string stair.

stepped flashing (stept), flashing along a roof slope against a wall or chimney, where the masonry joint entered must necessarily change at intervals to keep at a safe distance above the roof surface (16*i*).

ster′eobate, a substructure of a building without columns, in classical architecture.

stereochromy (ster′e o kro′ mee), painting on stone with pigments in waterglass.

stereotomy (ster e ot′o mee), the art of properly sizing and placing cut stones in a masonry structure.

stiacciato [It.] (stee ah chee ato), very flat, as low-relief sculpture.

stick, a long piece of wood, as a stick of timber.

stick′ing, the cutting of a molding in a woodworking mill.

stile, steps flanking a fence or wall, to aid in passing over it. 2. a vertical framing member of a paneled door or of paneling.

S-tile, a roofing tile of which the cross section resembles a prone letter S (6*b*).

stillicidium (stilla sid′eum), dripping eaves of a Doric building.

stilt′ed arch, or **stilted vault,** an arch (or vault) having some length of vertical intrados above the impost (1*b*).

stip′pling, in surface painting, the use of the brush point, a sponge, or the like, to secure a texture unlike that given by brush strokes or spraying.

stir′rup, an iron for the support of a joist at right angles to the line of its span (4*e*).

sto′a, in ancient Greek architecture, a portico or cloister.

stock, commonly used and commercially available patterns, as stock window sash, stock doors, etc.

stockade′, a space surrounded by logs driven into the ground as a palisade.

stoker, a mechanical device for feeding coal into a fire chamber.

stone, broken or cut rock as a building material.

Stone′henge, megalithic remains on Salisbury Plain, England.

Stone Mountain granite, a medium-grain granite formerly quarried in Georgia; widely used, of uniform light gray.

Stonington Pink Gray granite, *see* Deer Isle.

Stony Creek granite, a warm reddish granite of Connecticut, varying from medium to coarse grain, with bold veinings.

stool, an inside sill of a window.

stoop, a broad platform step at the entrance to a house.

stop, or **stop bead,** a strip on a doorframe or windowframe against which the door closes or the sash slides.

stop′cock, a valve in plumbing work to close a main or branch line of pipe.

store, a place in which merchandise is offered for sale; a place larger than a shop.

store′room, a room for miscellaneous storage.

storey, *see* story.

storm cellar, or **cyclone cellar,** an underground space for protection against violent windstorms.

storm door, an additional outside door in the doorframe, for better insulation against weather.

storm sash, or **storm window,** an additional sash covering the whole of a window opening, for better insulation.

storm sewer, a sewer designed for carrying away storm water as differentiated from sewage.

story, the space in a building between successive floor levels.

stoup, synonym for piscina. 2. a basin for holy water near the church entrance.

straight-grain, or **comb-grain** (strate grane, cohm), descriptive of lumber, particularly flooring, when the grain is clearly seen as continuous parallel lines.

strain (strane), stress carried to the point of deformation of a member.

strain′er, a globe of wire mesh inserted in a gutter at the top of a downspout to prevent clogging with leaves and other debris. 2. a pierced plate at top of a sink outlet.

S-trap, or **siphon trap,** the common trap in plumbing; an S-bend in the drain pipe beneath a fixture to provide a water seal against sewer gases.

strap hinge, one in which one leaf is a flat decorative strap and both leaves are attached to wall face of jamb and face of door rather than to the edges.

strap′work, a form of ornamentation employing interlaced raised bands.

stress, force exerted, as a load on a beam.

stress diagram, a graphic chart showing direction and amount of each stress in a structural unit.

stretch′er, a unit of masonry placed lengthwise in a course. 2. a frame on which may be stretched the canvas of a painter or the paper of a draftsman. 3. a litter.

stria (plural, **striæ**) (stry′ah, stry′ee), the ridge separating adjacent flutes in a column shaft; an arris (12).

striges (stry′jees), the channels of a fluted column (12).

strigil ornament (stry′gill), in Roman architecture, a fascia bearing a series of vertical reedlike flutings.

strike, in masonry, to cut off with a trowel stroke the excess mortar at the face of a joint.

stri′king plate, that member of a lock set or latch set that is fastened to the jamb to engage lock bolt or latch and at the same time to prevent damage by the latter to the wooden edge of the jamb.

string, the outer support of stair ends, or the member covering the same.

string course, a plain or molded horizontal continuous band on an exterior wall.

string′er, a horizontal framing timber supporting minor members at right angles to it. 2. the sloping outside strut or decorative end face of a stair.

stringybark, *see* yuba.

strip′ping, the removal of forms from poured concrete after it has set.

strix (striks), a channel in a fluted column (12).

struck joint, in masonry, where the excess mortar exuding between units is removed by a flush stroke of the trowel.

structural glass, *see* glass.

struct′ural terra cotta, or **hollow tile,** unit shapes for partitions, wall backing, floor arches, roof slabs, and fire protection of structural steel.

structure (struk′tyoor), a combination of parts put together to form a building, a bridge, or the like.

strut, a brace, or member under compression in a framework.

Stuart architecture, a section of Late Renaissance in England, covering the period 1625–1702, or the reign of Charles I (1625–1649), the Commonwealth (1649–1660), and the reign of Charles II (1660–1685), James II (1685–1689), and William and Mary (1689–1702). The architects leaving the greatest marks on this period were Inigo Jones and Sir Christopher Wren.

stucco (stuk′ko), plaster for exterior walls.

stud, an intermediate vertical member of a wood frame.

studio (stoo′dee o), the workroom of an artist, usually with high ceiling and north light.

study (stud′ee), a graphic preliminary representation of the solution of a problem. 2. a room devoted to mental activities.

style, characteristic form, as of a specific period in history. 2. distinctive or characteristic expression in any art.

sty′lobate, the main base of a building under the classical columns (11*j*).

sub′base, the bottom front strip or molding of a baseboard.

sub-base′ment, a story immediately below a basement, or one of several stories below a basement.

subcellar (sub sell′ur), a cellar beneath a cellar.

subcontrac′tor, one who contracts to carry through a definite part of the general contractor's obligation in building.

subdivision (sub′dih viz zhun), a plot of ground divided into building lots.

subfloor, a flooring of rough boards upon which a finish floor is to be laid.

sublet′, to enter into contract for the performance of work one has himself contracted to perform.

subsellium, *see* miserere.

sub′sidized hous′ing, housing for low-income groups, the construction costs or rental charges of which are at least partly borne by government or other authority.

sub′soil, earth below the layer of fertile topsoil.

substructure (sub′struk tyoor), foundation or structure below grade or below some arbitrary line, above which is the superstructure.

sub′urb, an outlying section of or near a city, predominantly for residential use.

sub′way, underground public transportation line.

sucupira (soo koo peer′ah) (*Bowdichia* spp.), a wood from Brazil and northern South America with a light tan-brown background, and often darker brown with narrow stripes; used chiefly for veneer, in which it resembles English fumed oak.

suite (sweet), a group of rooms and their connections to be used as a unit.

sum′mer, a heavy beam crossing a ceiling from girt to girt and supporting joists of the floor above.

sum′mer beam, an intermediate girder timber supporting the ends of floor or ceiling joists.

sum′merhouse, a rest house in a garden, or station point for a view.

sump, a receptacle or mere depression provided for the accumulation of unwanted water, which is usually removed therefrom by a sump pump.

sundeck, a deck or flat roof for sun bathing.

sun parlor, or **sun′room,** a room with abundant sunlighted glazing.

su′pa (*Sindora supa*), a wood from the Philippines, pale yellow, turning to yellowish brown with age; it is very hard and heavy, suitable for interior work and flooring.

su′perblock, a reconstruction on the gridiron plan combining a number of blocks by eliminating the dividing streets.

sup′ercap′ital, a block of stone above the capital of a column, as in Byzantine architecture.

supercilium (soo per sil′iyum), the molded lintel of a doorway. 2. in Roman architecture, the fillet crowning the cymatium (13).

supercolumnia′tion, the use of one classic order above another.

superinten′dent, a supervisor of construction.

su′permar′ket, a large retail food store of the serve-yourself type.

su′perstructure, structure above a foundation or grade line.

supervision (soo per viz′yun), the overseeing of construction to make sure of its conformity to drawings and specifications.

support′, that which upholds.

sur′base, the upper part of a baseboard, usually molded. 2. the molded top of a pedestal (12, 13).

surround′, an enframement.

surveyor (sur vay′or), one skilled in land measurement.

swag, a decorative form consisting of a simulated net-held mass of fruit and flowers sagging between two supports; usually in heavy bas-relief; pancarpi (16*j*).

swas′tika, a religious symbol dating back to the Bronze Age in Europe and still found in China, Japan, India, and among the Indians of North and South America; essentially a Greek cross with the arms ending in right-angled extensions running clockwise or counterclockwise.

Swenson Buff Antique, a muscovite-biotite granite of light to medium grayish buff color and fine to medium grain; quarried at Concord, N. H.

Swenson Pink, a biotite granite of light pink color, medium to coarse grain, with occasional waves of closely segregated black and pink stripes; quarried at North Berwick, Me.

swim′ming pool, an artificial pool for recreational swimming.

switch, an apparatus for making and breaking an electric circuit.

switch′board, a panel to which electrical lines are brought for the purpose of connecting or disconnecting circuits.

syc′amore, American (*Platanus occidentalis*), also called buttonwood or American plane tree; a tree of southern Ontario and the eastern U.S.A., south to Florida and Texas, the hard, reddish brown wood of which develops, in veneer, small flakes more numerous than in quartered oak.

syenite (si′en ite), rock of the nature of granite but containing little or no quartz.

symbolism (sim′bo lizm), representation, through an object or a form, of an idea, a person, or a place to be remembered.

symmetrical (sim met′re kal), having identical forms or masses on either side of an axial line.

synagogue (sin′agog), a meeting place for Jewish worship.

synecdoche (sin nek′do keh), a figure of speech in which a part is named for the whole, or the whole for a part, as a hearth for a home, or marble for a piece of sculpture. 2. a ciborium.

syn′odal hall, a meeting place for a synod or general gathering of the clergy and appointed representatives of a diocese.

syrinx (sir′inx), a tunnel-shaped rock-cut tomb of Egyptian antiquity.

systyle (sis′tile), a form of intercolumniation in classic architecture in which the columns were two diameters apart, center to center.

T

tabernacle (tab′ur nakl), a house of worship. 2. a receptacle for the consecrated elements of the Eucharist.

table tomb (ta′bl toom), a table-like tomb.

tab′let, an enframed or otherwise limited space, usually for an inscription.

tab′linum, a space in an ancient Roman house where family records and hereditary sculptured figures were placed.

tabularium (tab you la′reum), in ancient Rome, a depositary of public records.

tabulatum (tab you lah′tum), ancient Roman term for wood floors, wainscot, ceilings, etc., and even for balconies and other projections.

tachuelilla (tack you lee′lah) (*Zanthoxylum microcarpum*), a wood from Mexico, Costa Rica, Lesser Antilles, and South America, resembling yellow poplar with its satiny finish and ease of working; used for furniture, interior woodwork, and veneer.

tænia (tee′nea), the fillet separating the Doric frieze from the architrave (11*j*).

Tai-kih, in Chinese philosophy, the Great Uniter, bringing the world of opposites into fructifying union (5*bb*). *See also* Great Monad (5*aa*).

tailloir [Fr.] (tahl wahr), the abacus (12).

tail′piece, a subordinate joist, rafter, or the like, supported on a wall or sill at one end and headed into another timber at the other end.

talon [Fr.] (tal onh), literally, heel; a molding, frequently enriched, with a profile in variation of the cyma reversa (10*f*, *g*). *See also* ogee (12).

tambour [Fr.] (tam boor), literally, a drum; the naked bell of the Corinthian and Composite capitals (14*c*). 2. the wall of a circular temple surrounded by columns. 3. the vertical-sided drum supporting a cupola.

ta′mo (*Fraxinus sieboldiana*), a wood from Japan, varying in color from brownish tan through gray to almost white; in veneer the figure resembles a peanut shell.

tamp, to ram and concentrate, as in tamping freshly poured concrete in the form.

tanguile (tan geel′) (*Shorea polysperma*), a wood of the Philippines with heartwood pale to dark reddish brown with a purplish tinge; sapwood a very pale gray-brown; used for furniture, cabinetwork, and veneer.

tap, to connect a public service supply line with a branch to serve a particular building. 2. a faucet.

tar, a dark viscid oil, dry-distilled from resinous woods, coal, peat, and shale; used in roofing and as a road surface binder.

tarpau′lin, a waterproofed canvas covering for use in protecting unfinished work or stored materials against weather.

tarsia, *see* intarsia.

tar′tan, royal (*Argyrodendron trifoliatum* [= *Tarrietia argyrodendron*]), also known as brown tulip oak; a wood from New South Wales and Queensland, brown with a red tinge which, when quartered, shows a pattern of small flecks crossed by wavy, thin lines; used for flooring, joinery, paneling, and veneer.

tavel′la, a brick of 7″ x 3½″ face, used in ancient times.

tav′ern, a public guest house or saloon.

taxis (taks′iss), in ancient classic architecture, the quality of having proper correlation between size and use.

tax′payer, a building, possibly temporary, producing enough income to cover taxes and the building investment but not enough to provide also an adequate return on the land value.

tazza [It.] (tat′zah), the raised basin of a fountain.

teak (teek) (*Tectona grandis*), an East Indian tree, the wood of which is dark, heavy, and durable; used chiefly for fine flooring, decking, greenhouses, furniture, and interior finish.

tecassir (tek′aseer), in Mohammedan architecture, a gallery in a mosque, especially for the use of women.

tecto′rium opus [Lat.], a kind of wall plastering in ancient apartments.

tee, a pagoda finial, often gilded and hung with bells (16*e*).

tegurium (teg you′reum), a pointed roof over a sarcophagus, supported usually by colonnettes.

telamon (plural, **telamones**) (tel′ah mon, tel ah mo′nees), a columnar support in the form of a male figure; also called, in the plural only, atlantes.

temenos (tem′eh noce), the sacred enclosure in which a Greek temple stood.

tem′per, to mix and blend lime, sand, and water, or cement, sand, and water, to make mortar. 2. to thin with water either of the above mixtures to make them workable—a practice usually forbidden in specifications.

tem′pera, pigment in water or in a vehicle soluble in water; distemper.

tempered (tem′perd), descriptive of thoroughly mixed mortar or cement. 2. descriptive of case-hardened metals, particularly steel.

tem′pla [Lat.], purlins of a temple roof.

tem′plate, or **templet,** a pattern structure for repetitive marking or for a fabricating operation.

temple (tem′pl), a house of worship (16*n*).

ten′der, the bid of a contractor, as used by the English.

ten′ement, a building containing low-rent apartments. 2. an apartment in such a building.

tenia (tee′nya), *see* tænia (11*j*).

Tennessee marble, a group name for a great variety of

marbles of excellent quality. Ground tones vary from light warm gray and shades of pink and brownish pink to dark chocolate. All Tennessee marbles have more or less of a characteristic pinkish hue, although there are a black, a reddish green, and a buff marble as well. Traces of the marine animals whose remains were the raw materials of which it was made can often be discerned. Some varieties are: Antique Rose, Bond Pink, Bond Dark Cedar, Edward Pink, Craig Pink, Ellis Pink, Ross Pink, Acme Pink, Lawson Gray, Champion Pink, d'Or Fossile, Phantasia Rose, Phantasia Vert, Rochelle, and Imperial Black.

ten′on, a projection on the shoulder of a wood member, to fit snugly into a socket or mortise in another wood member, forming a joint (4*g*).

ten′penny, a size of nails, perhaps so-called because nails of this size sold in England at one time for tenpence a hundred.

tensile strength (ten′sil), the measure of a material's ability to withstand stretching.

tension (ten′shun), stress in a structural member caused by forces tending to draw it apart longitudinally, as in a tie rod.

teocalli (tee o kal′lee), a pyramidal temple in ancient Mexico.

te′opan, an Aztec form of the teocalli.

tepesuchil (ta peh soo′kil) (*Cordia alliodora*), also called laurel, palmwood, bonjon, a wood from tropical America, yellowish to brown, and resembling American walnut in color and density; texture uniform; used for furniture and interior finish.

tepidarium (teppi da′reum), an intermediate room in an ancient Roman bath, between the steam room and the cooling-room.

teram (tare′am), the scroll at the end of a step.

tercento (ter chen′to), designating Italian art of the fourteenth century.

ter′minal, or, rarely, **terminus,** an end feature, as the tip of a building, or a figure terminating a vista or an axis. 2. one end of an electrical conductor.

ter′minus, a station at the end of a railway.

ter′mite shield, a sheet of metal serving as a barrier to termites between a foundation wall and the woodwork above.

terne or **terne plate** (turn), sheet steel coated with an alloy of 80% lead and 20% tin; used chiefly for roofing.

terrace (tare′iss), a level space raised above the adjoining land, and usually flanked by a building.

ter′ra cot′ta, cast and fired clay units, usually larger and more intricately modeled than brick.

terras (tare ahss′), a blemish in a marble block, removed and replaced by a composition filling.

terrazzo (tare aht′so), a flooring surface of marble chips in cement, ground and polished after setting.

tes′sellated, formed of tesseræ.

tessera (plural, **tesseræ**) (tess′erah, tess′erye), an individual stone of a mosaic.

test, to measure the quality of a material by trial.

tes′ter, a canopy, as over a bed or a tomb.

testudo [Lat.] (tess too′do), an arched roof.

tetrapy′lon, a structure penetrated by two intersecting passageways meeting at right angles, as in various triumphal arches.

tet′rastyle, the type of classical building having four columns across its front.

tew′el, an opening for ventilation.

Texas Pink granite, of light pink, medium grain; quarried at Marble Falls, Texas.

tex′ture, surface conformation or quality independent of color.

thal′amus, or **thalamium** (thal ah′meum), in classical architecture, an inner room, often for women or for use as a bridal chamber.

thatch, a roof covering of rushes, straw, or the like fastened together to shed water.

the′ater, a building for the presentation of stage plays.

theod′olite, an instrument for the measurement of angles in surveying.

thermæ (thur′my), in classical architecture, the public baths.

Thermopane, trade name for an insulating double-glazing pane for window or door.

ther′mostat, an electric switch actuated by changes in temperature.

theseion (the′see on), a temple dedicated to Theseus.

thimble, *see* nipple.

thingan (*Hopea odorata*), a wood of India, Burma, and the Andamans similar to Philippine yakals.

thole, a votive niche or recess.

tho′lobate, the circular substructure of a dome.

tho′los, a circular building, or part of one.

three-deck′er, an early form of meetinghouse pulpit, having three parts: reader's desk, pulpit, and clerk's desk.

thresh′old, a doorsill. 2. the tread member of an entrance. 3. a saddle.

throat, of a fireplace, the narrowed passage at a plane between fire chamber and smoke chamber or enlarged base of the flue.

throat′ing, the undercutting of a projecting molding to form a drip.

throne, a seat of state for a sovereign or an ecclesiastical dignitary.

thrust, a force tending to push outward, as the thrust of a dome at its base, or that of a rafter on a plate.

thuja burl (thoo′yah) (*Tetraclinis articulata*), a wood from the Atlas Mountains, North Africa; light brown to nearly black, sometimes with tiny eyes similar to bird's-eye maple; used chiefly for veneer. *See also* sandarac.

thumb latch (thum latch), a door fastener opened by thumb pressure on a lever.

thumb tack, a short tack with a broad flat top, used for holding drawing paper and the like on a board.

thymele [Gr.] (thy me′lee), an altar in a Greek theater.

thyrone′um, a passage leading in from the entrance to a peristyle.

tie, a construction member in tension.

tie beam, or **collar beam,** a horizontal member in a roof structure, tying together opposed rafters.

tier (teer), one of a series of successively higher rows, as a tier of seats in an amphitheater.

tierce point [It., *di terzo acuto*], the pointed arch (1*i*).

tierceron (teer′seh ron), a vaulting rib starting from the intersection of two other ribs (8*h*).

tie rod, a construction rod in tension.

tige (teezh), a column shaft (15).

ti′gerwood (*Lovoa klaineana*), *see* walnut, African.

tig′na, tie beam of a timber roof.

tile, a unit of baked clay in various forms, for roofing or for wall or floor covering. Structural tile are units of baked clay, usually hollow, for self-supporting walls or partitions. Furring tile are rough-faced hollow units for use in backing up masonry walls. 2. an earthenware drain pipe.

bonnet tile, a roofing tile of approximately semicylindrical shape, used for covering the roofing along a hip.

English roofing tile, a flat, corrugated tile about 9″ x 16″, with interlocking, flush side joints (6*e*).

hip tile, *see* bonnet tile.

mission roofing tile, a clay tile 14″ to 18″ long, curved to the arc of a circle, slightly tapered lengthwise, laid alternately with the convex and concave side up (6*i*).

pan-and-roll roofing tile, a roofing tile in two shapes, one of flat rectangular section, the other a half-round section, for covering the joints (6*d*).

pantile, a curved roofing tile, somewhat like a prone letter S (6*a*).

S-tile, a roofing tile of which the cross section resembles a prone letter S (6*b*).

Spanish roofing tile, a rounded-top, interlocking side-joint tile about 9″ x 13″ (6*h*).

tim′ber, wood cut to shape for structural members.

tin, a white lustrous metal, used chiefly for coating sheet steel, as in "tin" roofing.

tinda′lo, *see* oro.

tin plate, bright sheet steel coated with tin. *See also* terne.

toe joint, in carpentry, the joint between a horizontal member and another at a vertical angle, as a rafter on plate.

toi′let, a bathroom fixture—the water closet.

tol′erance, acceptable variation from a standard size.

tollhouse (tole′houce), a collection lodge in connection with a tollgate.

tomb (toom), a structural resting place for the dead.

tondino (ton dee′no), Italian term for a molding of circular form.

tongue (tung), a tenon (4*g*).

tongue-and-groove, abbrev. t. & g., applied to boards having a tongue formed on one edge and a groove on the other for tight jointing; also called matched boarding, matched flooring, and the like (4*n*).

tooart, *see* tuart.

tooth ornament, a pyramidal form having no antecedents in classical architecture, based probably on the Norman nailhead and widely used in English thirteenth-century work and also on the Continent (9*o*).

tope, a Buddhist monument in a temple for preserving relics. 2. a large mound, enclosed and having gateways, as the Sanchi tope (600 B.C.).

topiary work (toe′pee ary), clipped boxwood, or other shrubs or trees, in ornamental or whimsical forms.

topography (toe pog′raffee), the physically detailed description of a piece of land.

top′soil, the fertile top layer of the earth's surface.

to′ran, a monumental gateway leading to a Buddhist temple.

torchère (tor share), an ornamental support for a flambeau or other source of light.

torii (to′re ee), the posts-and-curved-lintels gateway to a Shinto temple.

torque (tork), the resultant of forces tending to cause rotation.

torsade (tor sayd′), a ropelike molding.

torsion (tor′shun), the force tending to right a twisted rod, cable, or other long slender member.

to′rus, a large molding of convex semicircular profile, as usually found just above the plinth of a classical column base (12, 13).

tos′sut, the tunnel entrance to an Eskimo igloo.

totara (to tah′rah) (*Podocarpus totara*), a tree of New Zealand, the wood of which is deep red and very durable; used for panels and veneers; available in long, wide pieces.

toukul, or **tucul** (too kool), a type of native dwelling common to all parts of the African continent, distinguished by circular one-room plan and conical roof. Materials vary regionally, from mud brick to interlaced poles thatched with leaves, to timber or masonry; with roof nearly always of thatch.

tourelle (too rel′), a small tower, particularly one supported by corbeling.

tower (tau′ur), a tall structure, usually square or round in plan, rising to a greater height than its surroundings.

town hall, a building for the seat of government in a small community.

trabeated (tray′be ated), of post-and-lintel construction.

trabs, a wall plate.

tracery (trace′ury), the curving mullions of a stone window, as in Gothic architecture (8*g*).

trachelium (track e′leum), the necking of a Greek Doric column (11*j*).

trac′ing, a drawing on translucent paper or linen.

tradi′tional architecture, contemporary architecture that holds closely to forms established in an earlier period.

tram′mel, an instrument for describing a large circle or an ellipse.

transen′na, a lattice guard before a shrine.

tran′sept, either of the lateral arms in a church of cruciform plan.

tran′sit, an instrument for measuring angles on a horizontal plane, used in surveying.

Tran′site, trade name for a building board made of cement and asbestos, molded under pressure.

transition (tran sish′un), the slow change from one distinct style to another distinct style following it.

translucent (trans loo′sent), permitting the passage of light but not vision.

tran′som, an opening over a door or window, usually for ventilation, and containing a glazed or solid sash, usually hinged or pivoted.

transtra [Lat.] (trans′trah), horizontal roof timbers.

trap, a plumbing device for maintaining in a drain pipe a water seal against sewer gas.

trap′door, a door in a floor or roof.

trasco′ro, in Spanish churches, a part of the choir separated from the nave, as by a transept passage.

trash, waste matter resulting from a building operation.

trass, earth used in the making of hydraulic cement.

trav′erse, a gallery or loft of communication in a church or other building.

trav′ertine, or **Roman travertine,** a material that in composition is almost identical with that of onyx. It has a light creamy color, with irregular-shaped voids in fairly straight lines but ranging in size from pinhead to egg.

tray, a container, having low sides but no top; sometimes used as a drawer with no front closure, as to store linen.

trayle, an ornamental pattern of the Tudor period—a running vine with leaves and grape clusters; also called a vignette.

tread (tred), the horizontal surface of a step. 2. width measurement of a step.

tree′nail, a wooden pin used in securing together the ends of wooden framing. 2. a gutta, depending from a mutule in the Doric order. *See also* trunnel (11*j*, 12).

trefoil (tree′foyl), a three-lobed figure in various forms (9*b*).

treillage (trel′idj), latticework as a support for vines or espalier planting.

trel′lis, latticework as an outdoor screen, often a support for vines.

trem′ie, a movable form for placing concrete under water.

trench, a long, narrow, ditchlike excavation, for drainage, for drain pipe, or for a foundation wall.

tres′aunce, a passageway.

trestle (tres′sl), a post-supported and braced horizontal member, generally to support planking for scaffolding and the like; a sawhorse.

triap′sidal, having three apses.

trib′une, a dais for the magistrates' seats in the apse of a Roman basilica; hence a platform, dais, or rostrum.

triclinium (trik li′neum), in ancient Rome, the dining table and its couches.

triforium (try for′eum), a gallery or range of arches above the longitudinal arches bounding nave or choir in a church (7*g*).

triglyph (try′glif), a projecting rectangular block, vertically channeled and chamfered, occurring in series on an entablature of the Doric order (12).

trigonum (try go′num), a tessera of triangular shape.

tri′lith, a megalithic gateway, of two upright stones and a lintel.

trim, the enframement of doors, windows, and the like with molded wood or other material. Sometimes the term includes all standing finish woodwork indoors.

trim′mer, a short beam engaging the ends of several other beams or joists, usually to support a floor about an opening or at a chimney breast.

triptych (trip′tik), a union of three panels, the central one predominant, usually a base for paintings, and particularly altarpieces.

triquetra (trick et′rah), interlaced ornament of a three-point form (2*m*).

trium′phal arch, a large arched structure commemorating a national victory.

trochilus (trok′illus), Greek term for the scotia (11*c*).

trof′fer, a troughlike enclosure for light sources.

tropæum, or **tropaion** (tro pee′um, tro pi′un), a victory monument; in ancient Greece, a pile of captured arms; in ancient Rome (where it was called a trophy) a permanent structure ornamented with sculptured weapons, shields, prows of captured ships, and the like.

trumeau (tru mo), French term for an upright supporting member between two adjacent openings.

trunk, that part of a pilaster corresponding to the shaft of a column.

trun′nel, one of the short cylindrical, or truncated conic, projections carved on the underside of the regula and the mutule of the Doric cornice. Also called gutta. *See also* treenail (11*j*, 12).

truss, a combination of straight members so arranged and connected that the stresses in the members, due to loads on the whole, are direct stresses, either in tension or compression; used for beam action over larger spans.

- **fan truss** (4*k*).
- **Fink truss** (4*r*).
- **hammer-beam truss** (4*s*).
- **Howe truss** (4*p*, *q*).
- **king-post truss** (4*j*).
- **Pratt truss** (4*e*).
- **scissors truss** (4*m*).

try′lon, a tall, slim form, of triangular section, tapering to a point at the top. The term was invented to describe a dominant feature of the New York World's Fair of 1939.

T-square, a drafting aid by which parallel lines are drawn at right angles to the edge of the drawing board.

tuart (too′art) (*Eucalyptus gomphocephala*), a tree of Australia, the light yellow wood of which has a fine texture and interlocked grain and is very tough and dense; contains much tannin; used for ties and vehicles.

tuck pointing, decorative pointing of masonry.

Tudor architecture, designating the late phase of Perpendicular Gothic, when the four-pointed arch was a characteristic (2*c*).

Tu′dor flower, the conventionalized leaf, vine, or flower widely used in cresting of wood screens and the like; brattishing (9*a*).

Tuileries (twee′leh rees), the Paris palace of the French kings, built between 1564 and 1700.

tu′lip poplar, *see* poplar, yellow.

tu′lipwood (*Dalbergia frutescens*), a very hard wood from northeastern Brazil, with alternate stripes of red or violet and yellow; used for veneer and inlays.

tum′bling, *see* muisetanden (3*m*).

tung′sten-fil′ament lamp, an incandescent electric light source using a filament of tungsten wire having a high melting point and a low evaporation rate in a bulb filled with a mixture of argon and nitrogen.

tun′nel, an underground artificial passage.

tupelo, black, *see* gum, black.
water tupelo, *see* gum, water tupelo.

turbeh (toor′beh), a domed tomb structure of the Mohammedans.

turette′, a small turret.

turf (terf), sod.

turned work, woodwork cut on a lathe.

turn′stile, a rotating barrier through which one-way passage is effected, sometimes with counting or entrance-fee mechanism; as used in subways, supermarkets, and museums.

turn′table, a platform flush with floor or tracks, capable of being rotated horizontally.

tur′ret, a small tower, usually corbeled, at the corner of a building and extending above it.

Tus′can order, one of the classical orders, resembling the Doric but of greater simplicity; used in Roman and other Italian architecture.

tvärumstuga, *see* morastuga.

twining stem molding, a molding in which a conventionalized tendril winds about a stem (9*l*).

twist′ed column, a decorative column the shaft of which has the appearance of having been twisted along its vertical axis; also called wreathed column.

tympanum (tim′pan um), the space enclosed by the three molded sides of a pediment, or by the lines of a semicircular overdoor panel or the like.

type, the canopy sounding board over a pulpit.

U

uncial (un′shul), a form of lettering having the roundness and other characteristics of early manuscript writing.

unctorium (unk to′reum), in the ancient baths of Rome, a room or apartment used for anointing the body with oil.

un′dercroft, a vault under a church or chapel.

un′dercut, cut or molded so as to present an overhanging part, as a drip mold.

un′derground, beneath the surface of the ground, as drainage systems, electric conduit, etc.

un′derpass, one road or path crossing another at a lower level.

un′derpin′ning, a foundation replacing a former one or reinforcing it from below. 2. support for a structure by braced props, usually temporary.

undressed′ lumber, lumber which is not planed smooth.

union, a plumbing joint in which an outer-threaded sleeve draws inner-threaded pipe ends into close contact.

u′nit, or **British thermal unit,** abbrev. B.t.u., the amount of heat required to raise the temperature of one pound of water (at its maximum density) through one degree Fahrenheit.

u′nit heater, a combination of radiator and blower in a casing.

univer′sal joint, a joint that permits to one or both connected members free angular motion in any direction.

unveil (un vale), to disclose to public view, usually with ceremony.

upholster (up ol′ster), to equip with cushioning under a fabric, as an upholstered window seat.

up′percroft, a triforium gallery (*7g*).

up′set, to thicken an end or other part of a metal bar by hammering.

u′rinal (yu′rinnl), a plumbing fixture for use in urinating.

urn (ern), a vase of circular form, usually set on a pedestal. 2. a receptacle for ashes of the dead.

util′ity, or **public utility,** a continuing service available to all citizens of a community, as water, electricity, gas.

utility room, space in a dwelling where are grouped the heating plant and other utilities. 2. a room in a dwelling in which are grouped laundry equipment and the like.

V

V-joint, in woodworking, a tongue-and-groove joint in which one face of the boards is cut in a V instead of a butt joint.

vacuum system (vak′yoo um), a steam-heating two-pipe system having a thermostatic trap on the return end of each radiator and a vacuum pump on the return main, keeping the interior of the system at less than atmospheric pressure.

valley (val′lee), the line of intersection of two roof slopes, where their drainage combines.

valve (valv), a device to open or close a pipe, duct, or other passage.

vamure (va myoor′), the walk on top of a wall behind the parapet; the alure.

vane, a blade or banner form pivoted on a tower, steeple, or other high point to indicate the direction of the wind.

van′ishing point, a point to which lines in a parallel system converge in perspective drawing.

vaporarium (vapor ar′eum), synonym for caldarium.

vapor barrier, or **moisture barrier,** a material, usually in thin sheet form or combined with a sheathing material, designed to prevent the passage of moisture through a wall, with the aim of avoiding condensation within the wall.

va′por, or **vacuum-vapor, heating** (vak′yu um), a system in which steam rises through piping and radiators in which the air pressure is less than atmospheric.

vardastuga, the single-room log cabin of Sweden, a prototype of early Swedish buildings in America.

varel′la [It.], a pagoda (16*e*).

Varitone Mahogany, a medium-grain granite, reddish with black and gray spottings, quarried at Ortonville, Minn.

var′nish, a liquid composition which is converted to a transparent or translucent solid film after application as a thin layer.

vase (vaze), a container in various ornamental forms. 2. the bell of a Corinthian or Composite capital (14*c*). 3. synonym for echeum.

vault, that part of a structure roofed by arched masonry. 2. a roof structure of similar form but of otherwise supported plaster or the like.

vaulting shaft, a pillar from which spring vaulting ribs; the pillar may rise from the floor, from the capital of a pier, or from a corbel (7*g*).

vault light, the overhead, daylight-transmitting panel of an underground room; usually of rondelles set in a cement-and-steel frame in the sidewalk.

Veined Ebony, igneous rock of the gabbro or "black granite" class, of medium grain with pronounced darker veins, quarried at Mellen, Wisc.

velarium (veh la′reum), in the ancient Roman theater, the awning shelter over the seats.

velodrome (vell′o drome), a roofed or open banked race-track, as for bicycles.

veneer′, a thin layer of selected wood for glueing to a support. 2. a covering layer of material for a wall, as brick or marble veneer.

Vene′tian blind, a flexible and collapsible shade of thin slats, louver-like and adjustable as to angle.

Vene′tian dentil molding, a series of contiguous blocks, beveled oppositely and alternately.

Vene′tian door, in England a door with side lights.

Vene′tian window, early English term for the prototype of the Palladian window.

vent, an outlet for air. 2. a vent pipe in a plumbing system. 3. a ventilating duct.

ven′tilate, to provide free circulation of fresh air. 2. to carry off unwanted fumes or air, as by a ventilating hood over a range.

vera da pozzo (pot′so) [It.], a decorative curb for a cistern, particularly in Venice, resembling a well curb.

veranda (veh ran′dah), a long gallery-like porch, sometimes two-storied.

verd antique (vurd ann teek′), a boldly veined or mottled serpentine stone for decorative use; the *verde antico* of early Italian, Greek, or Egyptian origin was predominantly green.

Verdo′na, an Italian marble having a general over-all tinge of green, like a copper patina, with splotches of buff showing through.

verge, in Medieval architecture, the shaft of a column (15*g*).

vergeboard, or **bargeboard,** the vertical-face board following and set back under the roof edge of a gable, sometimes decorated by carving (7*e*).

vermicular (vermik′yu lar), or **vermiculated,** surface-cut to simulate undulating worm tracks, as in quoins or rustication.

vermiculite (ver mik′you lite), a hydrated magnesium-aluminum-iron silicate which is a micaceous material that exfoliates when heated, splitting into thin laminæ, and with further heating into long wormlike pieces (the Latin *vermiculare* means to breed worms) The exfoliated material is used as fill insulation, in place of sand in gypsum plaster, and as an aggregate in light-weight concrete and acoustical plaster.

Vermont marble, group name for a wide variety quarried in Vermont, many of them white or with a ground of white, although there may be considerable veining and clouding. Some are practically pure white. Vermont produces a very fine variety of verd antique, which, though classed as a marble, is a rock constituted largely of serpentine. Of many richly colorful Vermont marbles suitable for highly decorative work, a few are Best Light Cloud, Florence, Jasper, Light Vein, Metawee, Neshobe Gray, Oriental, Radio Black, Striped Brocadillo, Vermont Pavonazzo, Westland Cippolino, and Westland Green Veined Cream.

vernacular (ver nak′yu lar), indigenous; characteristic of a locality.

vesica, or **vesica piscis** (vess′eka pis′kiss), a lineal figure formed between two arcs of equal radius, each arc passing through the center from which the other arc is drawn (2*l*).

vestibule (vess′tih byool), a small room between an outside door and an inside one, the latter frequently opening into a hall.

vestry (vess′tree), a room in which ecclesiastical vestments, sacred vessels, and the like are stored, and in which the clergy and choristers robe for church services.

viaduct (vi′adukt), a bridge, usually of arched masonry, across a dip in the land.

vibration (vibra′shun), repeated motion back and forth of an elastic body.

vi′brator, an instrument for the puddling and compacting of concrete when first poured into the forms.

vicarage (vik′urage), the residence of a vicar.

Victo′rian, designating the art characteristic of the reign of Queen Victoria (1840–1901).

vignette (vin yet′), *see* trayle.

vihara (ve harr′ah), a Buddhist monastery.

vil′la, a country seat or suburban house.

vimana (vee mah′na), a small shrine-cell and its entrance porch in Hindu or Brahman architecture.

Vinal Haven granite, an even-textured, fine-grain, light gray granite of Maine, used for monumental work.

vinette (veye net′), a running ornament of leaves and tendrils.

viro′la (*Virola* spp.), also called banak; woods of tropical America, pale to deep reddish brown, frequently with a purplish hue; used chiefly for veneer.

vis, or **vise** (vice), early English term for a spiral staircase.

vise, a screw-actuated clamping device, usually fastened to a work bench.

visorium (ve sore′eum), that part of an amphitheater set apart for the seating of the spectators.

vista (viss′tah), a long-range view from a point.

vitrail [Fr.] (vee tray), glass in windows, particularly stained glass.

vit′reous enamel, porcelain enamel, a glossy composition fused upon metal.

vitrified (vit′re fide), surface-glazed, as certain clay products.

vivarium (ve vare′eum), a zoological garden.

vivo [It.] (vee vo), the shaft of a column.

volt, unit of electromotive force; the e.m.f. that, applied to a conductor whose resistance is one ohm, will produce a current of one ampere.

volute (vo loot′), a spiral ornament such as used as a pair in the Ionic capital (13).

vomitorium (vommit o′reum) (plural, **vomito′ria**), entrance or exit passage of an amphitheater.

voussoir (voo′swar), one of the stones of an arch lying between impost and keystone (1*b*).

W

wainscot (wane′skot), an overlining for interior wall surfaces, usually less than the full height of the story.

Wakeman Buff, a sandstone of fine grain and light buff color showing many faint variations commonly called "spider web"; quarried at Wakeman, Ohio.

waler (way′ler), a horizontal stiffener for concrete forms, sheet piling, and the like.

walk (wauk), a path or paved way for pedestrians.

walk′-up, multiple dwelling of not over four stories, without elevator service.

wall (waul), a vertical member of an enclosure.

wall′board, generic name for artificial board or sheeting, used in many varieties as a plaster base or as a substitute for plaster, wainscoting, or sheathing.

wall bracket, a source of artificial light on a side wall.

Waller stone, a sandstone similar in color and texture to McDermott sandstone, quarried in Scioto County, Ohio.

wallpaper, a special paper, plain or printed, for pasting upon a smooth interior wall surface as decoration.

wall plug, in electricity, a two-pronged connection to complete a circuit from an electrical socket or outlet.

wall rib, in Gothic vaulting, a half-rib projecting from the supporting wall to complete a motif in the vaulting.

wall shaft, in Gothic vaulting, a shaft, detached or attached, resting on a corbel to support a vault rib (7*g*).

wall space, plain wall surface between windows, doors, and like interruptions.

wall string, that one of the string pieces of a stair frame that is fastened against a wall.

wall tie, a bonding strip, usually of metal, serving to tie together two withes of a cavity wall, brick veneer to its structural framework, or facing masonry units to their backing.

walnut, African (*Lovoa klaineana*), **Congowood,** or **tigerwood**; a golden brown wood with dark streaks; used for furniture, veneers, gunstocks, and inlaying.

American black walnut (*Juglans nigra*), a hard, dark brown wood used chiefly for furniture and interior trim. It is the traditional material for gunstocks and is available for other architectural uses in limited supply.

Brazilian walnut, *see* imbuia.

California walnut (*Juglans californica* or *J. hindsii*), woods of California which produce veneers of tannish brown with prominent black and white stripes and black spots.

Circassian or **French walnut** (*Juglans regia*), a wood principally from southern Europe and Asia, tawny colored, with streaks of black or dark brown; used chiefly for furniture and veneer.

Queensland walnut, *see* oriental wood.

ward, a subdivision of a hospital or a jail. 2. a baffle in a lock preventing the full action of the key in the lock operation.

ware′house, a building for storage purposes.

warp, shape distorted by twisting, especially in too rapidly dried wood.

wash, the slight slope of a top surface to shed water. 2. an application of water color used in rendering.

washbasin, or **washbowl,** *see* lavatory.

wash′board, a baseboard.

wash-out closet, or **wash-down closet,** outmoded types of the water closet.

wash′room, a toilet room.

wash′stand, a lavatory.

wash′tub, a laundry plumbing fixture in which clothes and the like can be washed; also called laundry tray.

waste, refuse material resulting from a building operation. 2. a drain line of plumbing. 3. an overflow line in piping.

water back, a coil or chamber near the firepot of a range or heater, for hot-water supply.

water bar, a metal tongue in the bottom of a wood doorsill serving as a baffle to the entrance of water.

water-cement ratio, the proper mixture, with fine and coarse aggregates, for concrete making.

water closet, a bathroom fixture —the flushable toilet.

water hammer, a fault in plumbing whereby the surge of suddenly checked water is not properly cushioned against noise.

water heater, a device for heating water for the domestic supply through the plumbing system.

water meter, a device for recording the amount of water flowing through the piping.

water paint, a paint that contains water or water emulsion as the vehicle.

waterproof, made secure against flow or permeability of water, as a foundation wall or a ground floor.

water seal, the water remaining in a plumbing trap after the line has been flushed.

water table, the top level, at a given point, of the water which permeates the rock masses of the earth. 2. a projecting base course, beveled at the top for weathering.

watt, the common unit of electric power—approximately 748 to one horsepower.

wattle (waht′tl), interwoven twigs, wicker, bamboo, or such withes to form a screen or wall surface.

wave molding, a molding bearing a raised, incised, or painted conventionalized series of waves (10*b*).

wax, a paste of various ingredients, in proprietary form, for surfacing finished wood floors and other woodwork, linoleum, etc.

weather (weth′er), to undergo the changes in color, texture, or efficiency brought about by continued exposure to wind, rain, sun, frost, etc.

weath′erboard, a horizontal exterior wallboard laid with lower edge overlapping the next board below.

weathered joint, in masonry, a water-shedding slope to the outside of the upper part of a mortar joint.

weathering, the action described under **weather.** 2. a slight drainage slope given the top of a horizontal member, as a cap of coping, the exposed top edge of a belt course, or a water table.

weath′erstrip, a strip or interlocking strips of material that help block the passage of air around a door, window, or the like.

weath′ervane, *see* vane.

web, the middle plate of a girder or the middle section of an I-beam.

wedge, a V-shaped section to insert with force in a slot to induce splitting, or inserted between adjacent members to apply pressure.

weep hole, a hole for drainage, as through a retaining wall or at the bottom of a parapet.

weld, a joint made by bringing surfaces heated to plasticity into close contact.

well, an open space through one or more floors, as a stair well or an elevator well. 2. an underground source of water protected for convenient access.

well curb, a low wall protecting the opening of a well of water.

well′head, or **wellhouse,** a shelter over a well of water, usually with means of bringing water to the rim.

Wels′bach burner, a gaslight source depending upon the incandescence of an impregnated cotton-gauze mantle when heated by a Bunsen-type flame.

Welsh arch, a lintel form with a loose wedge in the middle (1*p*).

Welsh groin, or **underpitch groin,** a groin at the intersection of two cylindrical vaults, one of which is of less height than the other.

wet-bulb temperature, the temperature of a thoroughly wet body in air motion.

Weymouth Seam-Face granite, a Massachusetts stone with color blendings of brown or of golden yellow-green; of fine grain, giving fine and easily split seams, divided into plane sheets of 1″ to 8′ thick with no further dressing required.

whaler, *see* waler.

wheel window, a circular window, its divisions mainly radiating; a catherine wheel.

whispering gallery, an interior space having the acoustic property of reflecting a sound in one or more particular directions with surprisingly little loss of volume.

white bronze, a bronze made lighter in color by a larger proportion of tin.

white lead, common name for the paint pigment of lead carbonate and lead dioxide.

white′wash, a creamlike solution of slaked lime in water, applied as a paint.

white′wood, wood of the tulip tree, yellow poplar, cottonwood, or basswood trees; fine-textured and easily worked.

whit′ing, a chalk pigment used in paint and putty.

wick′et, a small opening in a door or gate.

wig′wam, the conical shelter of certain North American Indian tribes, built of poles covered by bark or skins.

Wilkerson sandstone, a medium-grain, hard, light gray, easily worked sandstone; quarried in Pierce County, Wash.

wind (wined), a twisting warp in lumber.

winder (wine′der), a wedge-shaped step occurring at a turn of a stairway.

wind′ing stairs, a spiral staircase.

win′dow, an opening in a wall for light and ventilation, with all its appurtenances.

case′ment window, having the sash hinged at jamb and opening out or in.

double-hung window, having two balanced sash, one sliding vertically over the other.

projec′ted window, having the sash hinged or pivoted at top or bottom to project entirely outward or inward.

win′dowbox, the space adjoining a window stile to permit the action of the sash weights. 2. a box for plants, usually at the outside of the windowsill.

windowpane, a unit of sash glass.

window seat, a built-in seat inside a window.

windowsill, the bottom member or group of members of a window opening.

window stile, an upright of the window frame, guiding the sash.

window stool, the inside front-molded horizontal shelf of a windowsill.

wine cellar, an underground room for wine storage.

wing, a secondary mass of a building, sometimes an addition.

winged disc, *see* feroher (16*b*).

wing wall, an abutment wall.

wiped joint, a soldered junction of lead pipes.

wire, flexible strand or strands of metal, chiefly used to conduct electricity.

wire cloth, woven wire screening.

wire-cut brick, that made by an extrusion process in which wire is used to cut the units.

wire glass, sheet glass in which wire mesh is embedded as reinforcement.

wire lath, a netting of galvanized wire used as a support for plaster.

withe, a partition, brick width thick, in brickwork, as between chimney flues or half a cavity wall (3*j*, *k*).

wood, the cellulose substance inside the bark of trees, cut into lumber and veneer for many uses in building.

wood block, blocks of wood, with grain vertical, used for paving or for industrial flooring.

wood brick, wood blocks of brick size inserted in the coursing for nailing purposes.

wood′work, that portion of a building that is wrought of wood, particularly the finish woodwork.

working drawing, a graphic representation of an object usually at a stated scale and with dimensions to enable artisans to build the object as designed.

work′manship, the quality of executed building.

work′shop, a room or a building where handicraft is carried on.

wreath (reeth), a twisted garland of simulated leaves, fruit branches, or flowers, usually circular and often tied at bottom with a ribbon.

wreathed column (reethd), one twisted in helical form about its vertical axis.

wrecking (rek′ing), dismantling or razing a building or other structure.

wrought (rawt), hammered into shape, as of ductile metals.

wrought iron (rawt), *see* iron.

Wyoming Valley stone, *see* Pennsylvania bluestone.

X

xat (zaht), a form of totem pole used by certain tribes of North American Indians.

xenodocheum (zeno do ka′ um), in ancient and modern Greece, an inn.

xoanon (zo′ah non), in ancient Greece, a primitive statue.

xyst, or **xystus** (zist, zist′us), in Greek architecture, a covered portico attached to a gymnasium, for winter exercise. 2. in Roman architecture, an open portico or walk around a garden or court; the cloister of later years.

Y

yacca (yak′ka) (*Podocarpus* spp.), woods from the West Indies, Mexico, Central and South America; whitish or yellowish in color; fine-textured; used for flooring, furniture, and cabinetwork.

yakals′ (*Shorea* spp. and *Hopea* spp.), woods from the Philippines; light yellow-brown, hard and durable; *see* thingan.

yali (yah′lee), a Turkish summer residence.

yamun (yah′mun), the official residence of a Chinese mandarin.

yaqua (yah′kah), the royal palm, as it is called in the West Indies, used for roof thatching.

yard, a unit of linear measure; 36 inches. 2. a piece of ground adjacent to and part of a residence or other building.

yar′rah (*Eucalyptus camaldulensis*), also called red river gum; an Australian tree with hard and durable red wood, some of which bends well; used primarily for construction; also prized for underwater or underground work.

yate tree (*Eucalyptus cornuta*), an Australian tree, the yellowish gray wood of which resembles ash in its toughness and elasticity.

ye′so, a gypsum whitewash widely used in Mexico. Not to be confused with gesso, which see.

yew, European (*Taxus baccata*), a wood from Europe and Asia, the sapwood almost white and the heartwood bright tan, becoming a warm brown upon exposure; may form burls; used chiefly for veneer.

yoke, a tie rod or similar tension member. 2. the head of a frame for a double-hung window.

yourt (yurt), a permanent or winter dwelling of the Eskimos.

yu′ba (*Eucalyptus obliqua*), an Australian tree, also called stringybark, messmate, and Tasmanian oak; light tan to golden brown in color; straight-grained and well patterned for veneer; it is also used for interior finish and flooring.

Z

zaccab (zak kab′), a form of plaster used in Yucatan; white earth mixed with lime and water.

zapo′ta (*Achras zapota*), the chicle tree of Central America, the wood of which is a deep, rich red or plum color with a hard, close texture; used where resistance to decay and rot is needed, and also for veneer.

zax, a slater's edged and pointed tool for cutting slate and punching nail holes.

zebrano, *see* zebrawood.

ze′brawood (*Brachystegia fleuryana*), also called zebrano, zingana; a wood from West Africa which, quarter-sawn, gives a veneer of light straw-colored background with parallel dark brown stripes; heavy, hard texture somewhat coarse.

zecca [It.] (zek′kah), a mint.

zeilenbau [Ger.] (zi′len bow′), row housing.

zenana (zeh nah′nah), in India, the apartments of the women.

zeta (za′tah), a room over a church porch, in which documents were kept. 2. a small chamber in ancient Greek architecture which was heated by air conducted through pipes in the wall from the room below.

ziggurat (zig′gyoo raht), a stepped-back temple tower of the Assyrians and Babylonians.

zig′zag molding, chevron molding (9*f*).

zinc (zink), a metallic element, in commercial form known as spelter; used for galvanizing sheet steel, for making brass, and, as an oxide, for a pigment for white paint.

zinc oxide, or **zinc white,** a white pigment used in paint.

zingana, *see* zebrawood.

zoc′co, zacco, zocco′lo, or **zoc′le,** variations of the word *socle*, the lowest member of a column or pilaster.

zoning (zone′ing), restriction as to size or character of buildings permitted within specific areas, as established by urban authorities.

zoöphorus (zo ahf′o russ), a sculptured frieze of men and animals.

zotheca (zo the′kah), a room or alcove, for living rather than for sleeping.

zwing′er [Ger.], a stronghold adjoining a city; a bailey.

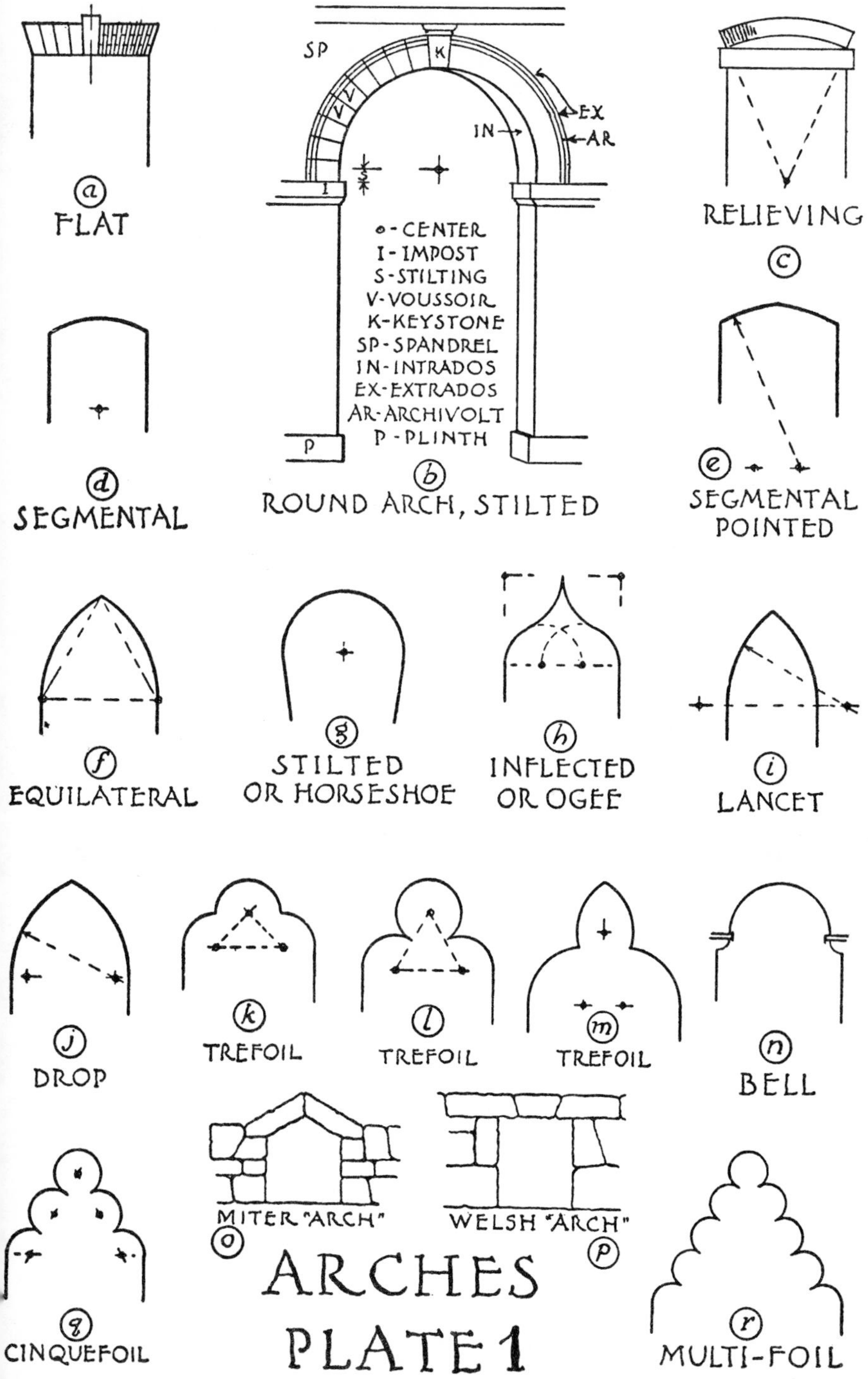
(a)
FLAT
SP
K
V
V
IN
EX
AR
S
I
o - CENTER
I - IMPOST
S - STILTING
V - VOUSSOIR
K - KEYSTONE
SP - SPANDREL
IN - INTRADOS
EX - EXTRADOS
AR - ARCHIVOLT
P - PLINTH
P
(b)
ROUND ARCH, STILTED
RELIEVING
(c)
(d)
SEGMENTAL
(e)
SEGMENTAL POINTED
(f)
EQUILATERAL
(g)
STILTED OR HORSESHOE
(h)
INFLECTED OR OGEE
(i)
LANCET
(j)
DROP
(k)
TREFOIL
(l)
TREFOIL
(m)
TREFOIL
(n)
BELL
MITER "ARCH"
(o)
WELSH "ARCH"
(p)
(q)
CINQUEFOIL
(r)
MULTI-FOIL

ARCHES
PLATE 1

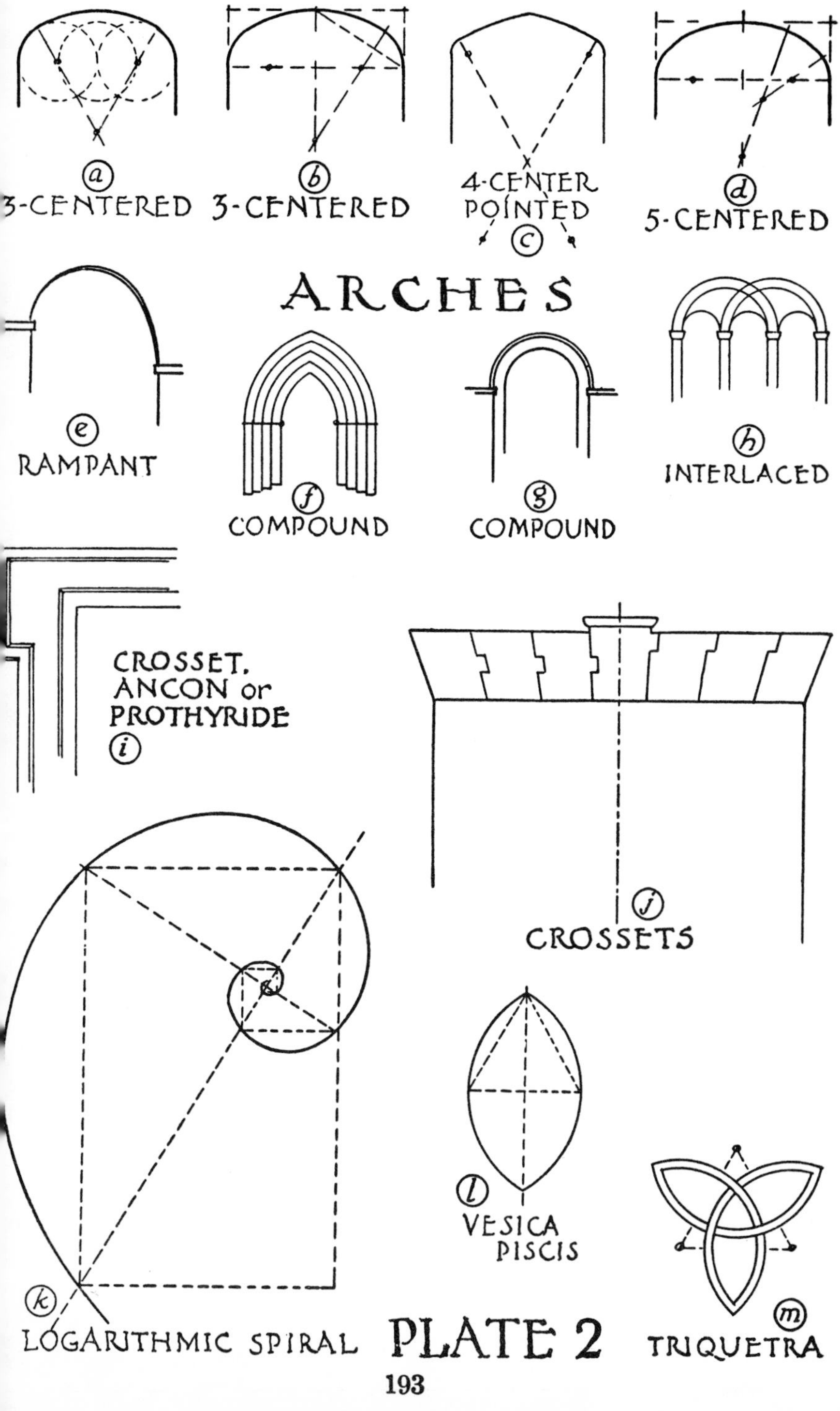
ARCHES
(a) 3-CENTERED
(b) 3-CENTERED
4-CENTER POINTED (c)
(d) 5-CENTERED
(e) RAMPANT
(f) COMPOUND
(g) COMPOUND
(h) INTERLACED
CROSSET, ANCON or PROTHYRIDE (i)
(j) CROSSETS
(k) LOGARITHMIC SPIRAL
(l) VESICA PISCIS
(m) TRIQUETRA

PLATE 2

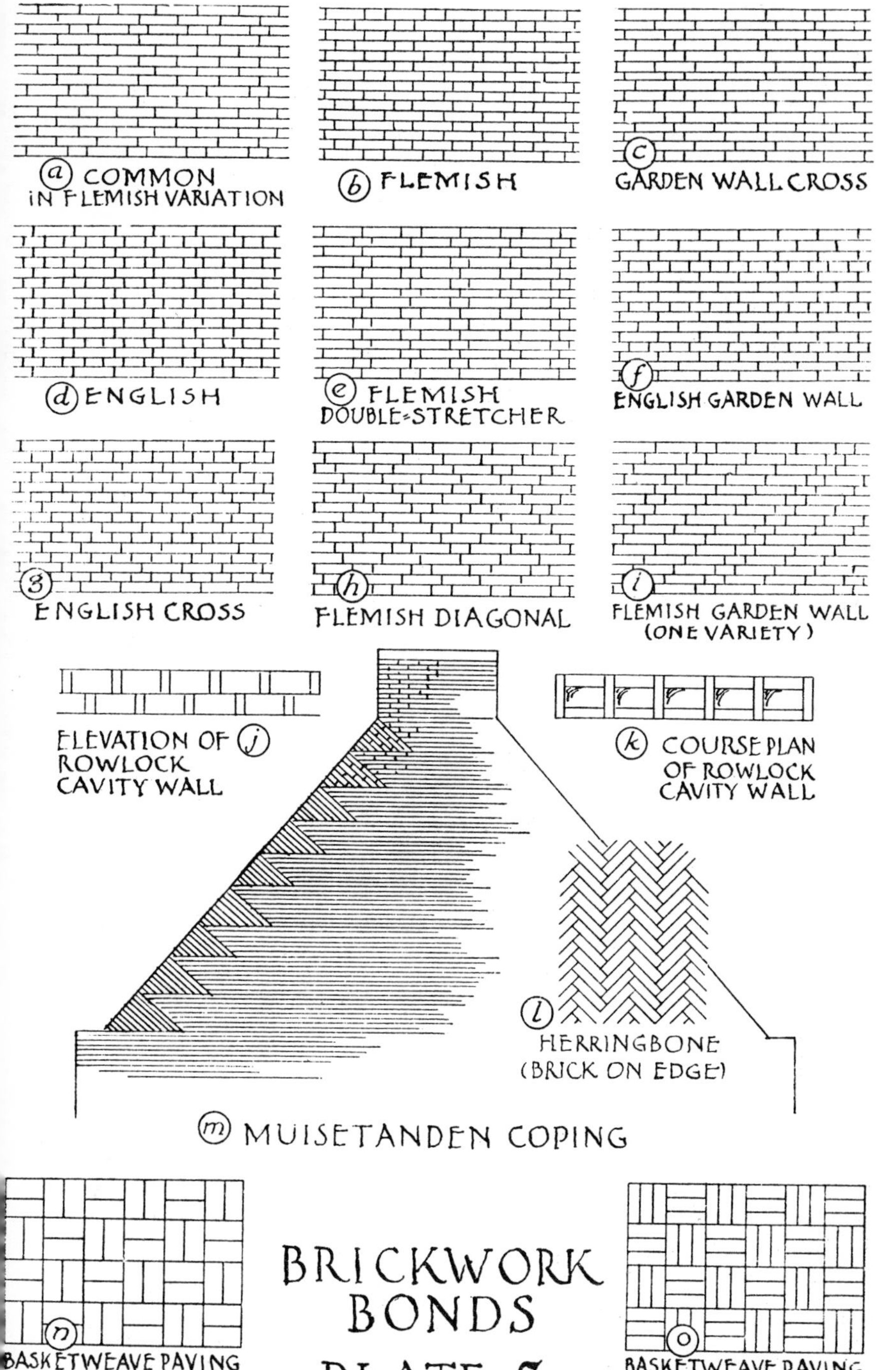
(a) COMMON IN FLEMISH VARIATION
(b) FLEMISH
(c) GARDEN WALL CROSS
(d) ENGLISH
(e) FLEMISH DOUBLE-STRETCHER
(f) ENGLISH GARDEN WALL
(g) ENGLISH CROSS
(h) FLEMISH DIAGONAL
(i) FLEMISH GARDEN WALL (ONE VARIETY)
ELEVATION OF (j) ROWLOCK CAVITY WALL
(k) COURSE PLAN OF ROWLOCK CAVITY WALL
(l) HERRINGBONE (BRICK ON EDGE)
(m) MUISETANDEN COPING
(n) BASKETWEAVE PAVING FLAT
(o) BASKETWEAVE PAVING ON EDGE

BRICKWORK BONDS

PLATE 3

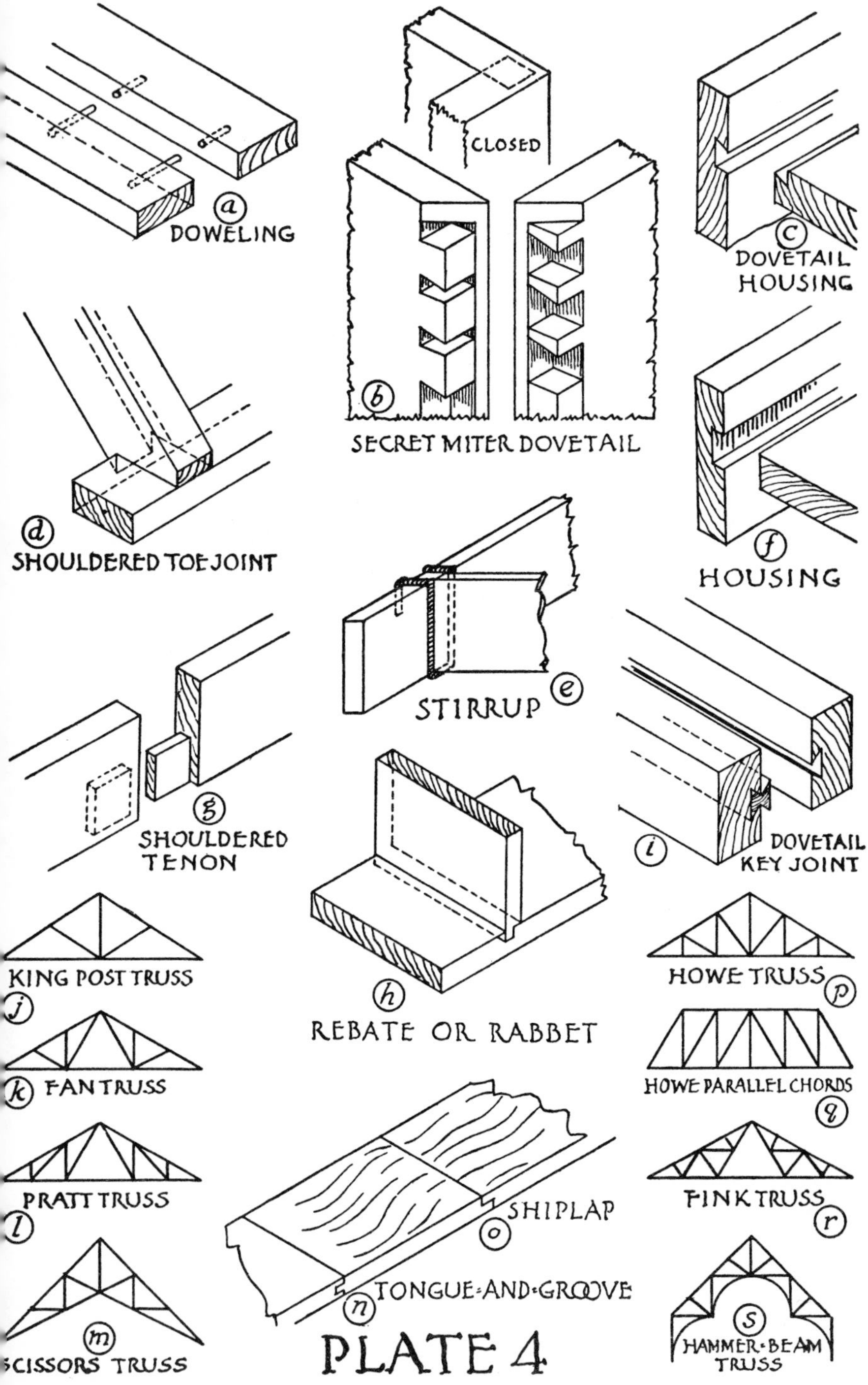
a
DOWELING
CLOSED
b
SECRET MITER DOVETAIL
c
DOVETAIL HOUSING
d
SHOULDERED TOE JOINT
f
HOUSING
e
STIRRUP
g
SHOULDERED TENON
i
DOVETAIL KEY JOINT
KING POST TRUSS
j
h
REBATE OR RABBET
HOWE TRUSS
p
k
FAN TRUSS
HOWE PARALLEL CHORDS
q
PRATT TRUSS
l
SHIPLAP
o
FINK TRUSS
r
TONGUE-AND-GROOVE
n
m
SCISSORS TRUSS
s
HAMMER-BEAM TRUSS

PLATE 4

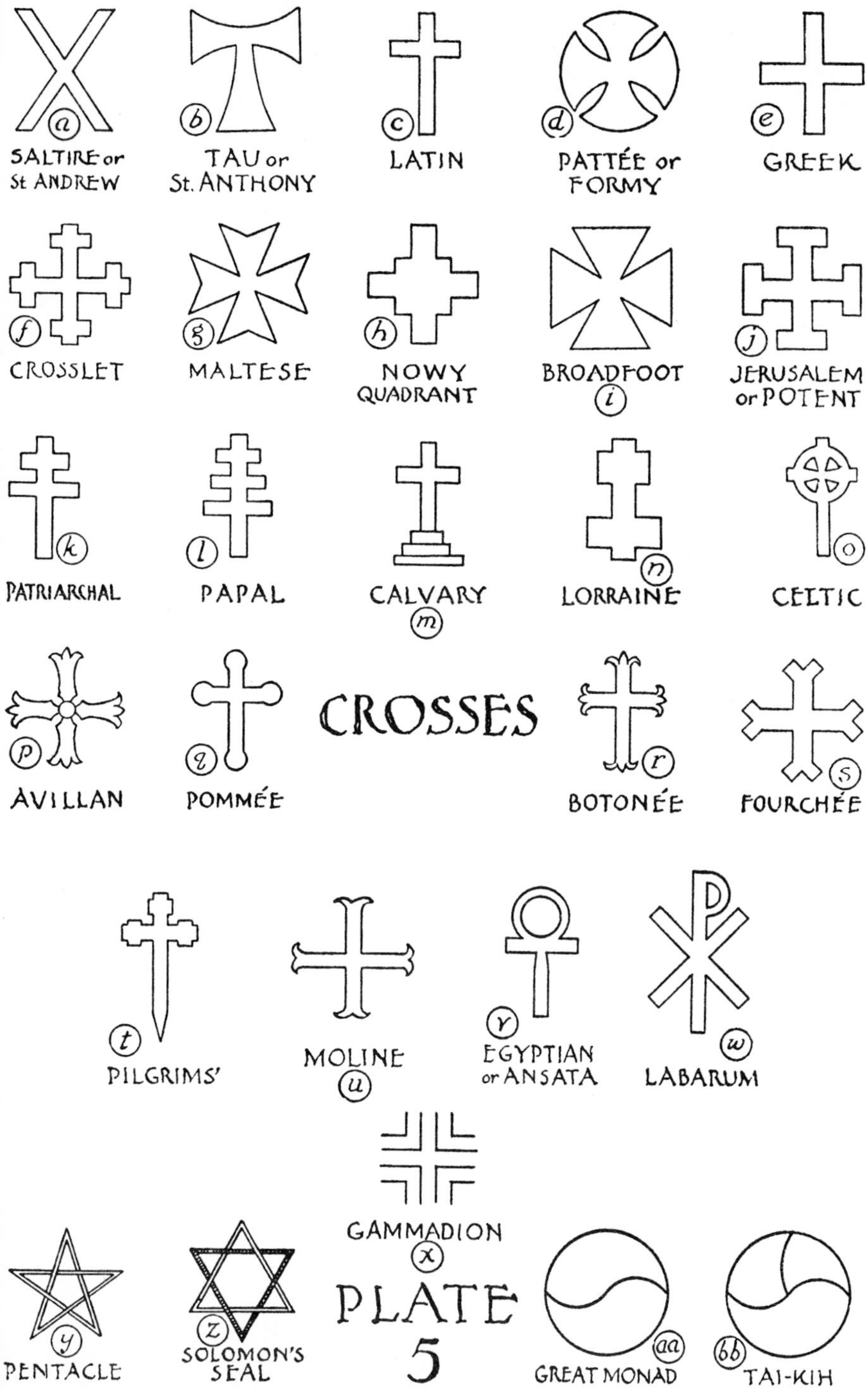

a
SALTIRE or St ANDREW
b
TAU or St. ANTHONY
c
LATIN
d
PATTÉE or FORMY
e
GREEK
f
CROSSLET
g
MALTESE
h
NOWY QUADRANT
BROADFOOT
i
j
JERUSALEM or POTENT
k
PATRIARCHAL
l
PAPAL
CALVARY
m
n
LORRAINE
o
CELTIC
p
AVILLAN
q
POMMÉE
CROSSES
r
BOTONÉE
s
FOURCHÉE
t
PILGRIMS'
MOLINE
u
v
EGYPTIAN or ANSATA
w
LABARUM
GAMMADION
x
y
PENTACLE
z
SOLOMON'S SEAL
PLATE 5
aa
GREAT MONAD
bb
TAI-KIH

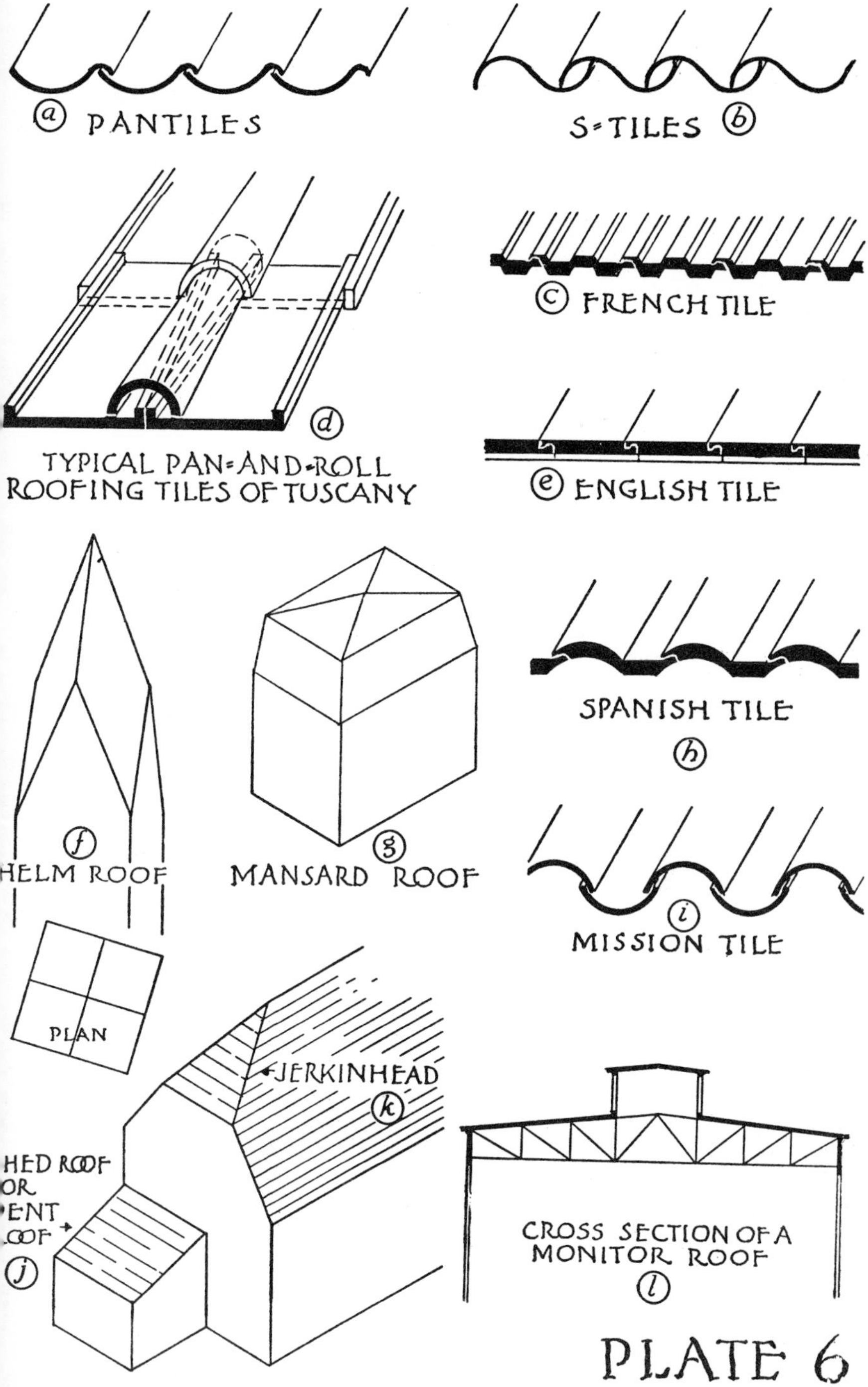

ⓐ PANTILES
S=TILES ⓑ
TYPICAL PAN=AND=ROLL ROOFING TILES OF TUSCANY
ⓓ
ⓒ FRENCH TILE
ⓔ ENGLISH TILE
ⓕ
HELM ROOF
ⓖ
MANSARD ROOF
SPANISH TILE
ⓗ
ⓘ
MISSION TILE
PLAN
JERKINHEAD
ⓚ
HED ROOF
OR
ENT
OOF
ⓙ
CROSS SECTION OF A MONITOR ROOF
ⓛ
PLATE 6

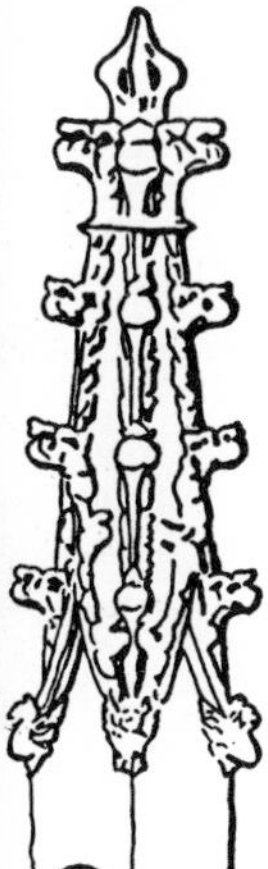

(a) PINNACLE, with CROCKETS

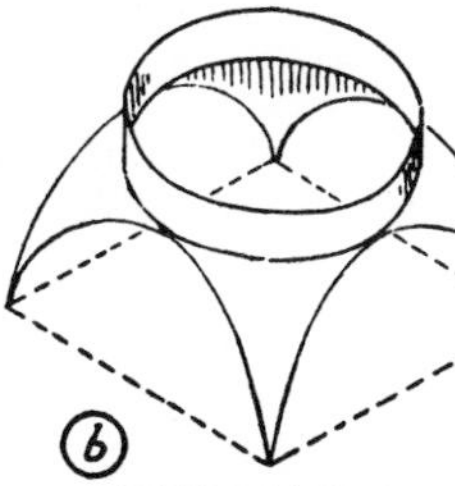

(b) PENDENTIVES SUPPORTING A DRUM

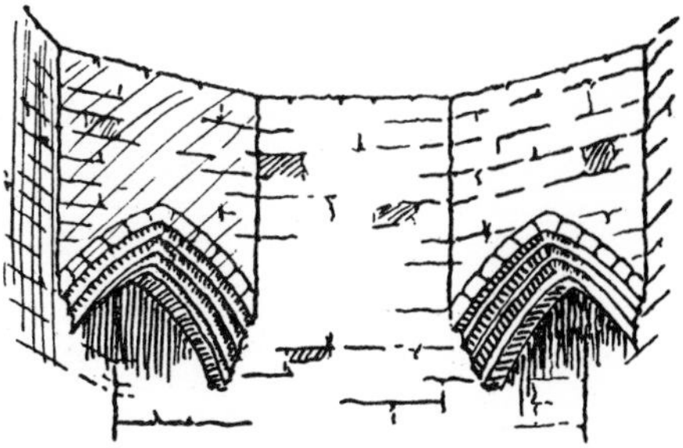

SQUINCHES (c)

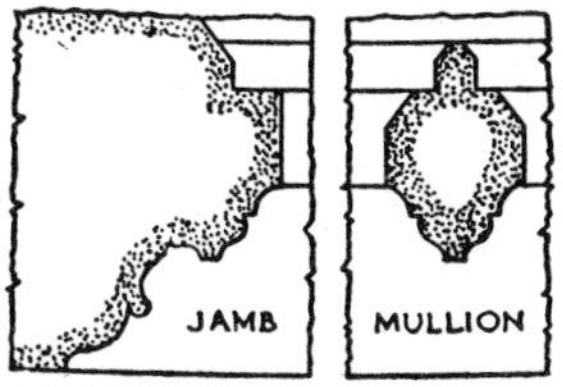

GOTHIC WINDOW SECTIONS (d)

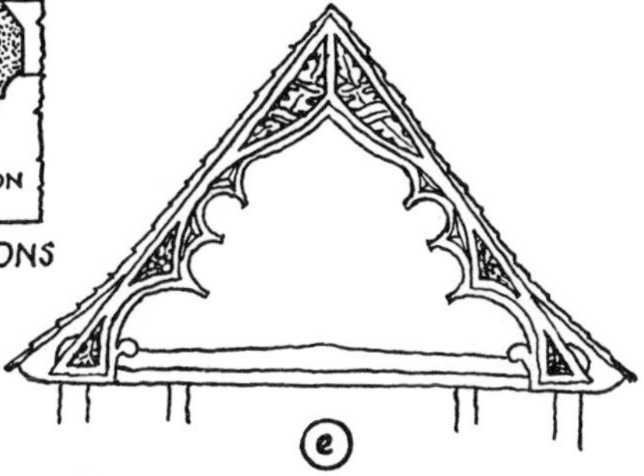

(e) GABLE WITH BARGEBOARDS

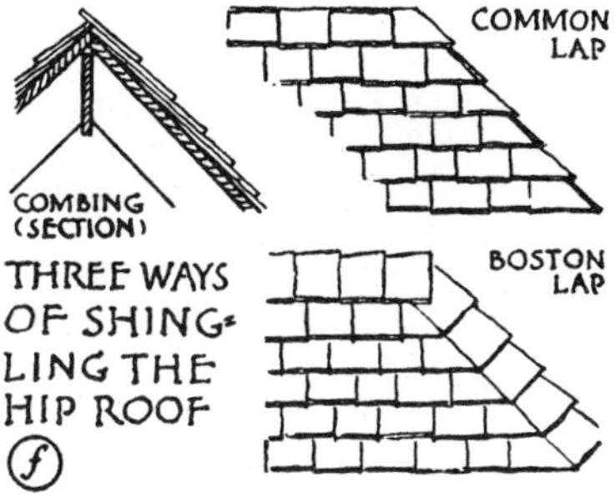

THREE WAYS OF SHINGLING THE HIP ROOF (f)

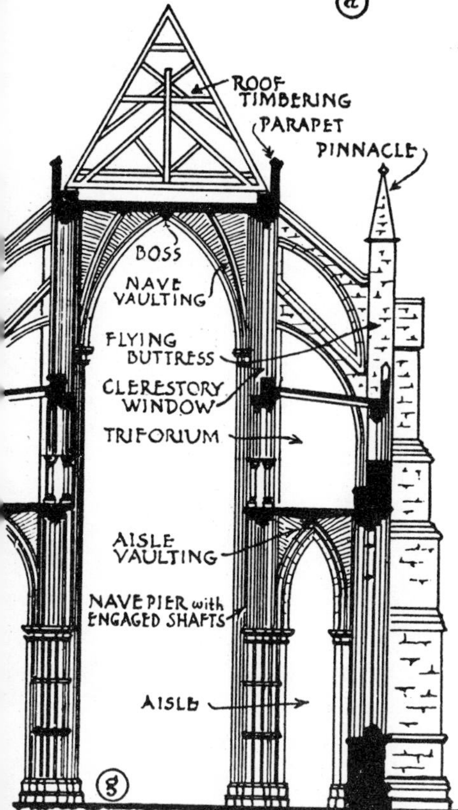

(g) GOTHIC CATHEDRAL, TRANSVERSE SECTION (SOUTH SIDE, WESTMINSTER)

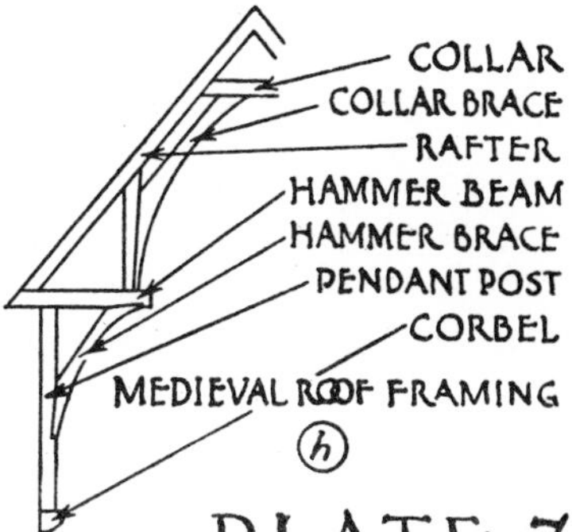

MEDIEVAL ROOF FRAMING (h)

PLATE 7

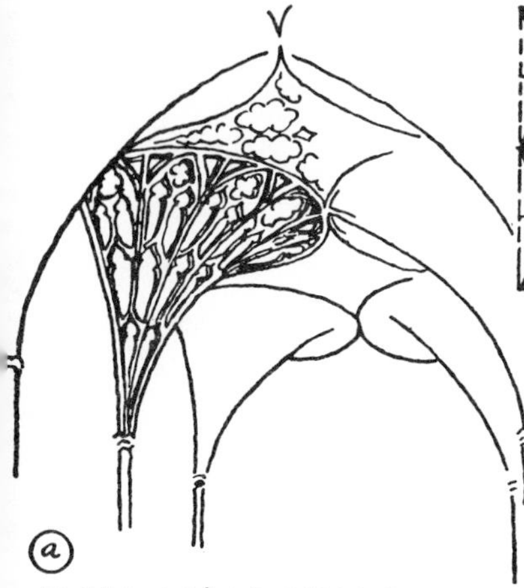

PLAN

(a) FAN VAULTING

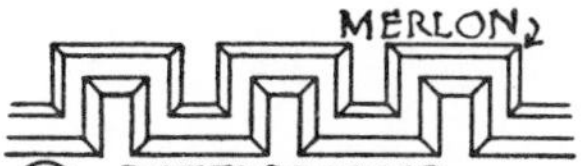

(b) BATTLEMENT

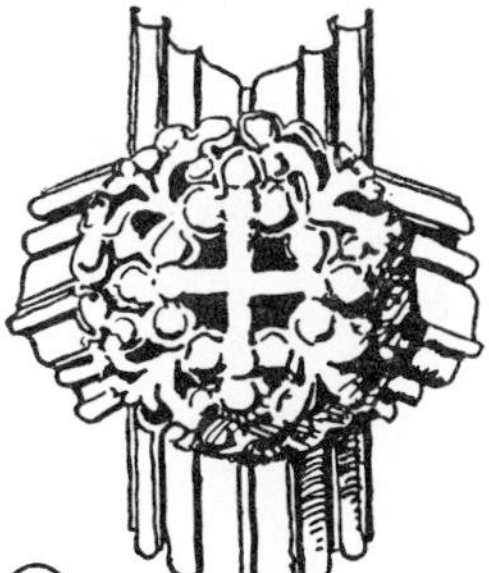

(c) BOSS AT THE JUNCTION OF VAULTING RIBS

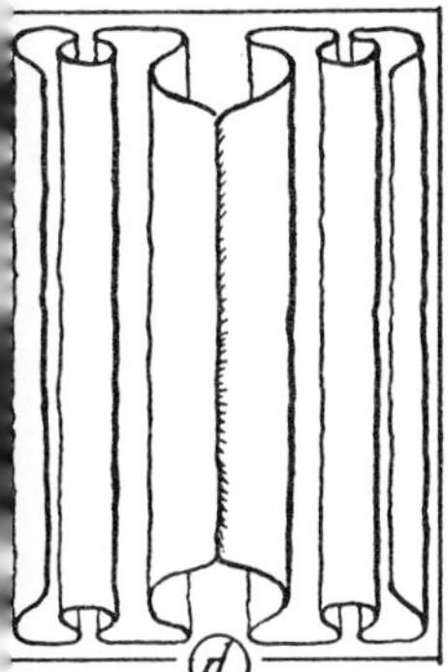

(d) LINENFOLD

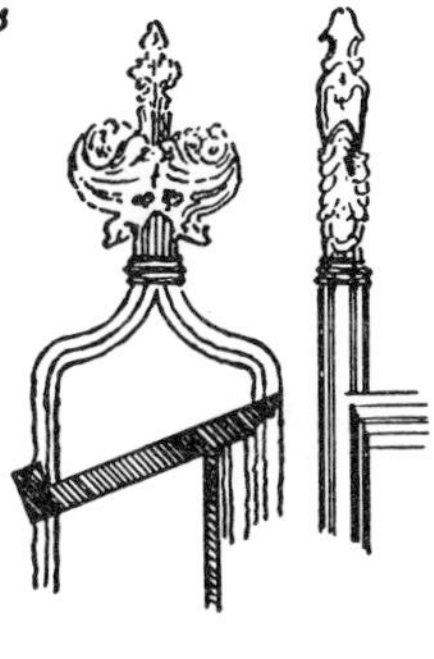

(e) POPIE

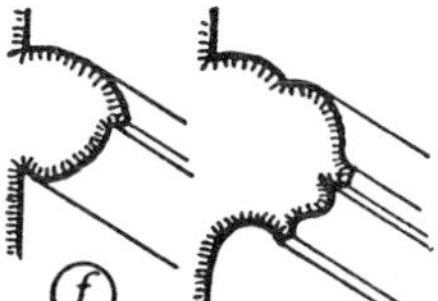

(f) ROLL MOLDINGS (VARIABLE)

(g) CUSPS IN TRACERY

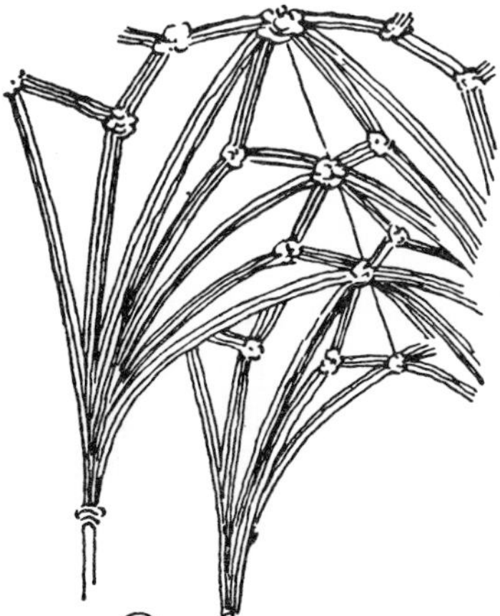

(h) LIERNE VAULTING

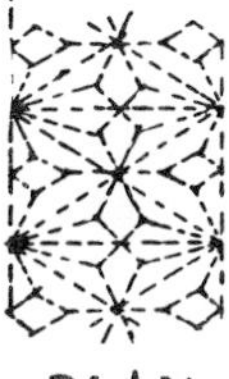

PLAN

PLATE 8